IMAGES
of America

HISTORIC PULASKI COUNTY

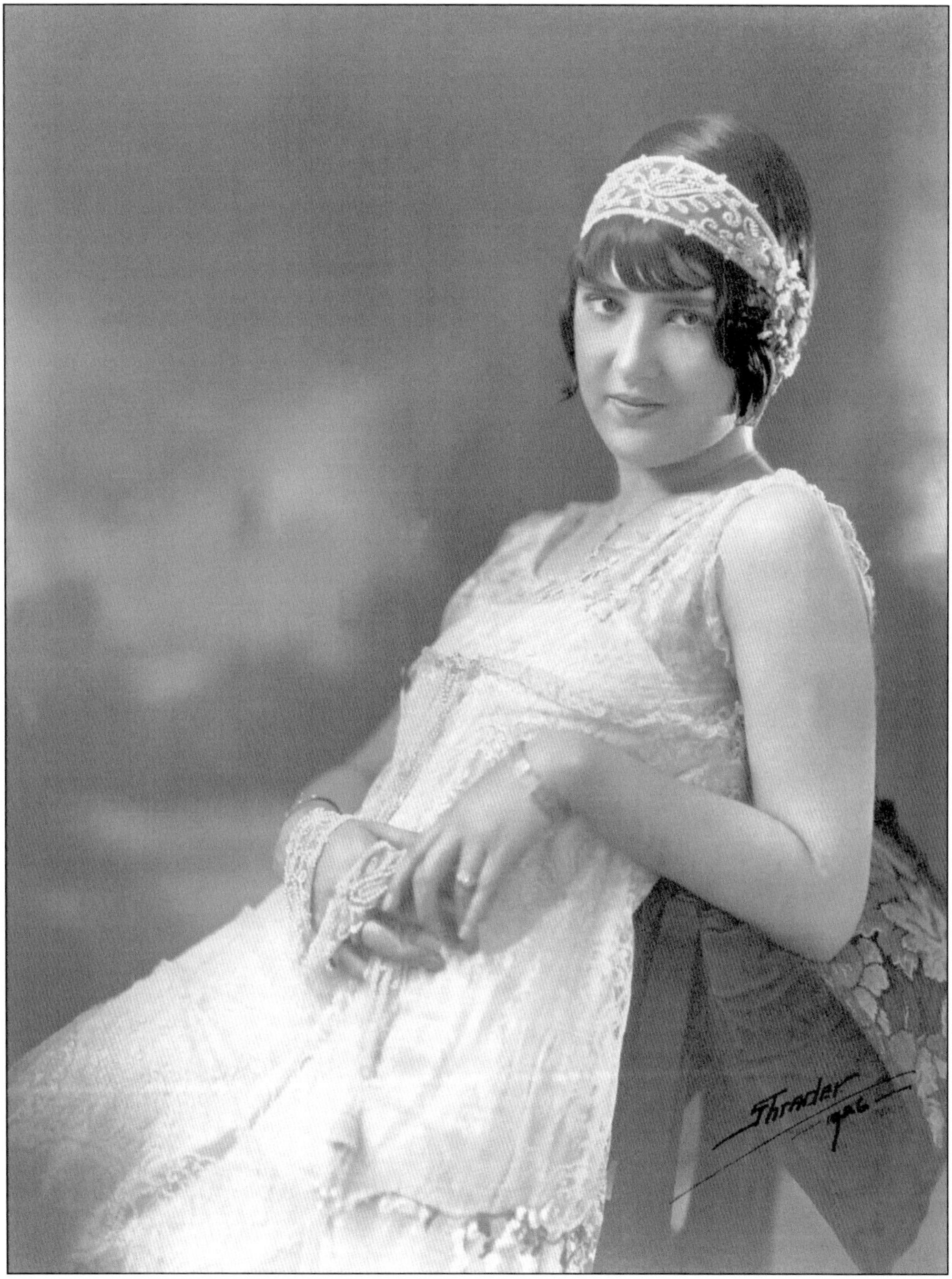

ROSLYN HOFFMAN PRITCHETT. This photograph was taken when she was 18 years of age in 1926. She was born in 1908 and died in 1953. (Arkansas History Commission.)

IMAGES
of America

HISTORIC PULASKI COUNTY

Paulette H. Walter
and Alan C. Paulson

ARCADIA
PUBLISHING

ISBN 978-0-7385-0006-5

Published by Arcadia Publishing
Charleston, South Carolina

Printed in the United States of America

Library of Congress Catalog Card Number: 99-066664

For all general information contact Arcadia Publishing at:
Telephone 843-853-2070
Fax 843-853-0044
E-Mail sales@arcadiapublishing.com
For customer service and orders:
Toll-Free 1-888-313-2556

Visit us on the Internet at www.arcadiapublishing.com

About the Authors

Polly Walter has taught journalism at the University of Central Arkansas since 1990. Prior to that she taught at the University of Alaska, and worked as photo editor and associate editor for *Alaska* magazine, *Alaska Journal*, and *Alaska Geographic*. She subsequently served as production manager and photo editor for *Mushing* magazine. A veteran journalist, her work has appeared in dozens of books, magazines, and newspapers such as the *Fairbanks Daily News-Miner*, *The Pioneer All-Alaska Weekly*, and the *Anchorage Daily News*. More recently, she edited and did most of the photography for the highly acclaimed book, *Roadside History of Arkansas* which was written by her husband, Al Paulson.

Al Paulson is an author and journalist specializing in the realms of history, science, and technology. Voted Alaskan Writer of the Year in 1977, he has written hundreds of magazine articles and a number of books. He has also worked as a biologist, conducting scientific research from the Arctic to the South Seas.

Walter and Paulson recently co-authored the book *Historic Faulkner County*, and they are currently collaborating on several books about Alaska and Wisconsin. Both are members of the Ozarks Writers League.

Contents

ACKNOWLEDGMENTS

We would like to thank Desmond Walls Allen of Arkansas Research for suggesting this project and subsequently providing invaluable assistance. Henryetta Vanaman has provided outstanding photographs for three of our last four books, including this one. Jimmy Bryant, archivist at the University of Central Arkansas, provided enthusiastic and generous support. Lynn Ewbank, Jane Hooker, and Mary Ann Stiles at the Arkansas History Commission were profoundly helpful. Finally, we appreciate all of the assistance provided by Linda R. Pine, Jane-Ellen Murphy, and John M. Jackson at Archives & Special Collections, University of Arkansas at Little Rock.

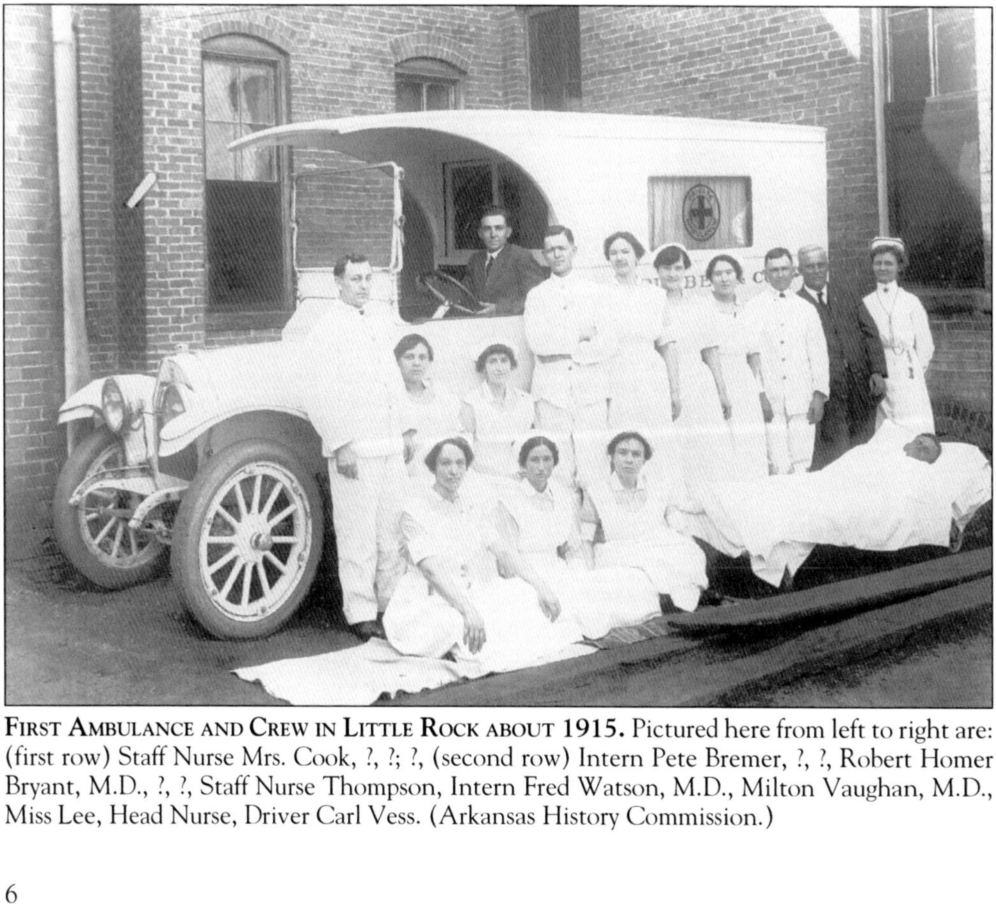

FIRST AMBULANCE AND CREW IN LITTLE ROCK ABOUT 1915. Pictured here from left to right are: (first row) Staff Nurse Mrs. Cook, ?, ?; ?, (second row) Intern Pete Bremer, ?, ?, Robert Homer Bryant, M.D., ?, ?, Staff Nurse Thompson, Intern Fred Watson, M.D., Milton Vaughan, M.D., Miss Lee, Head Nurse, Driver Carl Vess. (Arkansas History Commission.)

INTRODUCTION

The recorded history of the area begins long before there was a Pulaski County or even an Arkansas. Early French explorers traveling up the Mississippi and Arkansas rivers observed that this spot had one of the first two rock outcroppings to be encountered upriver of New Orleans. According to legend, French explorer Jean-Baptiste Bernard de La Harpe called this landmark *Le Petit Rocher*, "The Little Rock," in 1722. Since the first settlers to the area did not appear until 1806, when John Gozel led seven families to the area from Carolina, Little Rock may be the only city in the United States that was named a century before the place got its first home. In 1807, brothers John and Jacob Pyeatt settled about 12 miles north of Little Rock at Crystal Hill, founding a community called Pyeattstown. The first known document to actually use the name "Little Rock" was a land deed dated 1814 and recorded in 1821 that refers to "little rocks bluff."

Remarkably, Pulaski County is older than Arkansas. It was one of five counties created by the Missouri legislature in December 1818, back when the land that would eventually be known as Arkansas was part of Missouri Territory. The legislators named the county in honor of a Polish nobleman, Count Casimir Pulaski, who joined the American Revolution in 1777. Despite the fact that he was only 29 at the time, his experience in Europe earned him a commission as a brigadier general. Pulaski formed a cavalry unit and fought with distinction until he was killed during a charge at the Battle of Savannah in 1779.

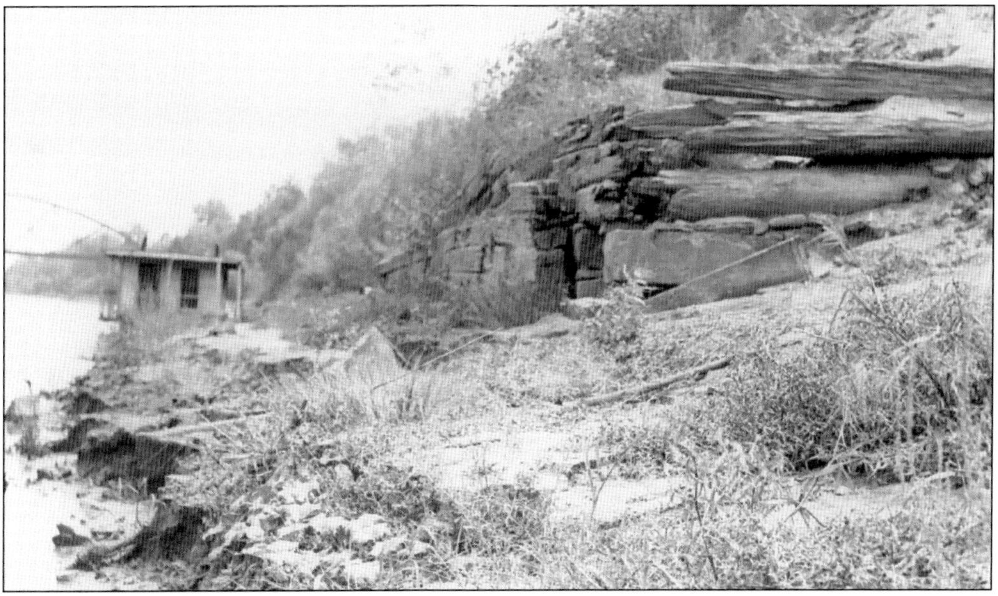

THE "LITTLE ROCK" ALONG THE ARKANSAS RIVER. Early French explorers noted that this spot was one of the first two rock outcroppings seen when traveling up the Mississippi from New Orleans. According to legend, French explorer Jean-Baptiste Bernard de La Harpe called this landmark *Le Petit Rocher*, "The Little Rock," when he journeyed past it in 1722. (Arkansas History Commission.)

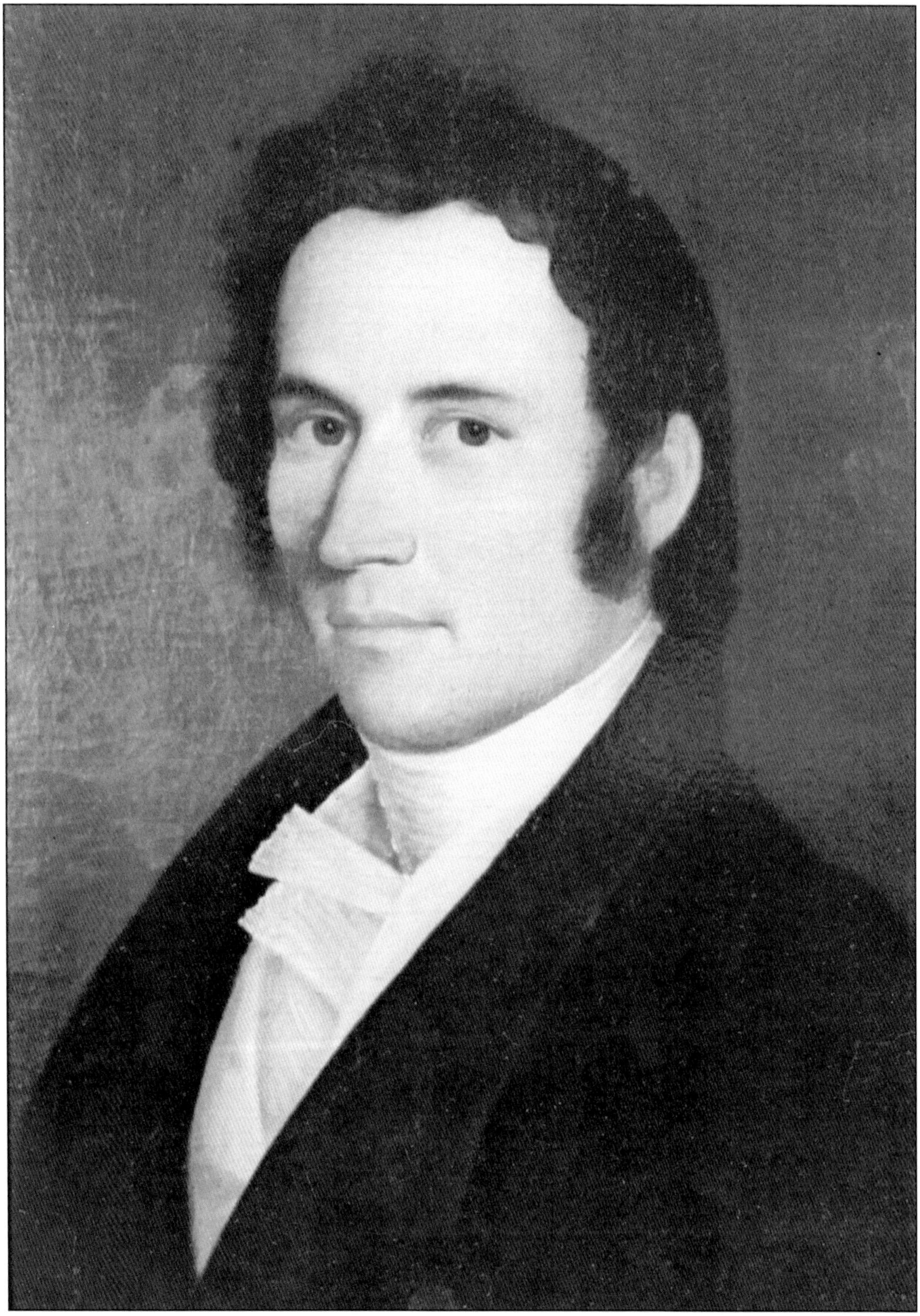

WILLIAM WOODRUFF (1795-1885), FOUNDER OF THE ARKANSAS *GAZETTE*. Woodruff's paper would remain the oldest continuously published newspaper west of the Mississippi until its demise on October 18, 1991. Established at Arkansas Post in 1819, the *Gazette* moved to Little Rock in 1821. (UCA Archives.)

One

The Antebellum Years

Congress split off the southern half of Missouri to form Arkansas Territory in 1819, and Little Rock became the permanent seat of Pulaski County in March 1822, nine months after the legislature moved the territorial capital from Arkansas Post to Little Rock. The riverfront town prospered with the growth of steamboat traffic, which gradually increased after Arkansas became a state in 1836. In 1830, for example, the town was lucky to see one steamboat per week. By 1858, about 10 boats arrived per week to deliver goods and haul the area's principal exports—cotton and corn—back to New Orleans. By 1860, Little Rock had grown to a population of 3,727.

With the election of Abraham Lincoln to the presidency, regional politics became increasingly polarized. Nevertheless, Little Rock was by no means a hotbed of secessionist fervor, even after South Carolina, Mississippi, Florida, and Alabama left the Union. Support for secession grew slowly, until legislators decided to call a popular election on the issue.

A group of ardent secessionists did not wait for the election, however, marching on the U.S. Army Arsenal in Little Rock. The commander surrendered the arsenal to avoid bloodshed, and the secessionists secured the arsenal's cache of weapons and munitions.

The debate changed completely after hostilities erupted during the U.S. Navy attempt to reinforce Fort Sumter in Charleston Harbor. Slavery was no longer the issue for most Southern voters, since Lincoln essentially declared war on the secessionist states. With war visited upon the South, the only question for Arkansas voters became which side to join. Folks pretty much sided with their kith and kin.

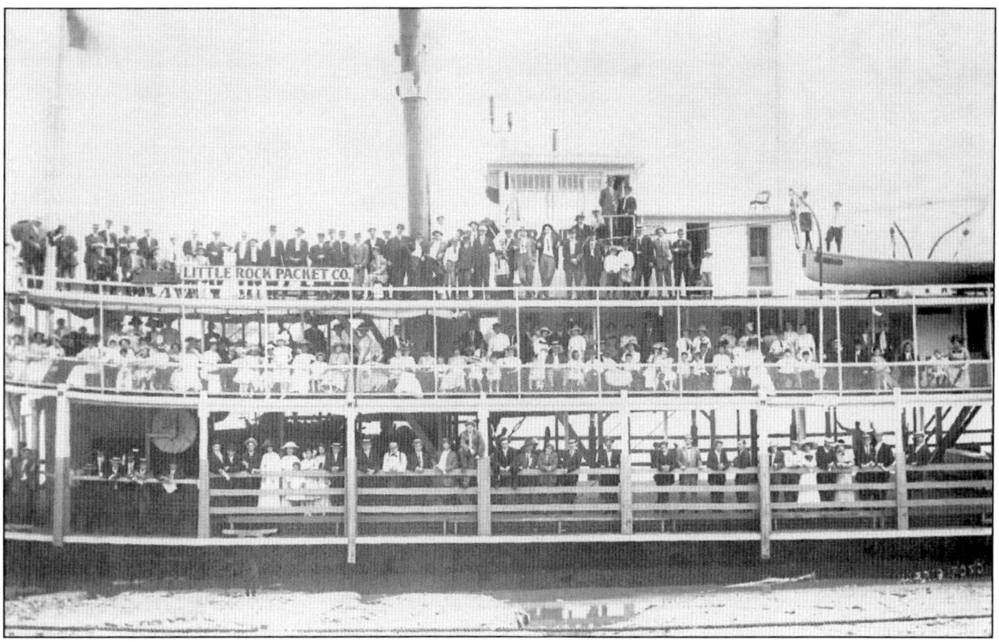

Wharf Scene Showing the Steamboat Choctaw. (Arkansas History Commission.)

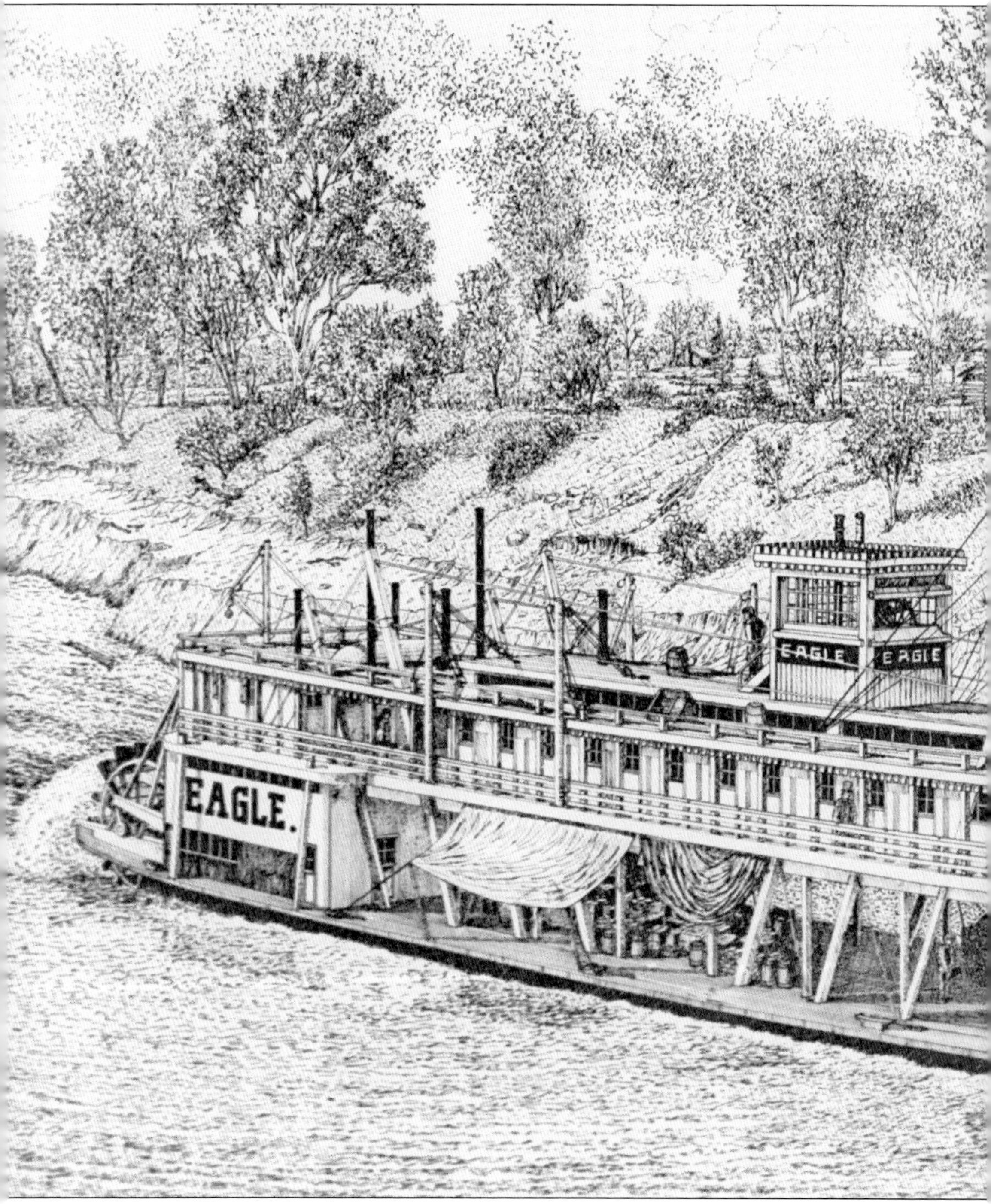

First Steamboat Arrives in Little Rock, 1822. When it became the capital of Arkansas Territory in 1822 (replacing Arkansas Post in that capacity), Little Rock was a very small town. Even three years later, the community only had 60 buildings; all were simple log cabins except for six brick and eight frame structures. The territorial legislature met in a 10 by 10 foot log cabin. So it was quite a surprise when Capt. G. Morris brought the 118-ton *Eagle* about

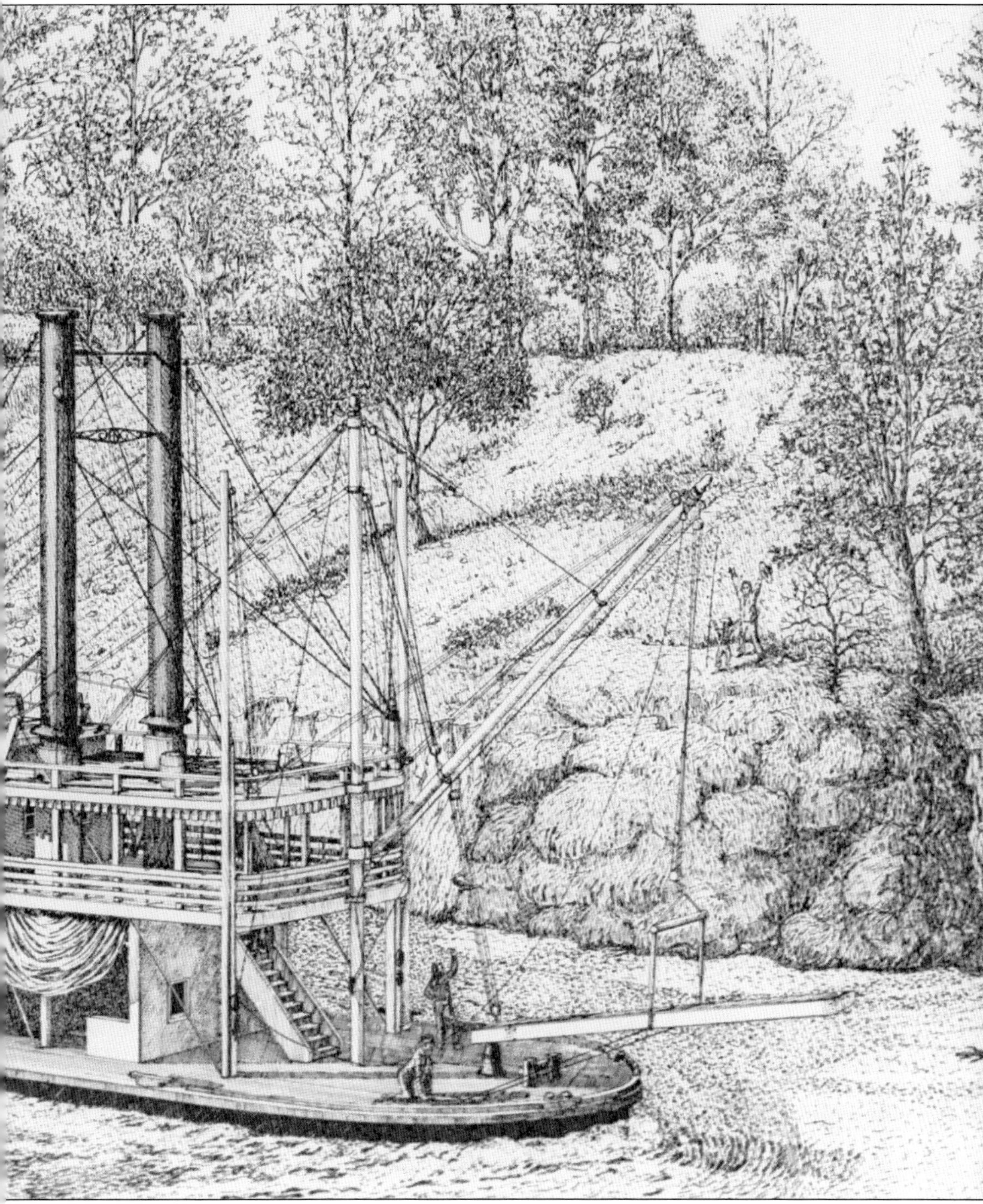

300 river miles north from New Orleans all the way to Little Rock. Early on the morning of March 16, 1882, he nosed the *Eagle* ashore at the sleepy village and announced his arrival with the scream of his steam whistle and a salute of gunfire. It was the first time a steamboat had come up the river farther than Arkansas Post. (Drawing by Richard DeSpain, Arkansas History Commission.)

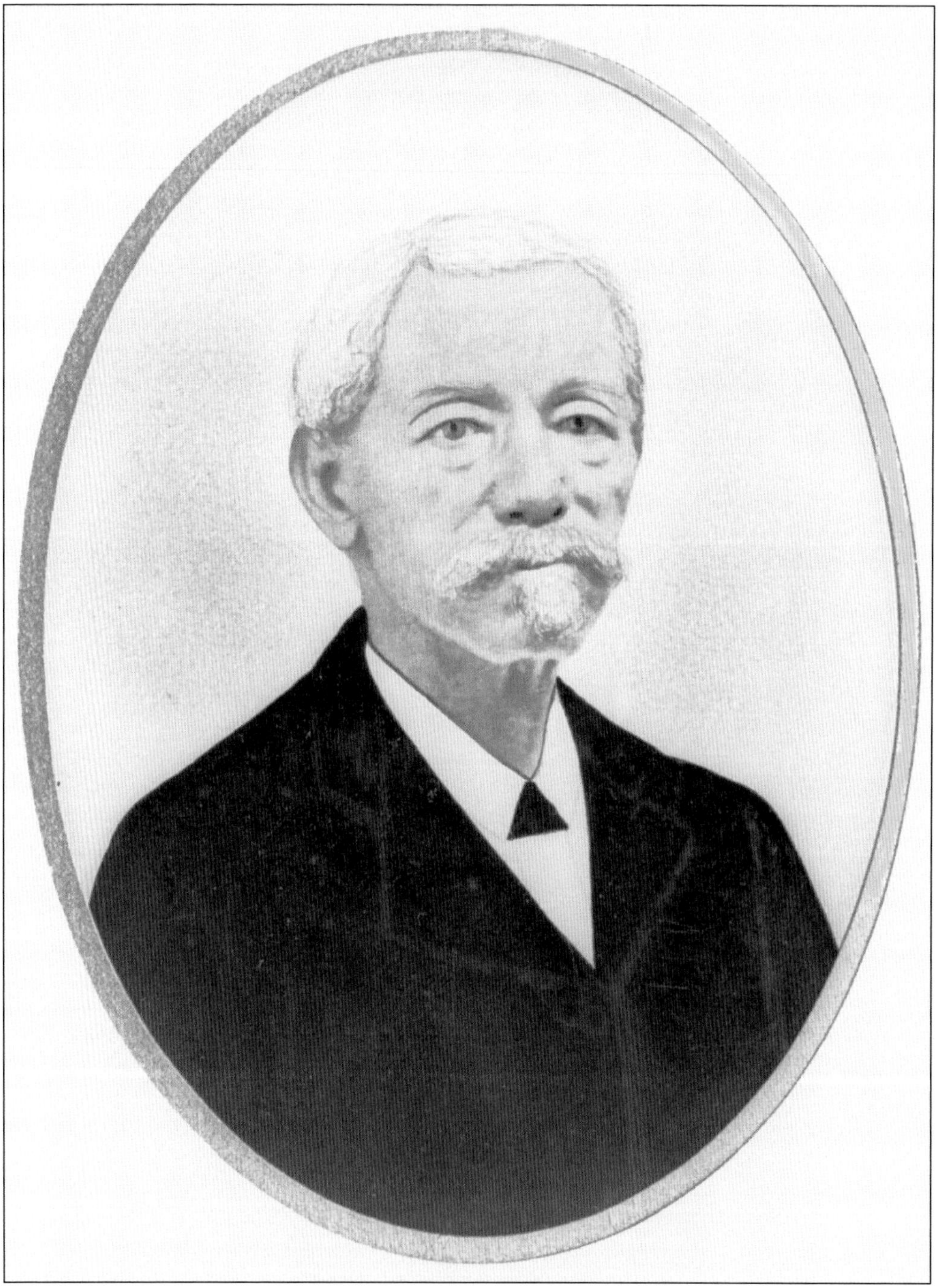

NATHAN WARREN. One of the few free black businessmen in antebellum Pulaski County, Warren was a man of tremendous industry. He worked very hard during the 1840s and early 1850s to earn enough money to buy the freedom of his family members. Warren became Little Rock's confectioner, and he soon had blacks and whites alike eating out of his hand. Also a gifted fiddler, he was always in demand for social events of all sorts. (Arkansas History Commission.)

LOGAN JAMES ABOUT 1850.
(Arkansas History Commission.)

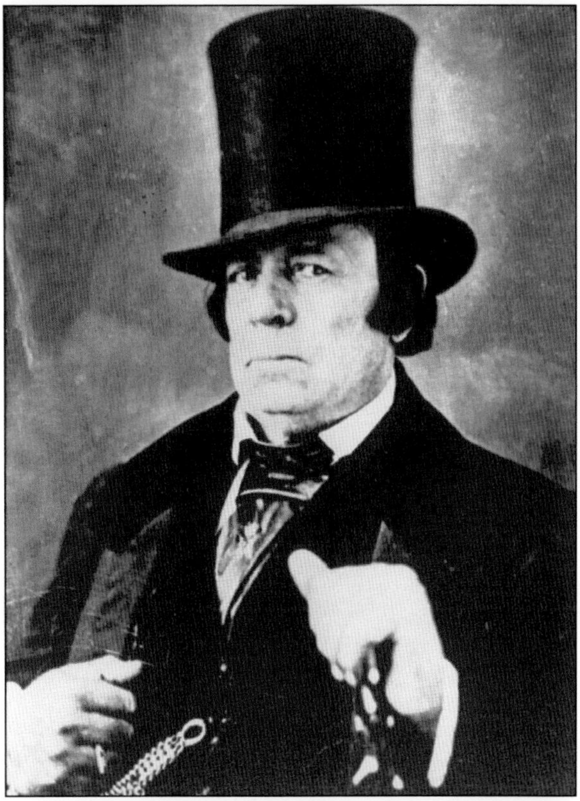

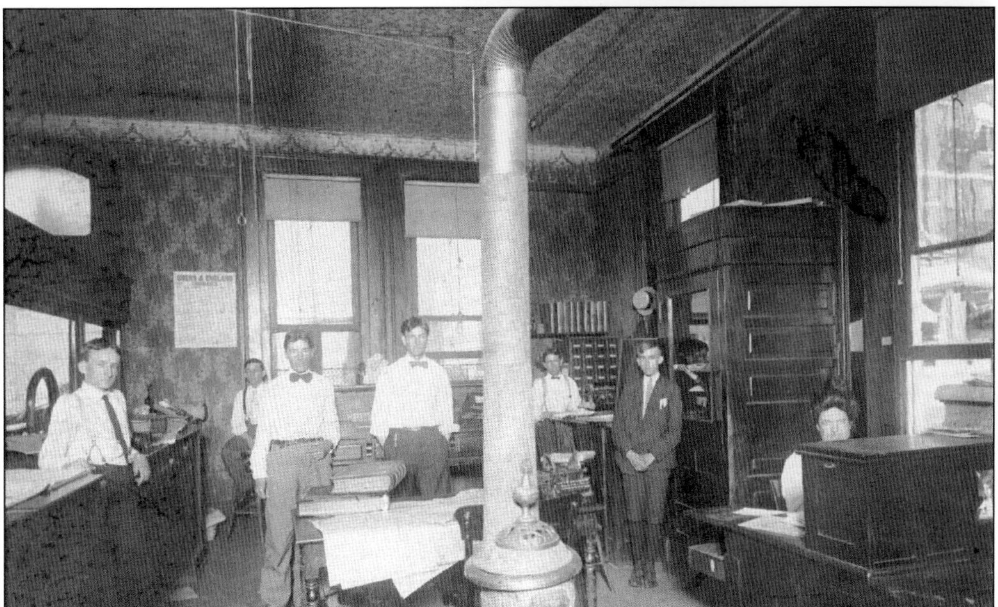

BURT WEBER'S FATHER, AN ACCOUNTANT AT THE *ARKANSAS GAZETTE*, C.1906. The *Gazette* was established at Arkansas Post in 1819, the year when the post became the capital of Arkansas Territory. The *Gazette* remained the oldest paper west of the Mississippi River until its demise on October 18, 1991. (Arkansas History Commission.)

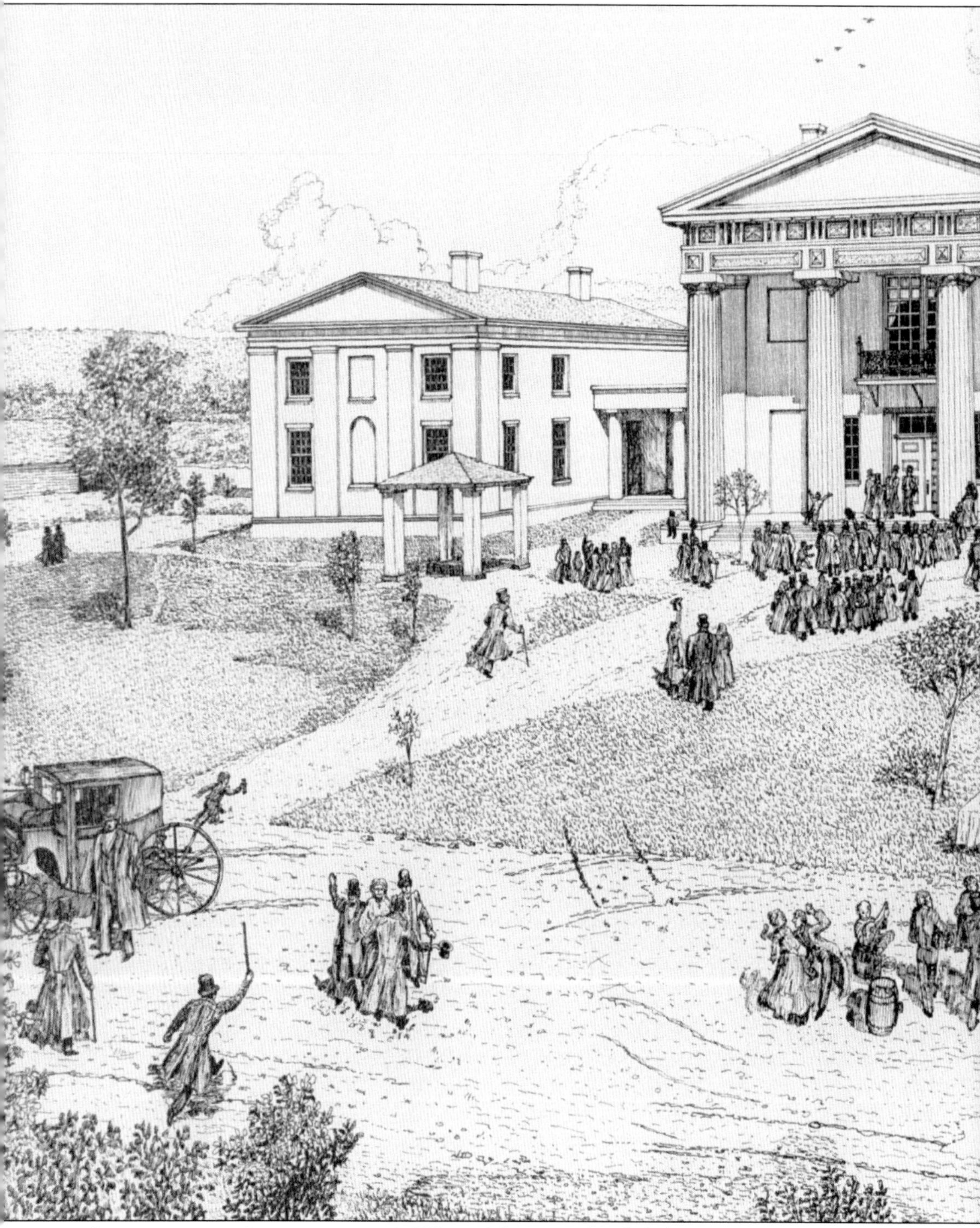

Statehood for Arkansas, 1836. When Arkansans decided they wanted to live in a state rather than a territory, Arkansas Territory had a population of about 52,000, and Little Rock had about 600 residents. On January 4, 1836, 42 delegates convened in a small log Baptist church to begin drafting a constitution, which was an important step down the road toward

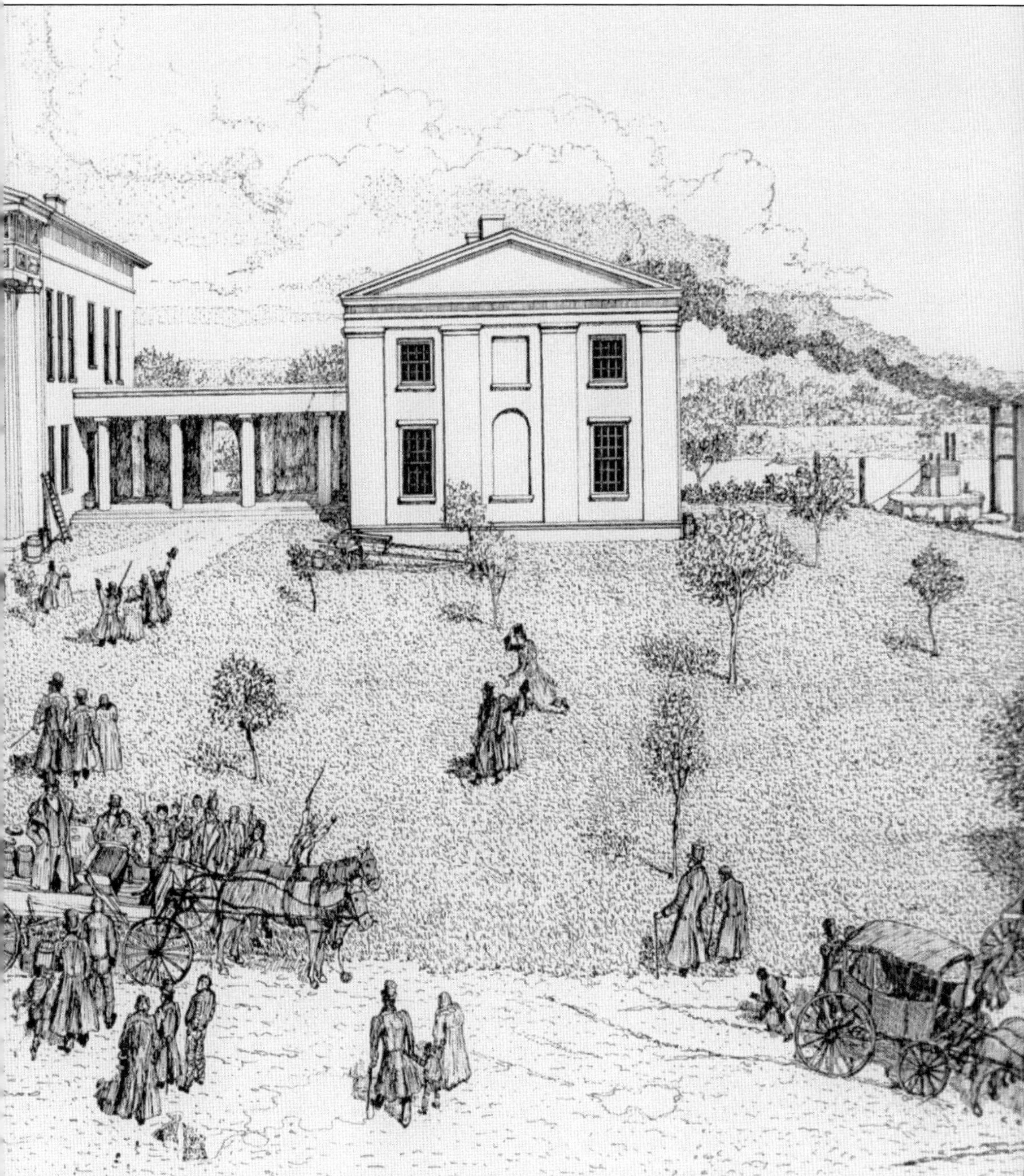

statehood. Several days later, the convention moved to the more spacious presbyterian church, completing their task on January 30. Arkansas became the 25th state on June 15, and James S. Conway was inaugurated as the first state governor on September 13. (Drawing by Richard DeSpain, Arkansas History Commission.)

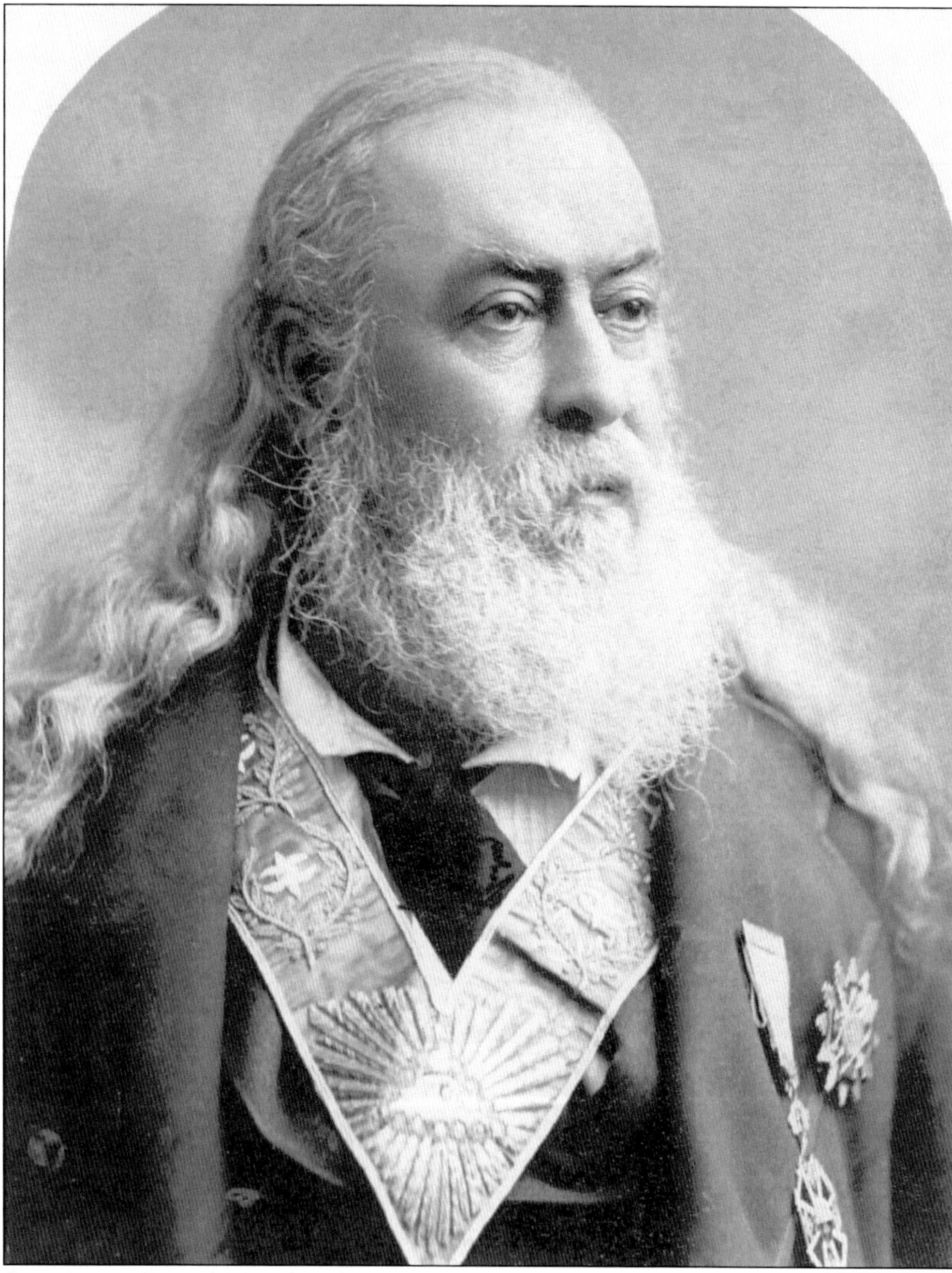

GEN. ALBERT PIKE, CSA. Pike subsequently became Sovereign Grand Commander of Scottish Masons of the United States. He is pictured here in a Bradley & Rulofson photo. In 1835, Pike said of Little Rock, "There is no more intelligent, shrewd, sensible, and at the same time generous and hospitable community in the world." Pike would go on to become an important Arkansas politician, a prolific writer of poetry, a general in the Confederate army, and an influential member of Scottish Rite Masons thanks to his personal charm, as well as his writing of a seminal book on Masonic law and symbolism. In short, he was one of the most colorful Arkansans of the 19th century. (Arkansas History Commission.)

Two

WAR BETWEEN THE STATES

The year 1861 passed without any fighting on Arkansas soil, and Pulaski County emptied out as men rushed off to fight in the East. New Orleans and Memphis fell to the Federals in 1862, driving hordes of refugees into Little Rock. Union gunboats blockaded the Mississippi, strangling the flow of supplies to Arkansas. By the end of 1862, there wasn't a single egg or pint of whiskey left in town. Then war came to Arkansas with a vengeance. After a great deal of fighting, Federal troops under the command of Maj. Gen. Frederick Steele marched on Little Rock, pushing through the last Confederate resistance on September 10, 1863.

Little Rock adapted quickly to Federal control, largely because of Steele's conciliatory policy toward the residents. He arranged to feed the town's hungry population, and he imported skilled hospital personnel to relieve the exhausted lady volunteers who had been tending wounded Union and Confederate soldiers for months. Finally, Steele offered full pardons to anyone who would swear allegiance to the Union—but Steele lost the moral high ground with the execution of a youngster.

David O. Dodd was traveling with his father, who was a sutler for the 3rd Arkansas Infantry in Mississippi, while his mother and sisters remained in Little Rock. After the Federals captured their hometown, David's father obtained the paperwork necessary for David to cross Union lines and bring his family back to Confederate-held territory. On his way back, David was caught with a note written in Morse code that detailed the disposition of Federal forces in Little Rock. He was hanged as a spy at the age of 17.

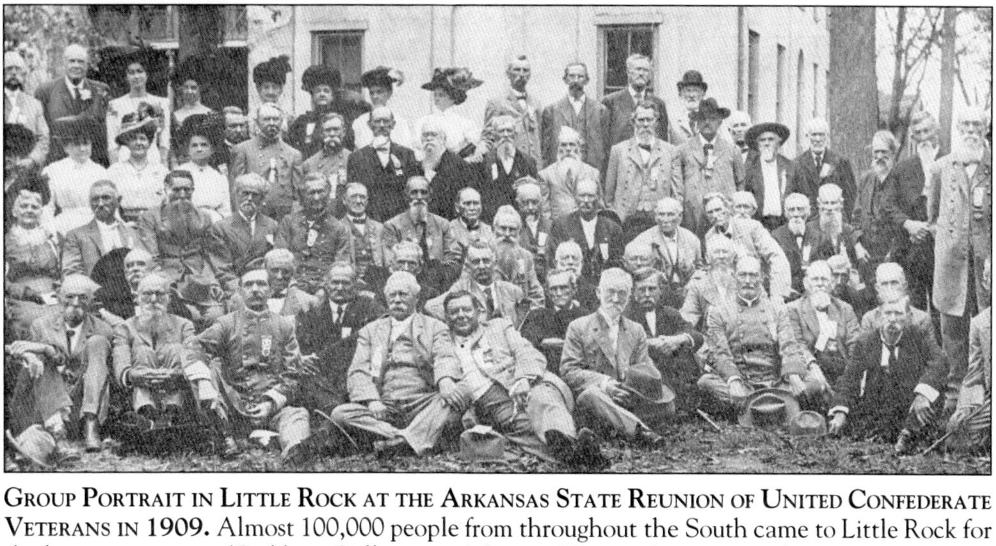

GROUP PORTRAIT IN LITTLE ROCK AT THE ARKANSAS STATE REUNION OF UNITED CONFEDERATE VETERANS IN 1909. Almost 100,000 people from throughout the South came to Little Rock for the historic reunion. (Stebbins Collection, Arkansas History Commission.)

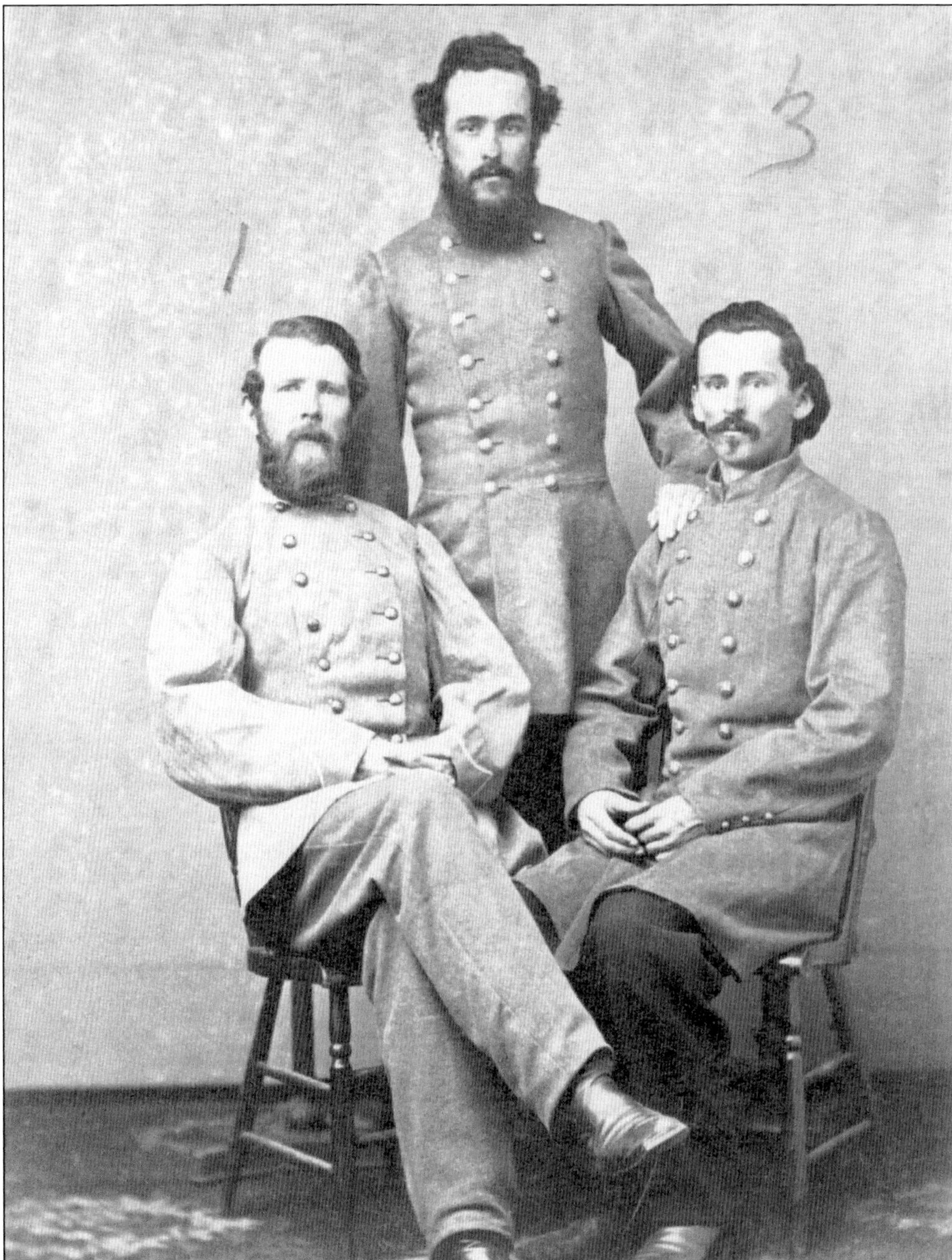

CAPTAINS BEHEN, FOOTE, AND ROBERTS, CSA. A *Carte de Visite* featuring a photograph was a popular form of calling card in the mid-1800s. This one, produced by Brown's Gallery on Main Street in Little Rock, is unusual in that it features three people rather than just one. The rear face of the card is signed "With regards of Foote, Roberts, and Behen." (Arkansas History Commission.)

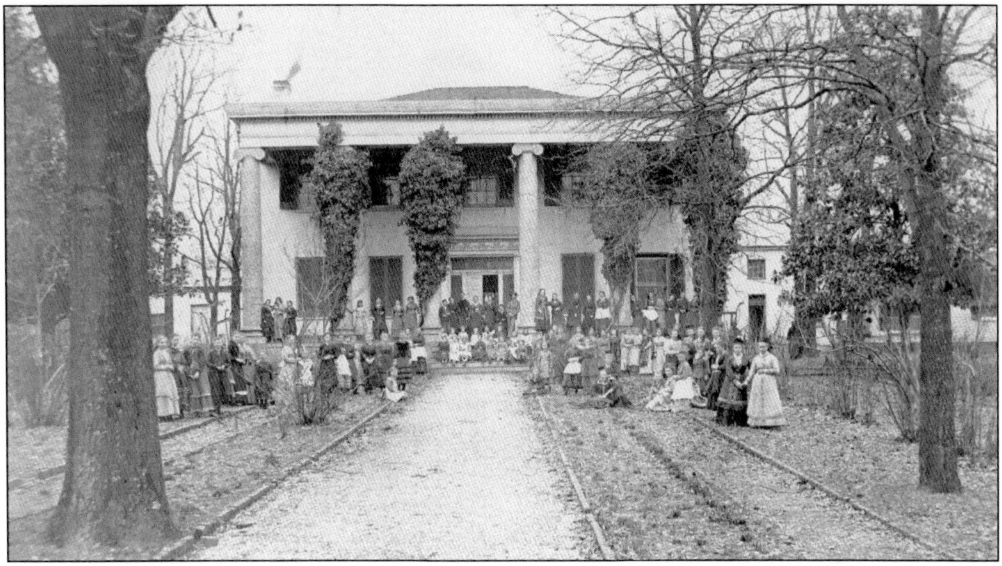

Albert Pike Mansion in Little Rock. Built in 1839 in the Greek Revival style, writer and poet John Gould Fletcher grew up in this house and wrote the poem "The Ghosts of an Old House" about his reminiscences there. Congressman D.D. Terry subsequently lived at the house, which eventually became a branch of the Arkansas Art Center called the Decorative Arts Museum. (Arkansas History Commission.)

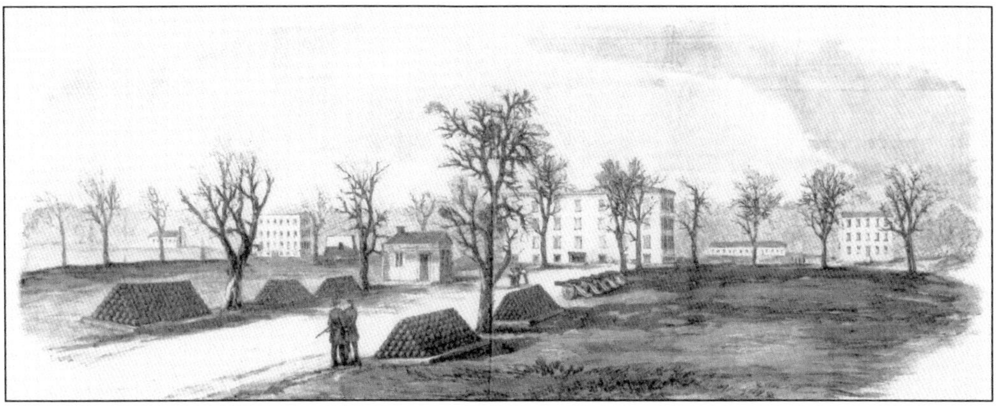

U.S. Arsenal in Little Rock, Surrender to State Troops in February of 1861. This drawing shows the Workshop on the left, the Magazine just left of center, Bragg's Battery to the right of center, and the Commandant's House to the far right. (Arkansas History Commission.)

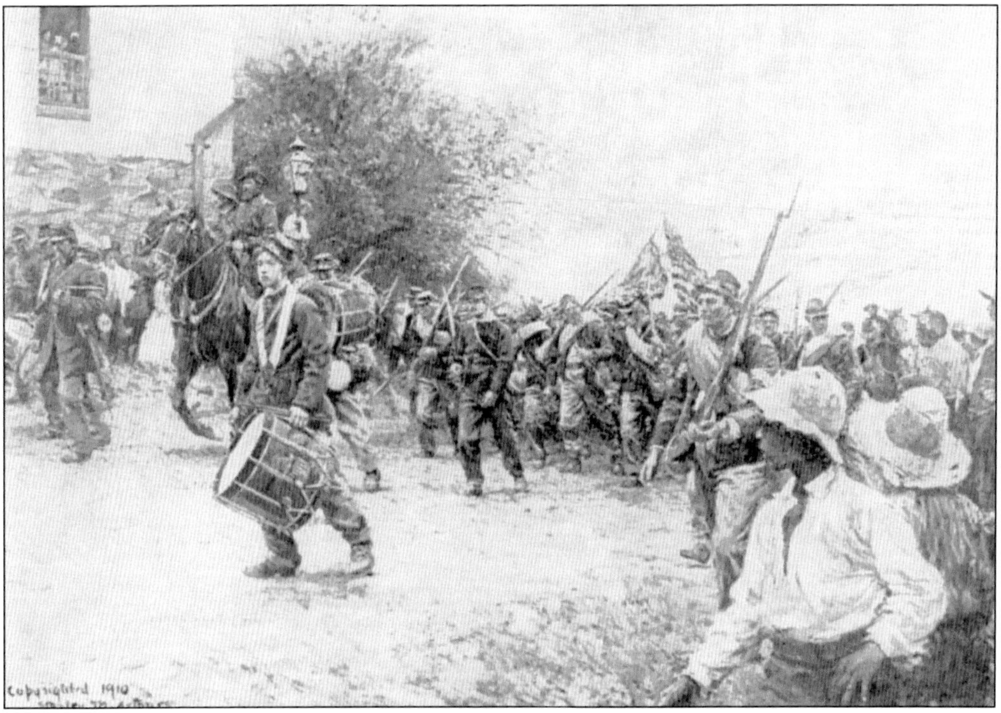

Federal Troops Entering Little Rock in 1863, From a Painting by Stanley M Arthurs. After a great deal of fighting, Federal troops under the command of Maj. Gen. Frederick Steele marched on Little Rock, pushing through the last Confederate resistance on September 10, 1863. (UCA Archives.)

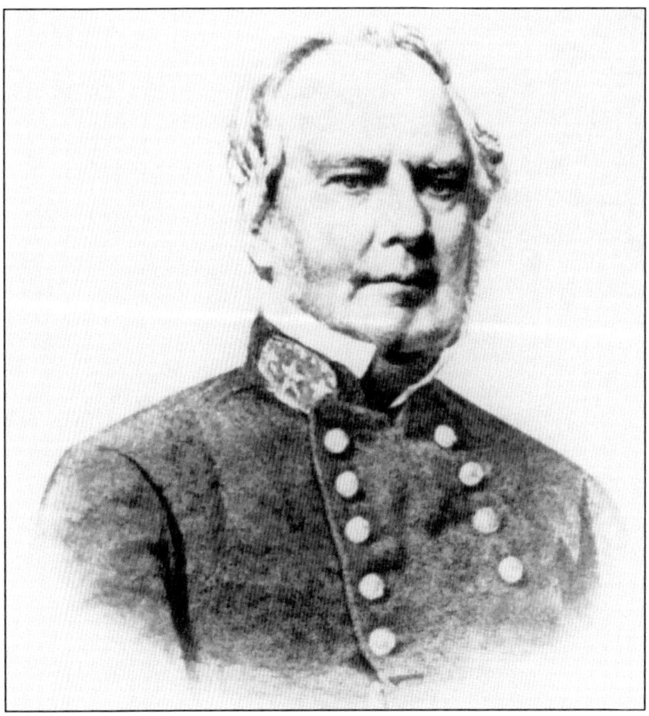

Maj. Gen. Sterling Price, CSA. Price was a likable 290 pounds of Missouri vanity, known affectionately as "Old Pap" by his men. When Maj. Gen. Frederick Steele marched out of Little Rock in 1864 to destroy the Confederate Trans-Mississippi forces, Price encircled the Bluecoats and cut their supply lines. Steele was forced into a bloody retreat to Little Rock, thus ending large-scale military operations in Arkansas. (Arkansas History Commission.)

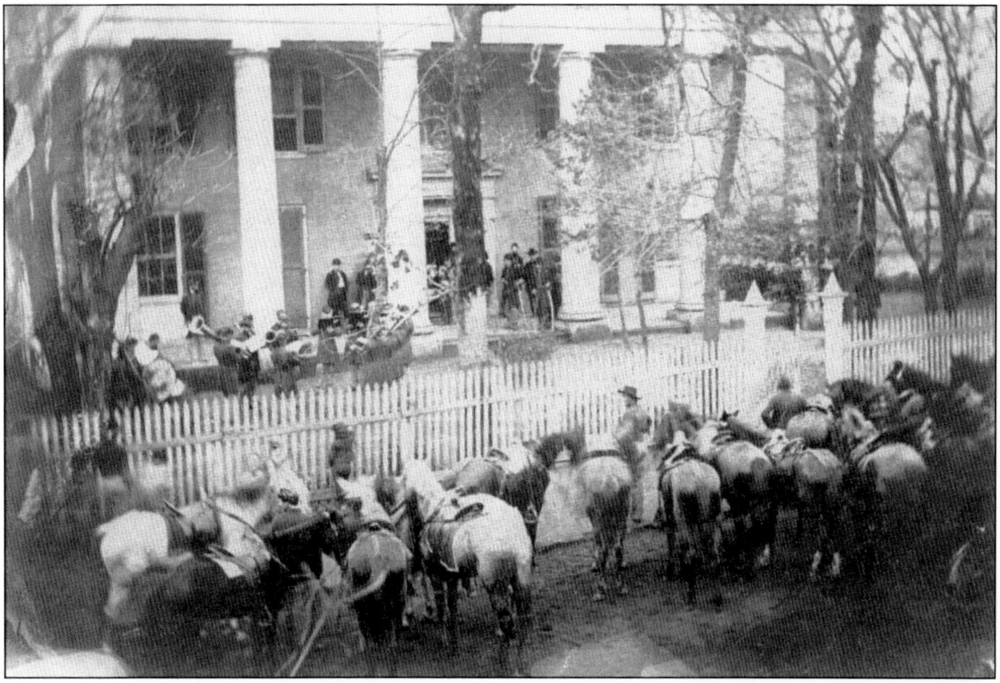

UNION TROOPS AT THE W.E. WOODRUFF HOUSE ON EAST 8TH STREET IN LITTLE ROCK, C.1864. The residents of Little Rock readily adapted to the Federal occupation and got along fairly well compared to many occupied communities in the South, at least until General J. J. Rogers replaced Major General Frederick Steele after Steele's ill-fated Red River Campaign. (Arkansas History Commission.)

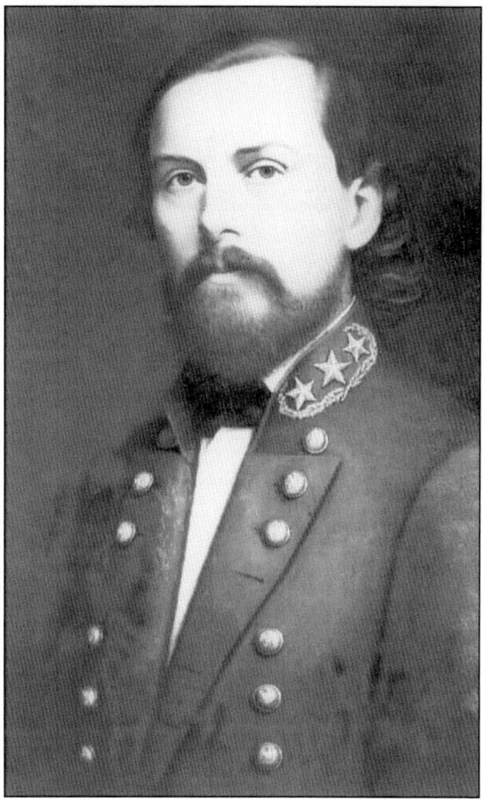

GEN. THOMAS C. HINDMAN, CSA. When the Federals advanced along the White River in a bid to capture Little Rock, Hindman asked hungry Arkansas families to destroy every ounce of food and forage, and to burn every bridge in an effort to slow the Federal advance. He threw the state into chaos, and the newspapers and residents of Little Rock subjected Hindman to extreme daily ridicule. (Arkansas History Commission.)

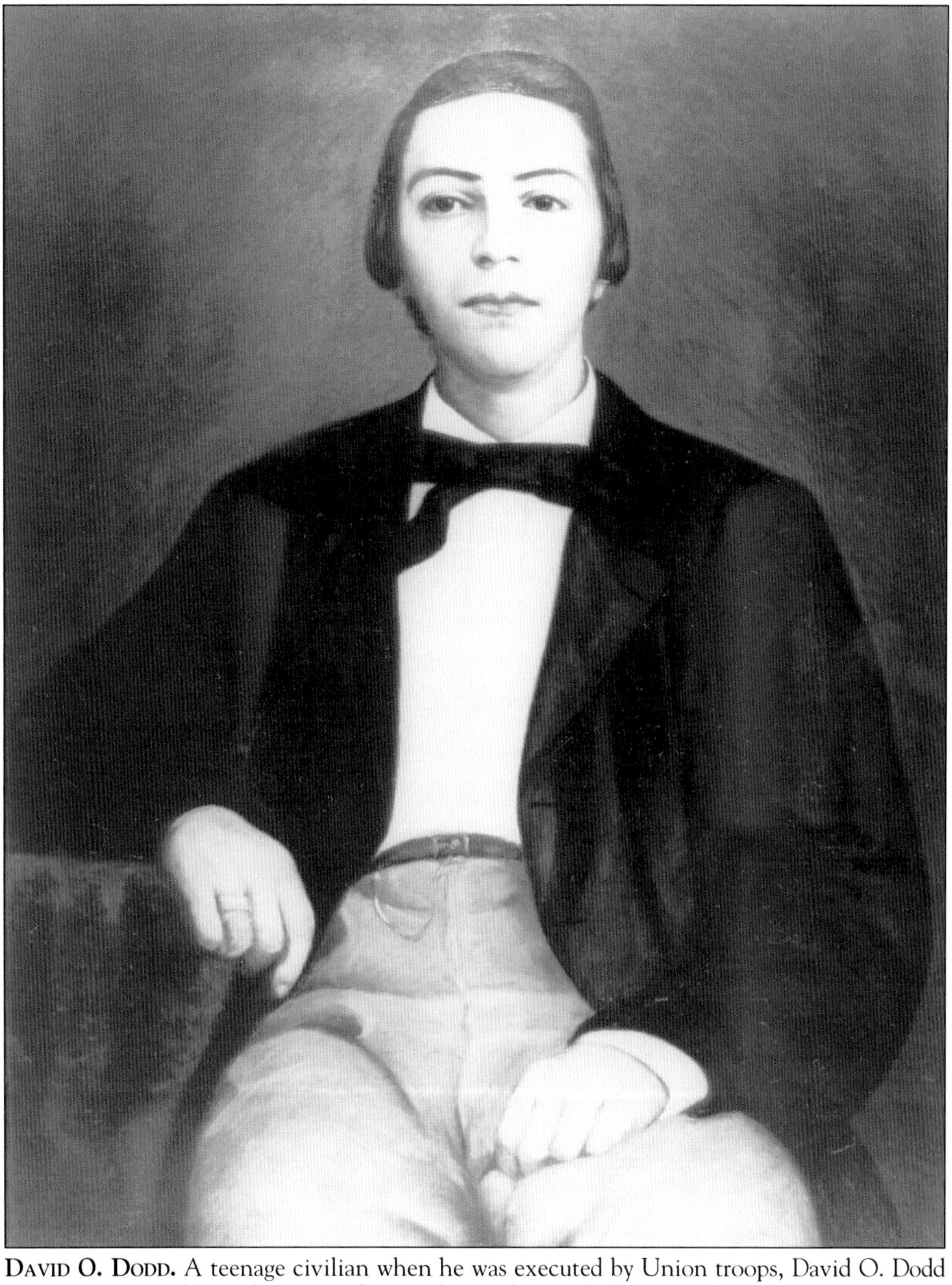

David O. Dodd. A teenage civilian when he was executed by Union troops, David O. Dodd became the most famous hero in Arkansas during the Civil War. Caught with a note in Morse code that detailed the disposition of Federal forces in Little Rock, Dodd was hanged as a spy at the age of 17. (UCA Archives.)

Three

RECONSTRUCTION AND THE BROOKS-BAXTER WAR

Many problems fueled the argument for political change in the early 1870s. Political incompetence and corruption—as well as outright fraud—generated runaway government debt. Then cotton prices plummeted by 50 percent. Worst of all, entrenched officials could deny voter registration to anyone who publicly supported the Confederacy, whether or not they actually carried arms against the Union. Change only became possible when Congress passed the Amnesty Act of 1872, which restored voting rights to disenfranchised supporters of the Lost Cause throughout the South.

Ironically, the quest for change would spawn a second civil war, this time between rival gubernatorial candidates in Arkansas. Citizens in favor of reform supported Methodist minister Joseph Brooks. Former governor Powell Clayton, then a U.S. senator, had been prosecuted by Brooks for election fraud, so he supported Elisha Baxter of Batesville. The 1872 balloting showed that Baxter beat Brooks, but Brooks claimed that election officials (who were all Clayton's men) actually threw out ballots from four counties that Brooks should have carried. Tensions mounted until the Pulaski County court declared that Brooks was the legal governor of Arkansas. He immediately raised a band of armed supporters and evicted Baxter from the statehouse. Baxter retreated and began raising his own army. The Brooks-Baxter War had begun, and soon each army numbered about 2,000 men. Skirmishes followed over the next month, but President Ulysses S. Grant finally stepped in before a full-scale civil war erupted. Grant declared Baxter to be the rightful governor, thereby ending the fracas. Two years later, Arkansans drafted a new constitution and turned their attention to the future.

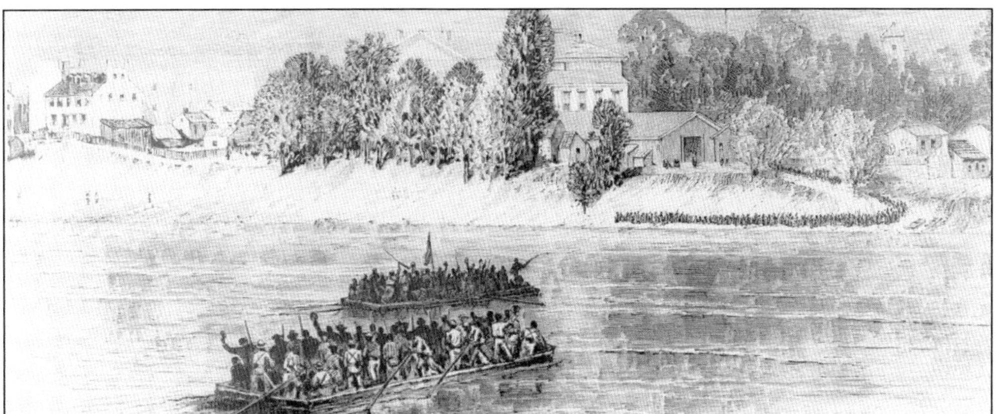

THE BROOKS-BAXTER WAR. This engraving from the May 2, 1874 issue of *Frank Leslie's Illustrated Newspaper* had the caption, "Anarchy in Arkansas—reinforcements for 'Governor' Brooks crossing the river at Little Rock." (UALR Library Archives.)

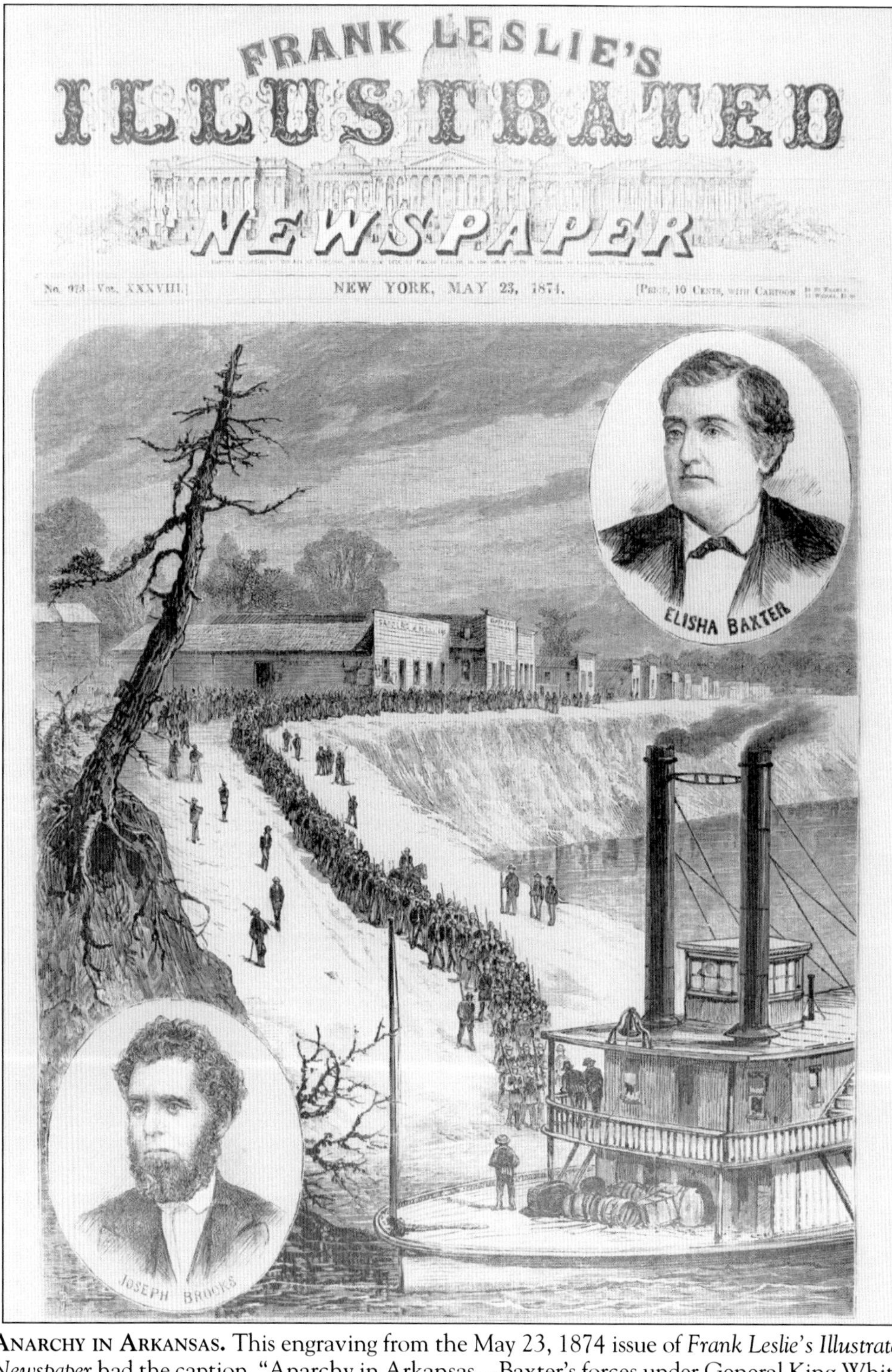

Anarchy in Arkansas. This engraving from the May 23, 1874 issue of *Frank Leslie's Illustrated Newspaper* had the caption, "Anarchy in Arkansas—Baxter's forces under General King White, embarking at Pine Bluff near Little Rock, for New Gascony, to attack Brooks troops." Note also the inset portraits of Mssrs. Brooks and Baxter. (UALR Library Archives.)

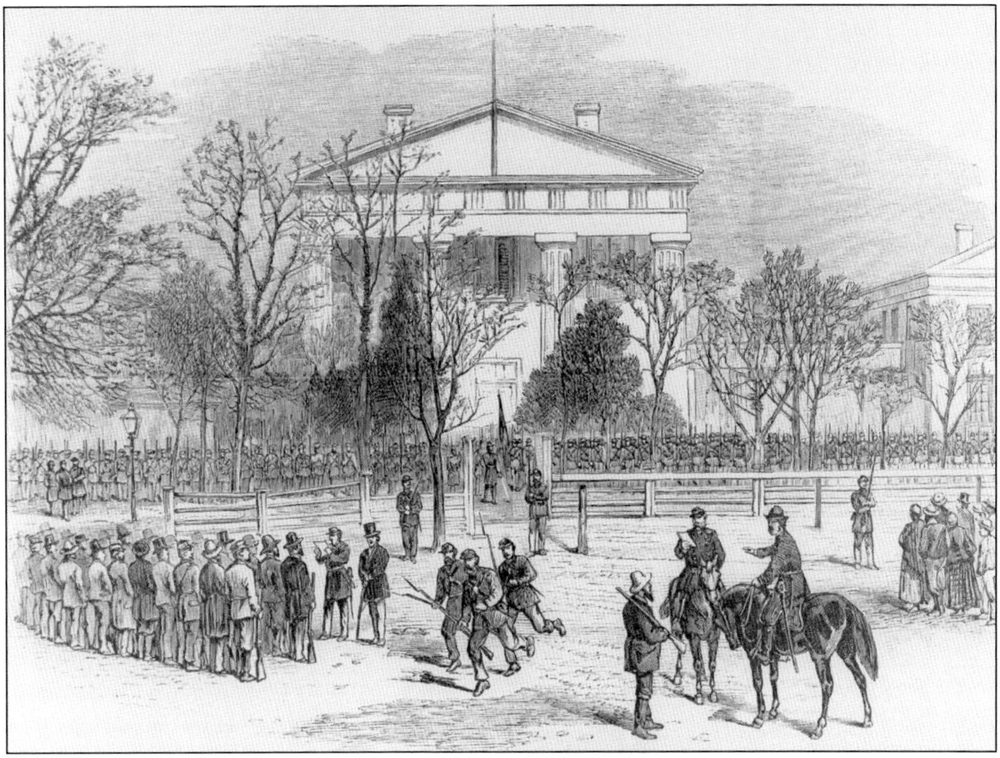

The "War" Continues. This engraving from the May 2, 1874 issue of *Frank Leslie's Illustrated Newspaper* carried the caption, "The Baxter-Brooks imbroglio—the capitol building at Little Rock defended by the troops of Pseudo-Governor Brooks." (UALR Library Archives.)

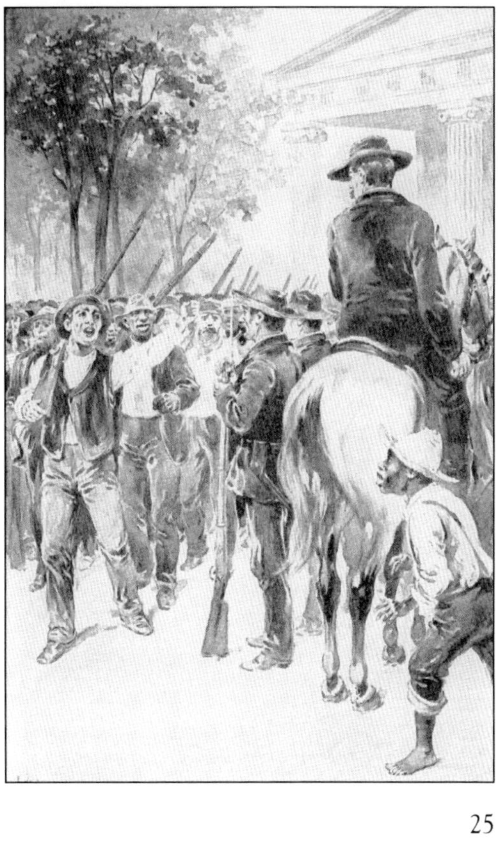

The Brooks-Baxter War in 1874, From a Painting by C. Kendric. This is the artist's view in front of the State House in Little Rock. A crowd is gathered to debate what became the most hotly contested election in Arkansas history. (UCA Archives.)

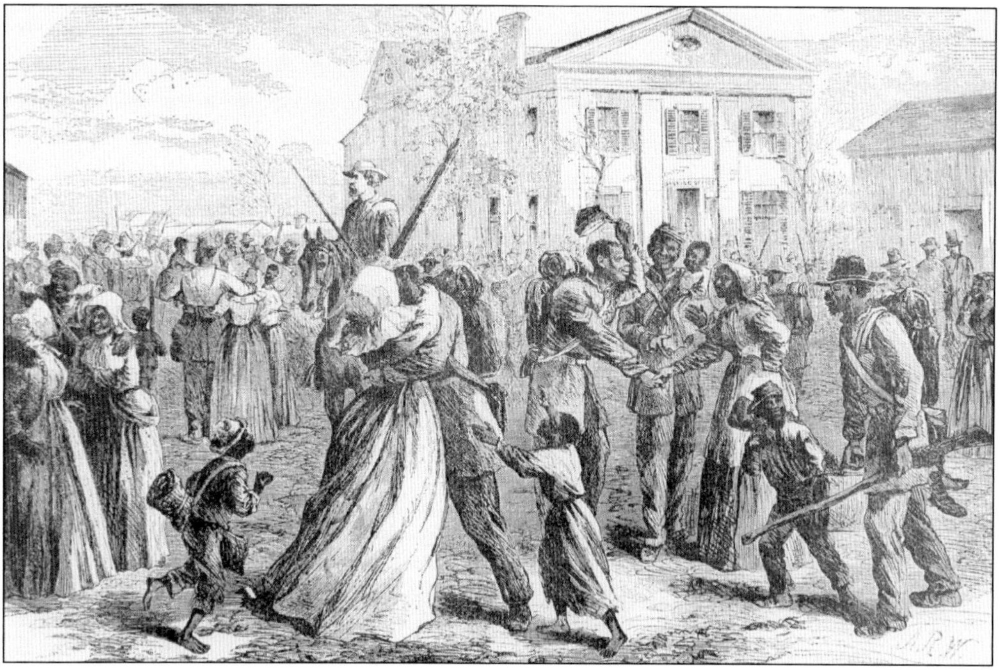

MUSTERED OUT UNION NEGRO VOLUNTEERS AT LITTLE ROCK IN 1866. This image was copied from an 1866 lithograph published in *Harper's Weekly*. (UCA Archives.)

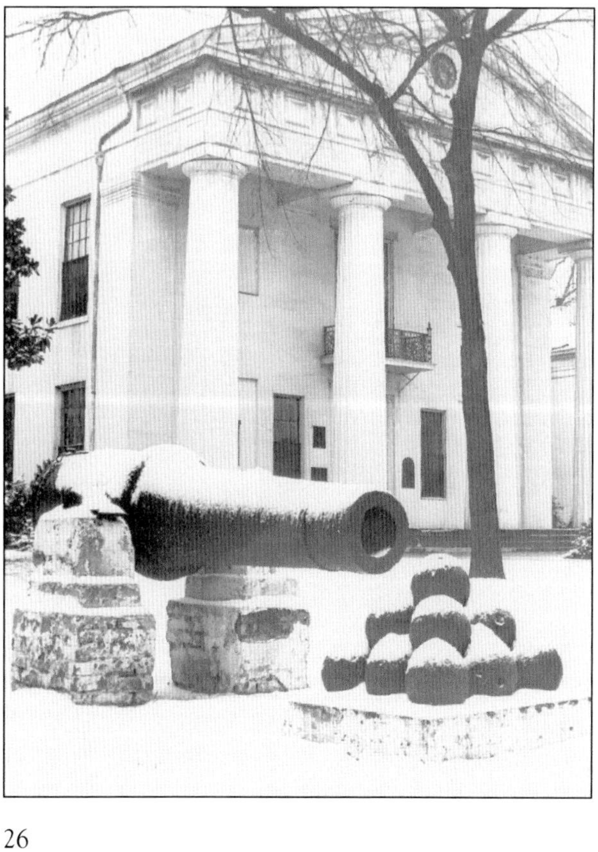

THE OLD STATE HOUSE IN LITTLE ROCK. Commonly described as one of the best surviving examples of Greek Revival architecture in the South, this building served as the state capitol from 1836 until 1911. The canon on the grounds, called "Lady Baxter," was last fired to celebrate the end of the Brooks-Baxter War in the 1870s. (Arkansas History Commission.)

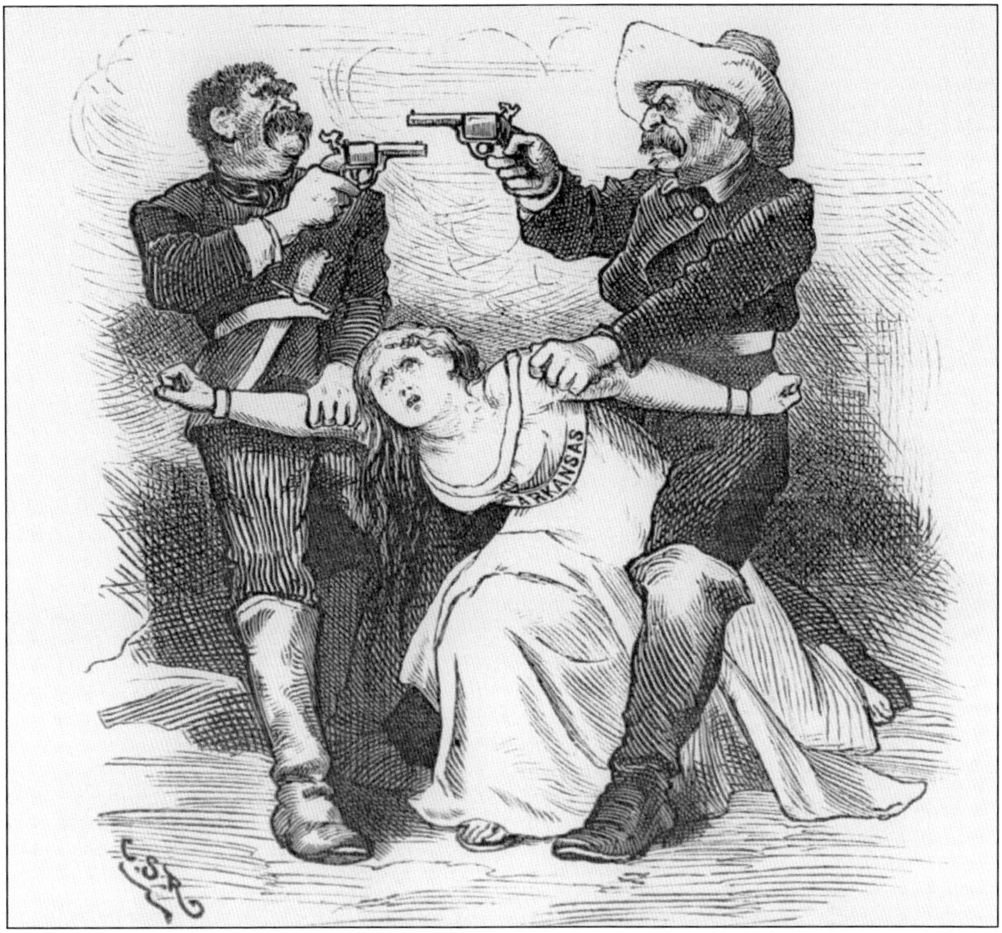

Choosing Not to Choose Sides. This political cartoon from the May 14, 1874, issue of *Harper's Weekly* entitled, "A plague o' both your houses!" suggests that not all Arkansans joined one of the factions in the Brooks-Baxter War. (UALR Library Archives.)

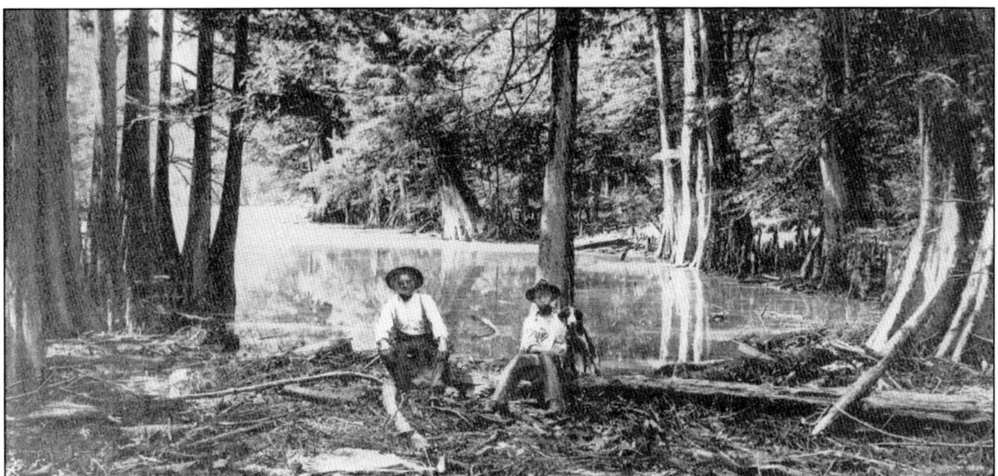

Cypress Brake Near Little Rock. (Arkansas History Commission.)

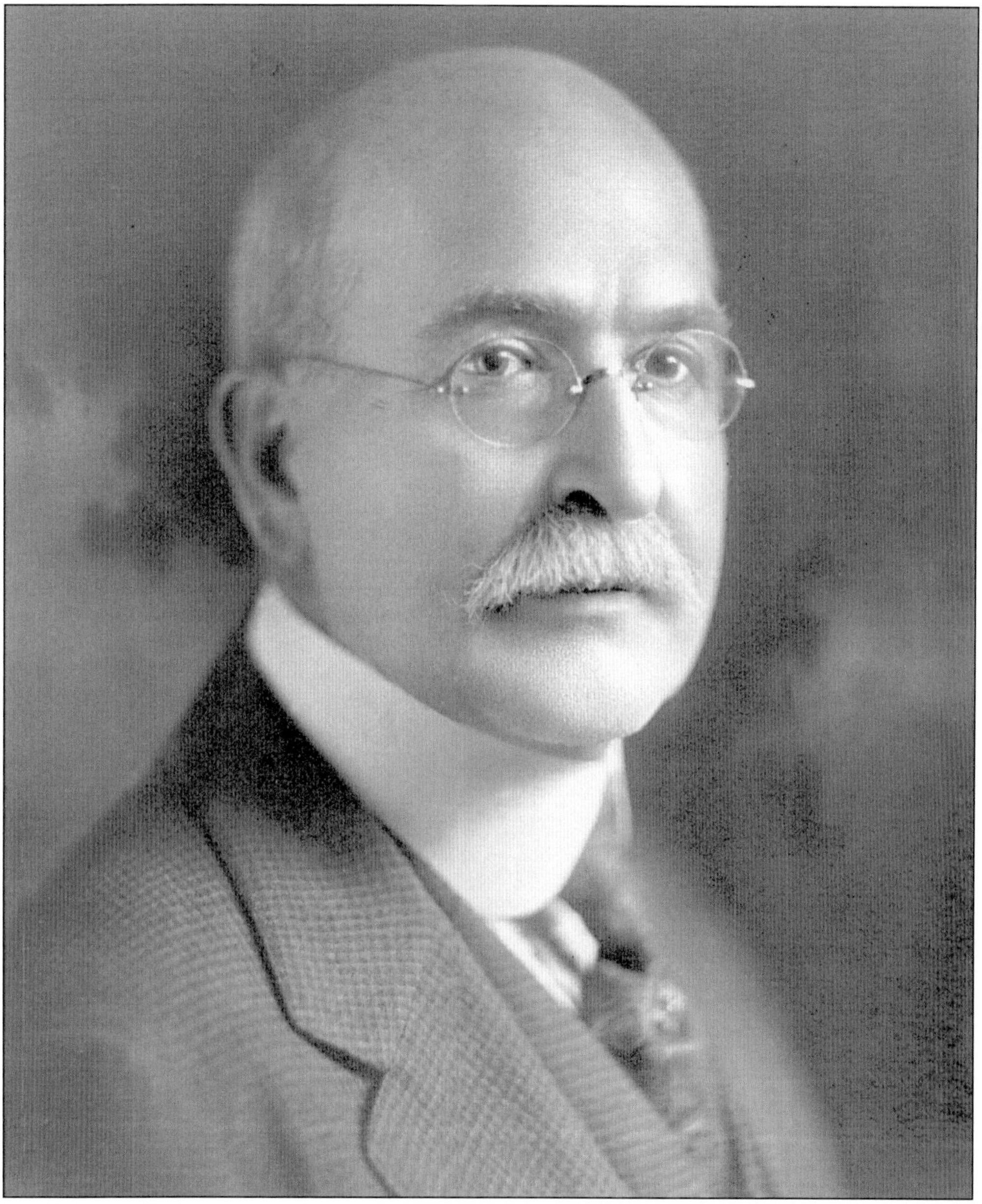

Dr. William B. Hughes, a Renaissance Man. After working as the sheriff of Monroe County for two years, Hughes studied law and was admitted to the Arkansas bar in 1857. After serving in the 23rd Arkansas Infantry as a captain and later lieutenant colonel, he served as a state legislator in 1866–67. Hughes became the state attorney general in 1874, simultaneously working as a delegate to the constitutional convention. He subsequently worked as a lawyer in Little Rock and was elected governor in 1884. He went on to earn a medical degree, and worked as a general practitioner in Little Rock. Next, Hughes studied eye, ear, nose, and throat specialties in New York, London, and Vienna, whereupon he returned to Little Rock to practice as a medical specialist. Most of all, Hughes was known for his sterling character, likable demeanor, and his ability to earn the respect of people in each of his chosen professions. (Arkansas History Commission.)

Four

Little Rock Prospers, Farmers Founder

After Arkansas got its new constitution, Little Rock's economy gradually improved, and a small but successful black middle class began to emerge. The economy really took off during the last two decades of the 19th century, thanks to the advent of railroad service connecting Little Rock with the rest of the country. While the city's population tripled and the community prospered, most Arkansans (about 90 percent) still lived on farms. The farmers were having a very tough time.

Cotton was still the principal cash crop throughout the state. While cotton earned 25 cents per pound in 1860, it only brought 5 cents by the mid-1890s, since the world market was glutted. Because it cost more than 5 cents per pound to produce cotton, Arkansas farmers were in a world of hurt. Farmers organized and became politically active throughout the South. A lawyer from Russellville who became governor, Jefferson Davis, had a unique ability to speak to the very soul of the powerless farmers who wanted to strike back at the system, appealing to them with vicious attacks upon bankers, blacks, businessmen, news editors, and the political establishment. He coined the term "redneck" as a badge of honor to differentiate hardworking farmers from their citified oppressors who wore high starched collars. The net result was a series of Arkansas laws that disenfranchised blacks and thereby removed their political power.

These so-called Jim Crow laws spawned an era of social segregation that would last through the Gilded Age and two world wars, until the Civil Rights Movement of the 1950s began effecting serious change on the political landscape.

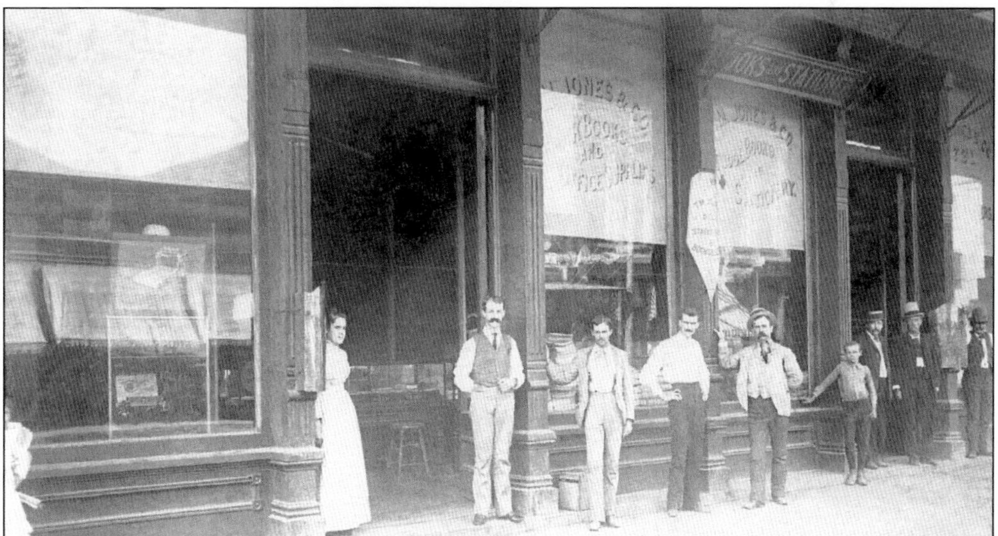

The Exterior of T.M. Jones & Company, about 1900. The man with the moustache standing at the door is T.M. Jones. The store sold general-interest books, law books, stationery, and office supplies. (Arkansas History Commission.)

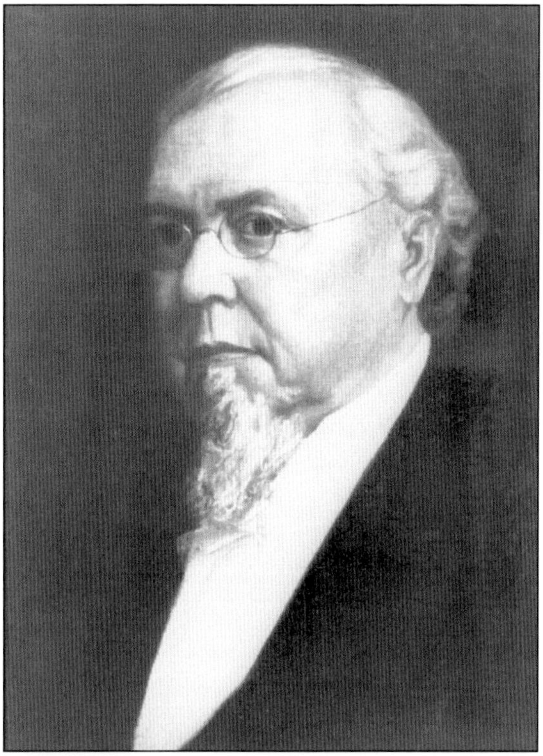

Dr. Philio Oliver Hooper in 1876. One of the most influential physicians of the 19th century, Hooper was a member of the Grand Lodge of Arkansas, International Order of Odd Fellows; he was also a Mason. Living on his own from the age of 16, Hooper graduated from Jefferson Medical School in Philadelphia in 1856. He married Georgia Carrol of Conway County two years later. After serving the Confederacy with distinction, he worked to establish the Arkansas State Medical Association to protect the public from the growing number of quacks and incompetent medical practitioners. He went on to help establish the Arkansas State Hospital and was the first dean of the University of Arkansas Medical School. (Arkansas History Commission.)

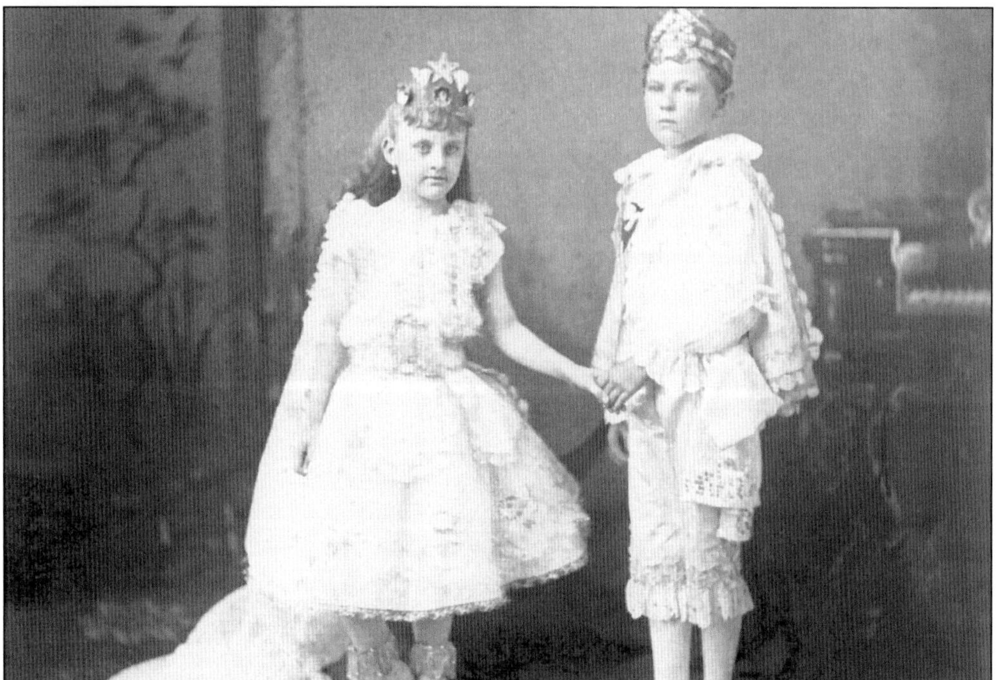

Dancing School Students, c.1910. Charles Knox Lincoln earned the title "King of the Dancing School," while Hattie Waters earned the title of "Queen". (Arkansas History Commission.)

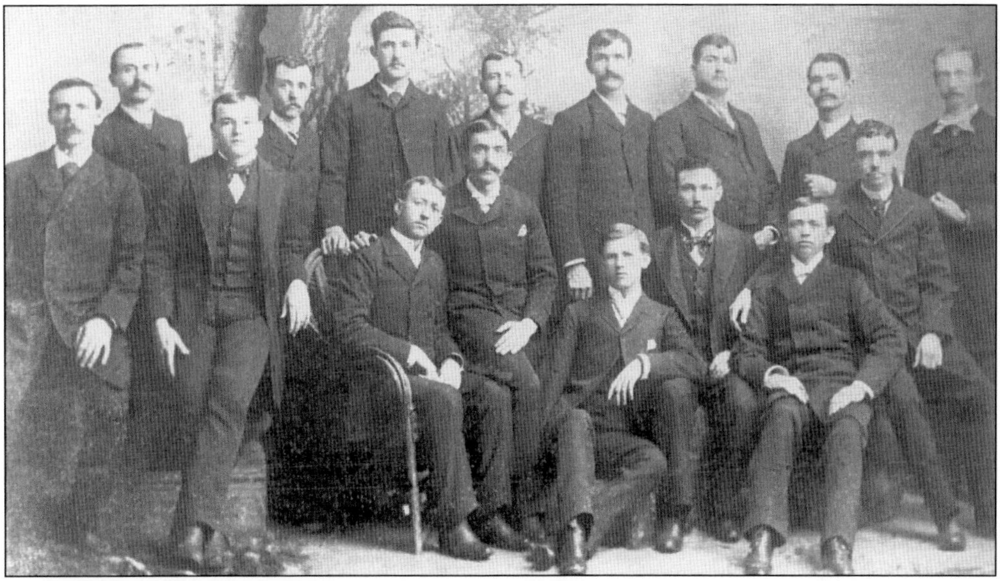

University of Arkansas School of Medicine, Class of 1890. The medical school was built in Little Rock rather than Fayetteville because the state capital could provide better facilities, doctors, and clinical opportunities. The medical students in this photo include Joseph G. Adams, David E. Evans, Columbus E. Gannaway, Fred A. Hipolite, George K. Mason, Louis E. McCurry, Frank P. Payne, Isaac M. Paynor, John W. Pipkin, Hassel Prothro, John W. Ringgold, Robert J. Smith, Moore F. Stanfield, Calvin B. Stark, George A. Waters, and Neal Wood. (Arkansas History Commission.)

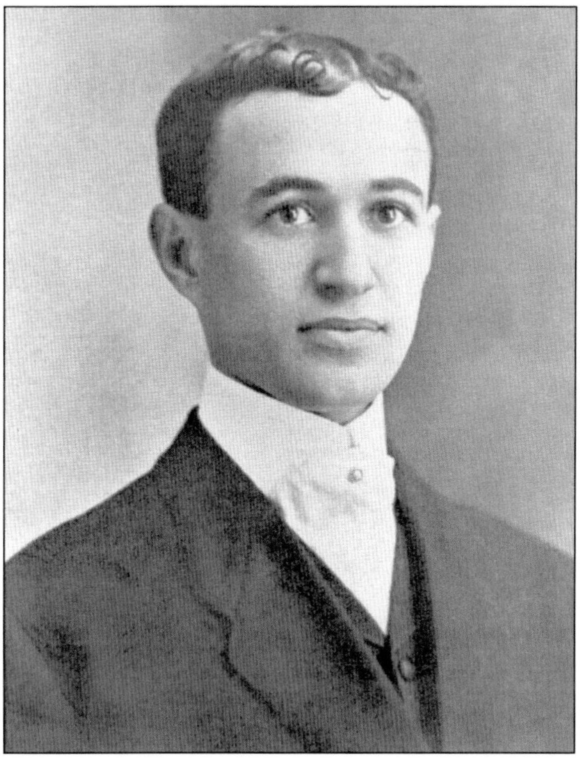

Ike Kempner, a Retail Merchant and Jewish Leader in Little Rock. (UCA Archives.)

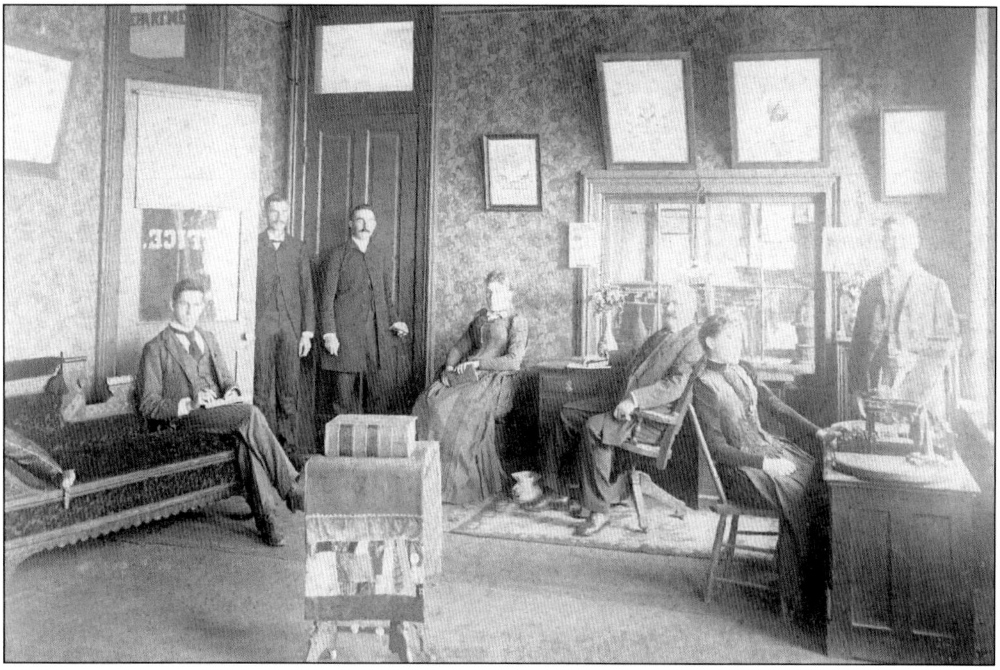

Draughon's Business College. The school was founded in 1874 as the Little Rock Commercial College. The privately owned college was located at 203-1/2 Main Street in Little Rock. Miles A. Stone, who died in 1937, is at the desk in the center of the photograph. His sister, Mattie Stone (Mrs. Will) Bigger is on his right at the end of the desk. Will Bigger worked in the silver department at Pfeifer's. (Arkansas History Commission.)

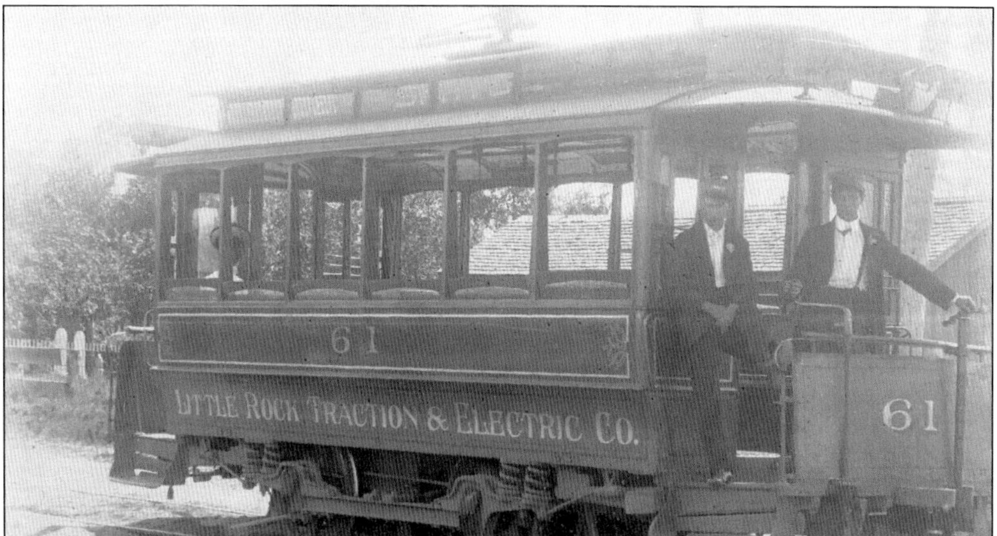

Streetcar Number 61 of the Little Rock Traction and Electric Company. The first streetcars used mules to pull coaches along a rail system. A second company began service in 1888 using steam-powered streetcars. The first electric-powered streetcar appeared in Little Rock on November 24, 1891. The new company bought out the two older ones and expanded service with 28 electric cars that cost $3,300 each, dramatically improving the quality of life for the residents of Argenta and Little Rock. (Arkansas History Commission.)

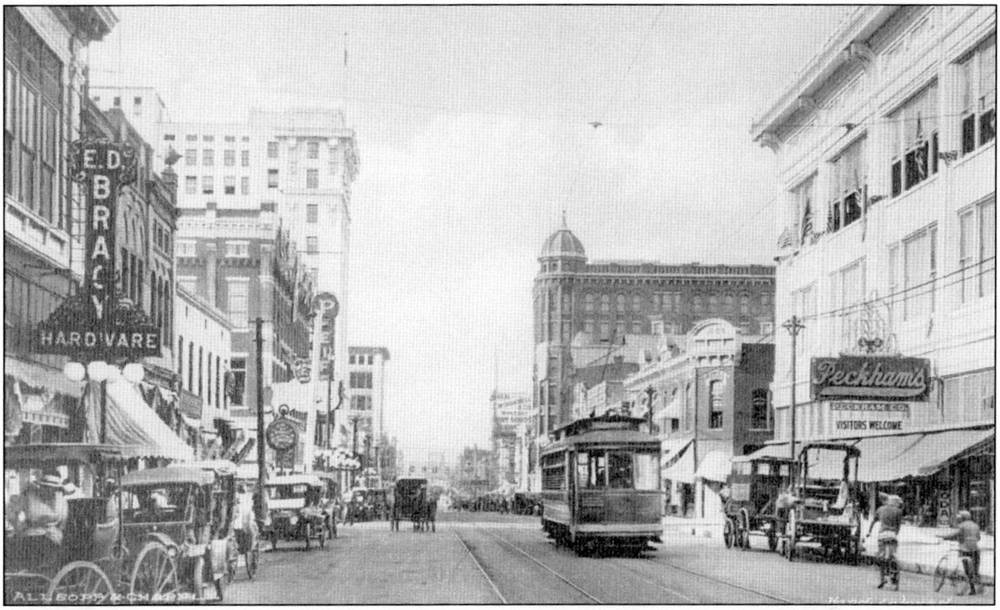

MAIN STREET, LOOKING NORTH, IN DOWNTOWN LITTLE ROCK ABOUT 1900. Printed by the Albertype Company of Brooklyn, New York, this was one of several dozen sample cards sent as a proposal to Freeman's Souvenir Shop at 3315 Roosevelt Road in Little Rock on April 12, 1948. Also shown is Albertype's rate card, which was provided so Miss B. Freeman could order custom postcards for her shop. The Albertype Company was established in 1887 and provided custom postcards to "Many of America's Religious Institutions, Hotels, Resorts, Book, Stationery and Drug Stores, Schools, Colleges, Academies, Museums, Historic and Religious Shrines, Scenic Wonders and many other places." (Arkansas History Commission.)

The Albertype Company

ESTABLISHED IN 1887

250 ADAMS STREET, BROOKLYN 1, N. Y.

THE FINEST AMERICAN MADE

VIEW POSTCARDS

TO ORDER BY THE ALBERTYPE PROCESS OF PHOTOGRAPHIC REPRODUCTION

		EACH	1.000	2.000	3.000	5.000	CARDS OF A SUBJECT
PLATINO-PHOTO-BLACK	Full size or with margins	@	$12.00	$11.50	$11.00	$10.50	Shipment in 5 weeks
OLIVE-BLUE	....	"	12.50	12.00	11.50	11.00	" " 6 "
SEPIA-ON-IVORY	....	"	13.00	12.50	12.00	11.50	" " 6 "
SEPIA-DOUBLETONE	....	"	15.00	14.50	14.00	13.50	" " 7 "
HAND-COLORED	....	"	20.00	19.75	19.50	19.25	" " 8 "

Per 1000 Cards

Terms: Net 30 days. F.O.B. Brooklyn, New York City

Above prices are based on regular view cards of buildings and scenery. For special postcards of Private Residences, Flowered Subjects, Portraits, Paintings, Museum Objects, Drawings, Etchings and Advertising subjects, please ask for quotations, stating style and quantity desired.

When ordering postcards please send photographs with desired titles written on reverse side; if films write on margin or envelope. We remove defects if not difficult, Special Retouching at a moderate charge.
Descriptive caption at top of message space $1.00 to $2.00 extra per thousand cards.
Do not write on the face of the view. Proofs are not possible in our process due to its special nature.
If Handcolored postcards, give color directions, or duplicate photo, tinted for guide.
Present day paper stocks are good but variable, we use the best we can buy suitable for our process.

VIEW BOOKLETS, VIEW ALBUMS, VIEW FOLDERS and SCENIC PICTURES of various sizes by estimate.

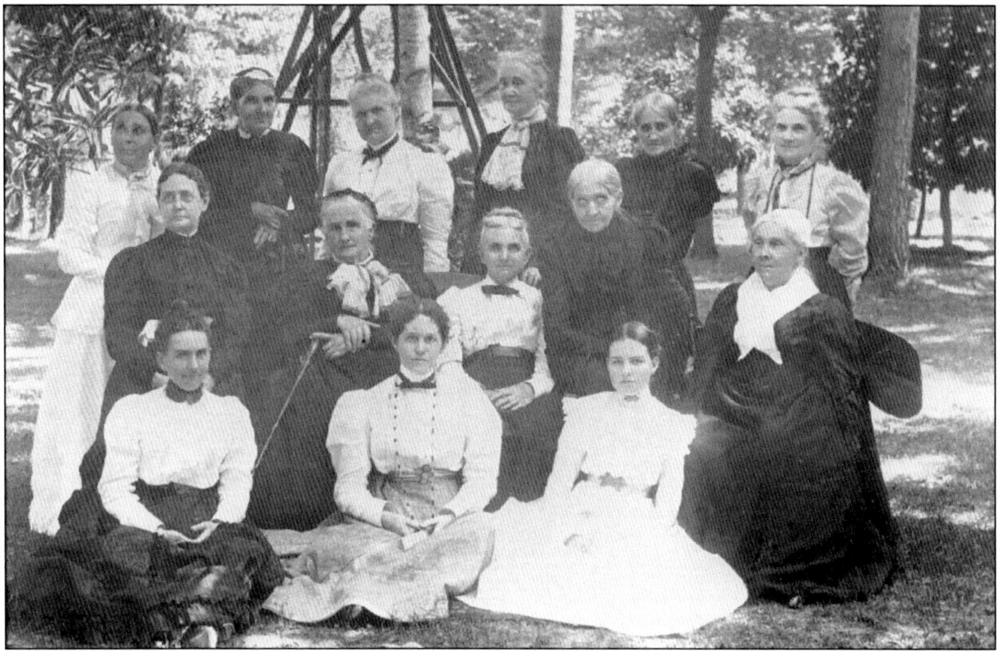

Spend-the-Day Party. This was a birthday party held for Mrs. John M. Rose c. 1890 at her home. She is in the center of the front row. Others in the picture include Mrs. O'Neal, Mrs. Van Etter, Mrs. Boone, Mrs. Suell, Mrs. John Peay, Mrs. Carroll, Mrs. McAlimont, and Mrs. Deshon. (Arkansas History Commission.)

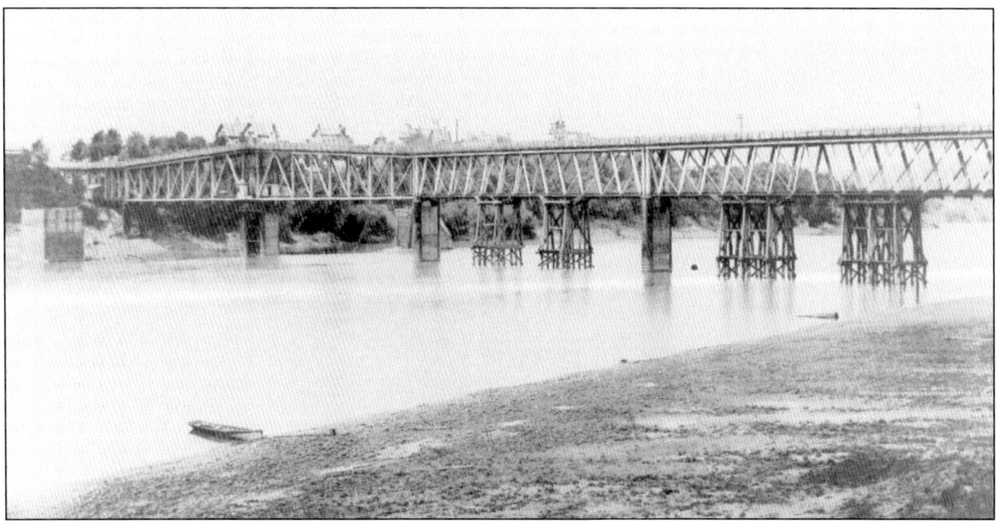

Baring Cross Bridge in 1890. English banker Alexander Baring financed the construction of a vehicular and railroad bridge over the Arkansas River to connect Argenta with Little Rock. Railroad shops were built at the north end of the bridgehead and soon a village called Baring Cross developed there as well. Argenta eventually absorbed the community. The bridge continued in service until 1927, when a flood washed it away. It was replaced two years later. (Arkansas History Commission.)

ROSE CITY CARRIAGE WORKS. The Carriage Works shares the building with Upton and Webster. (Arkansas History Commission.)

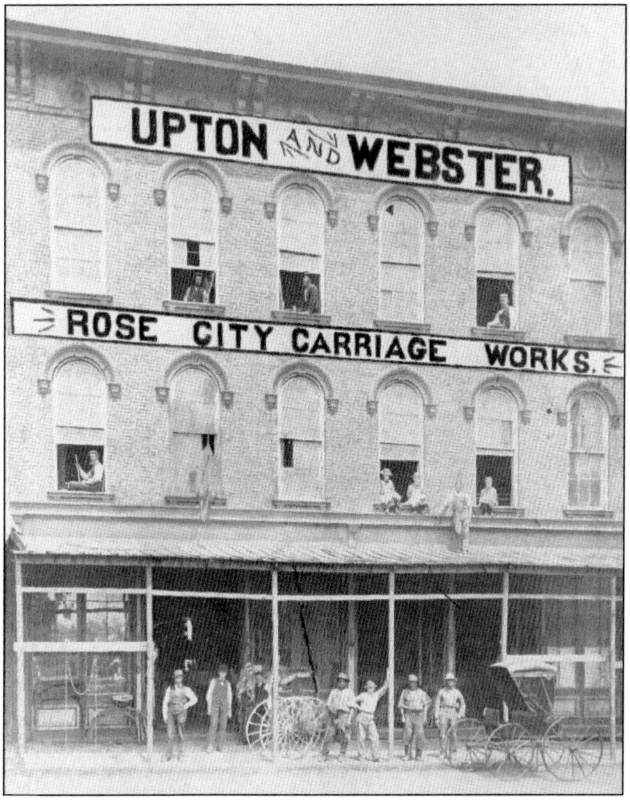

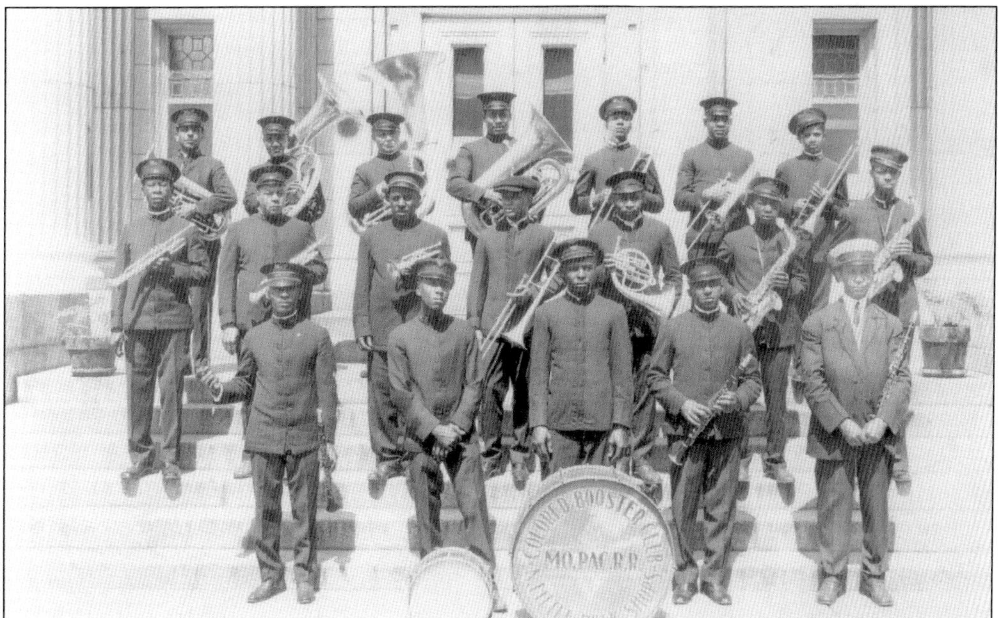

MISSOURI PACIFIC RAILROAD'S COLORED BOOSTER CLUB SHOP BAND OF NORTH LITTLE ROCK. Booster bands, city bands, and even family bands were popular throughout Southern society at the turn of the 19th century. (Arkansas History Commission.)

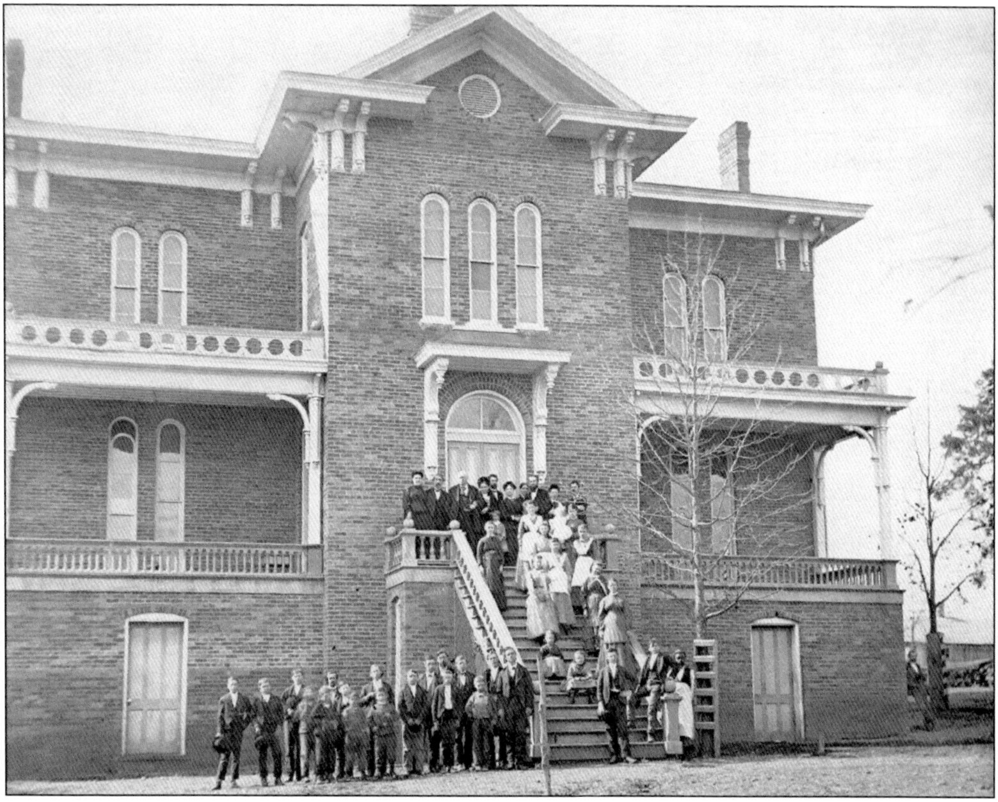

The Deaf-Mute Institute in Little Rock about 1880. Subsequently renamed the Arkansas School for the Deaf, the school's site at Markham Street and Park Avenue commanded a broad view of the Arkansas River and Big Rock. Before 1868, when this land was donated to the state to educate deaf-mutes, the brush-covered bluff was prime habitat for hunting wild turkeys. (Arkansas History Commission.)

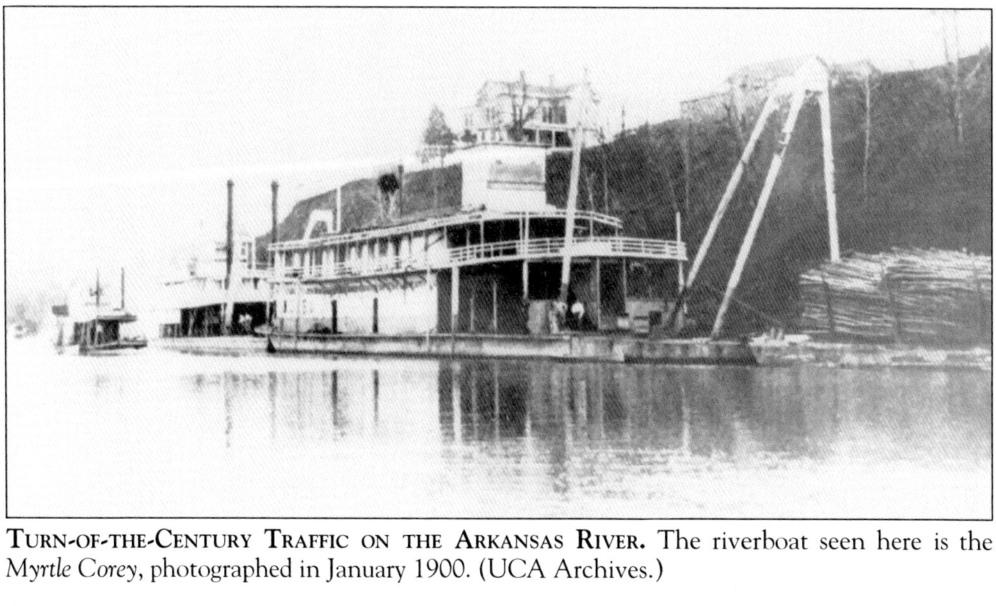

Turn-of-the-Century Traffic on the Arkansas River. The riverboat seen here is the *Myrtle Corey*, photographed in January 1900. (UCA Archives.)

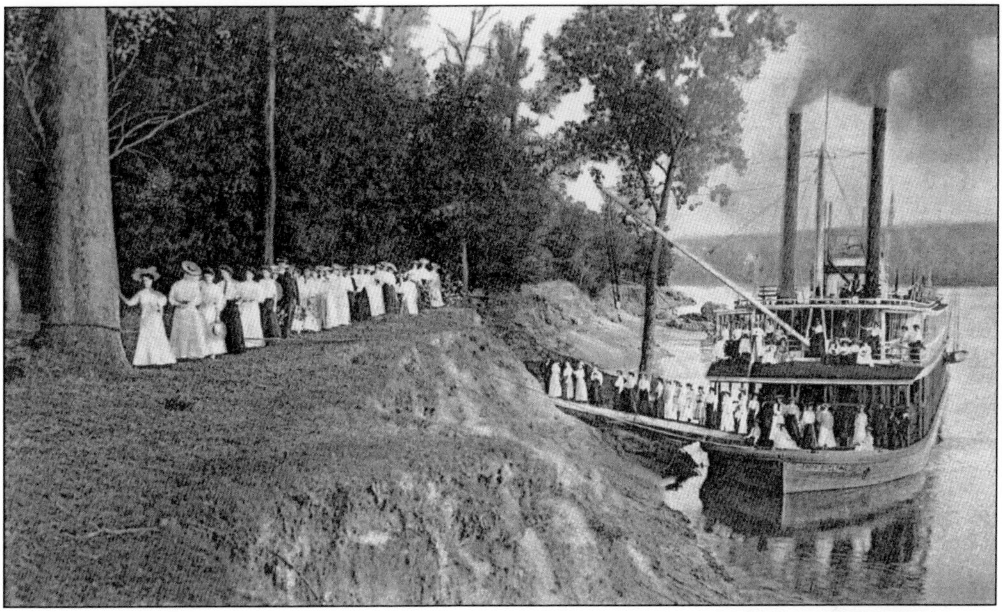

Postcard of an Excursion Boat on the Arkansas River at Little Rock c.1900. (Arkansas History Commission.)

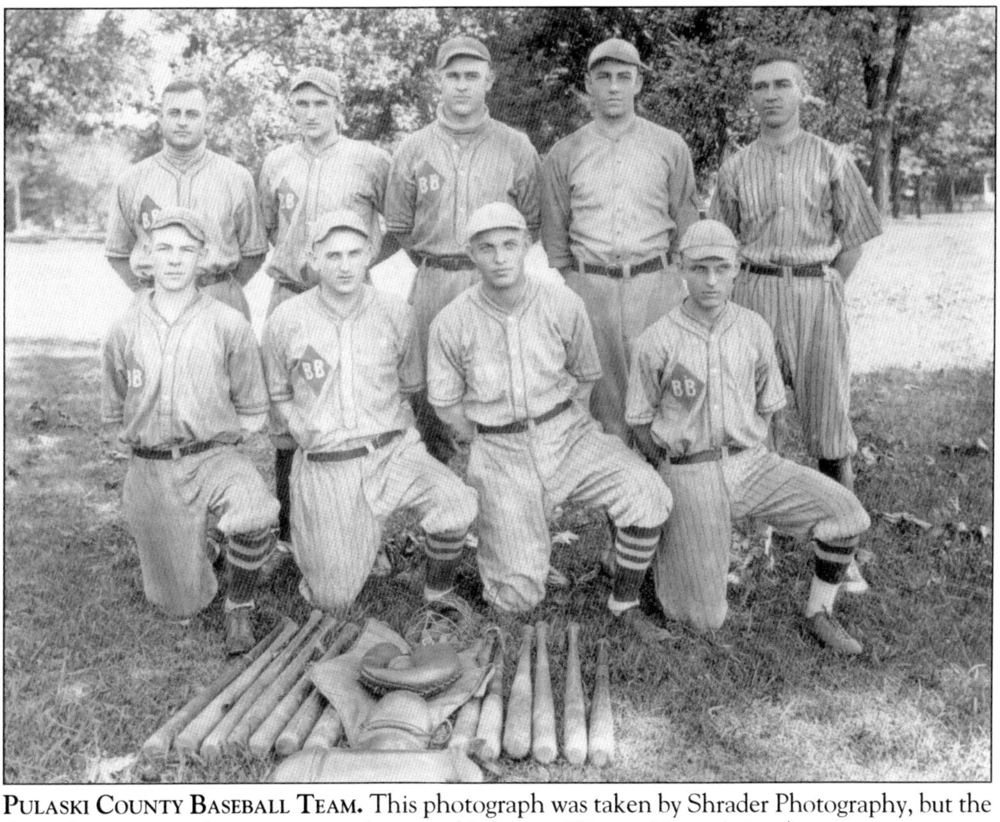

Pulaski County Baseball Team. This photograph was taken by Shrader Photography, but the date when it was taken remains unknown. (Arkansas History Commission.)

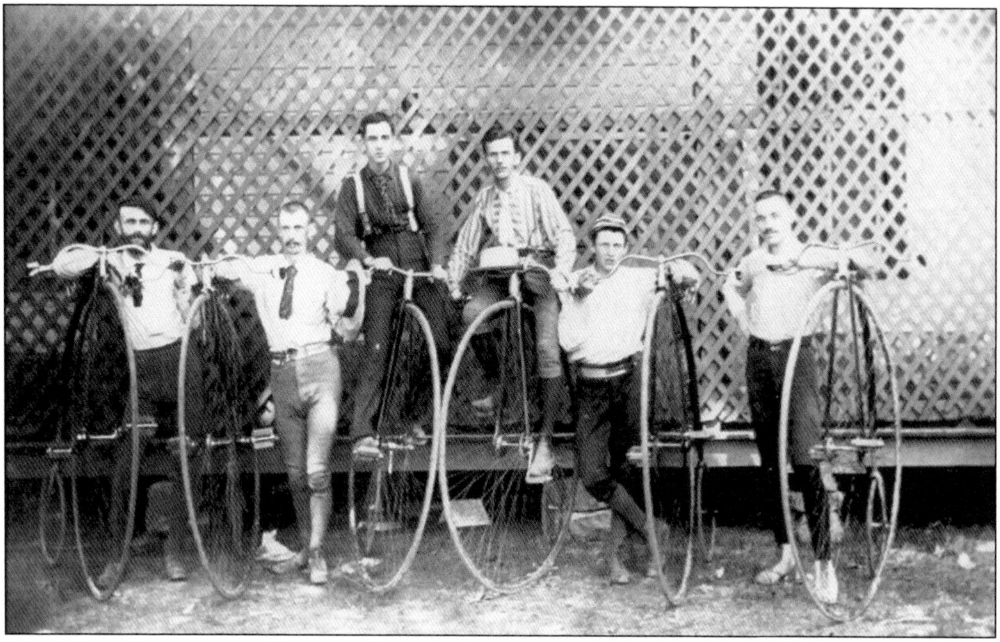

Men With Velocipedes (Bicycles) in the Late 1880s. Many sermons of the day condemned velocipedes—cycling on Sunday was viewed by some as a desecration of the Sabbath. (Arkansas History Commission.)

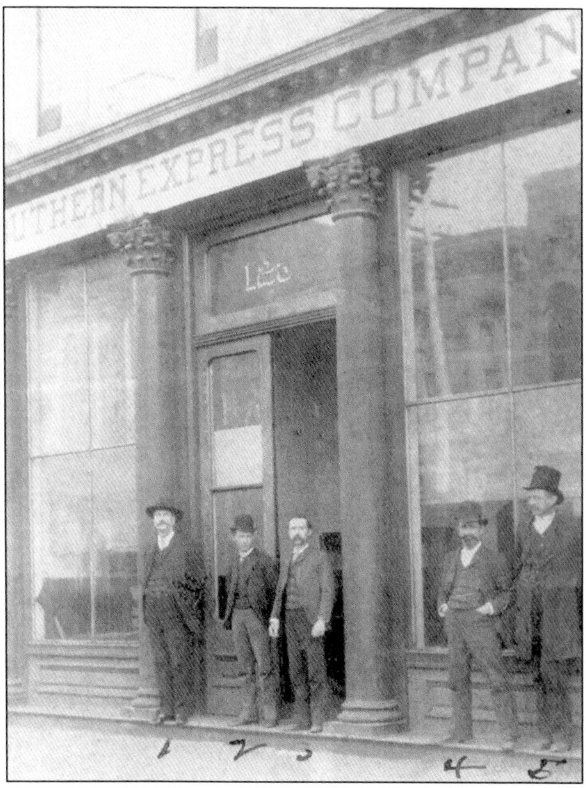

Southern Express Company in 1884. The numbers written on the photograph represent (1) John F. Boyle, (2) Thomas F. Oury, (3) J.M. Bracy, (4) J. Menkus, and (5) F.M. Fulk. The Southern Express Company was located at the corner of Markham and Louisiana streets. (Arkansas History Commission.)

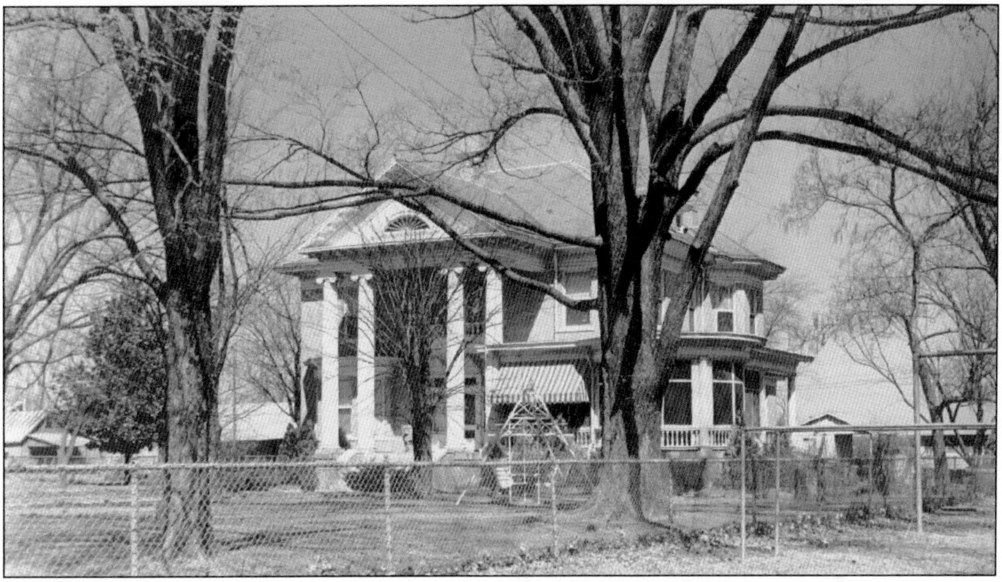

THE HOUSE OF CHARLES N. ALEXANDER. Alexander was a plantation owner, and this house was located just east of Little Rock in Young township. He came to the area in 1879, raising cattle and cotton on 2,500 acres. A founding member of the Little Rock Country Club, he remained a formidable golfer well into his eighties. He also served as a director of the Exchange National Bank and was president of the Rose City Cotton Oil Mills. (Arkansas History Commission.)

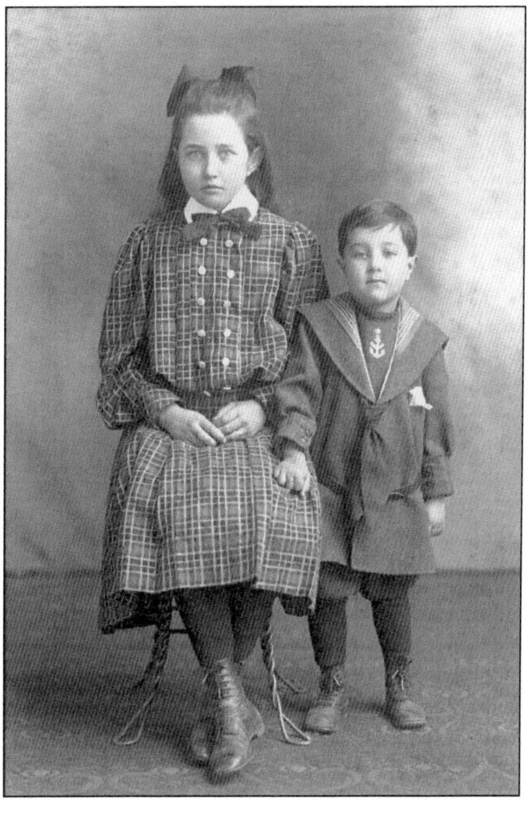

OLIVE AND JACOB KAUFFMAN, DATE UNKNOWN. (Arkansas History Commission.)

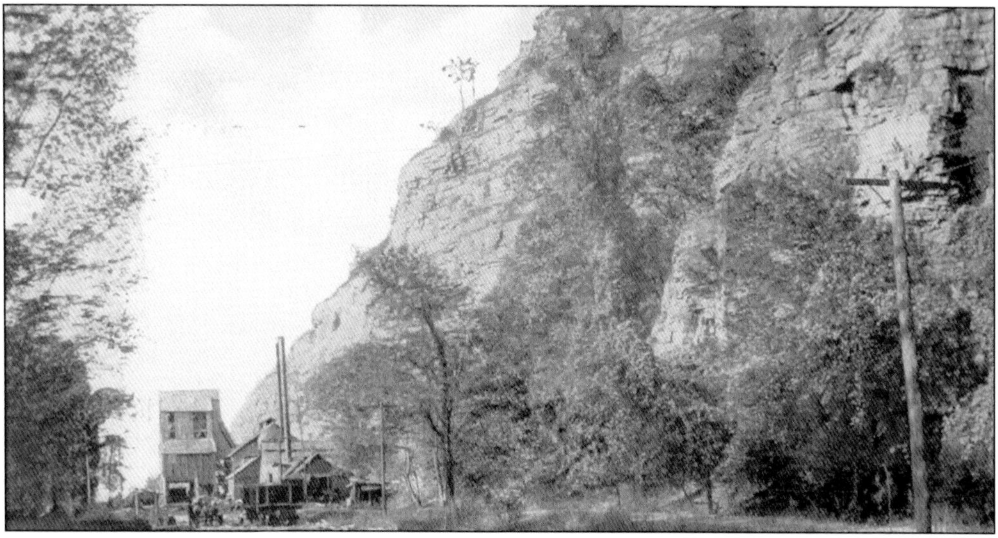

The Rock Crusher at Big Rock. Called *Le Rocher Français* by French explorer Jean-Baptiste Bernard de La Harpe in 1722, this landmark lies just upstream from *Le Petit Rocher* on the north shore of the Arkansas River. J.H. Smith of 1607 Main Street sent this postcard to Mrs. H. Spurlick, Box 402, Pine Bluff on August 13, 1912. It required 2 cents for postage. (Arkansas History Commission.)

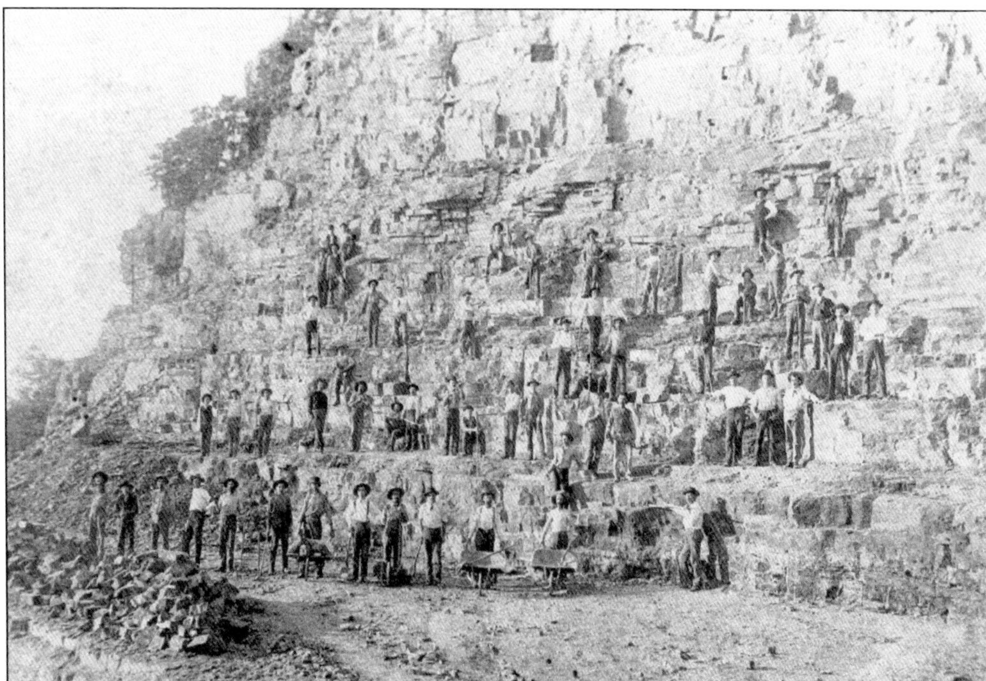

View of W.S Works in 1892 at Big Rock. Charles Ed Owens, overseer; Andy Amrhien, foreman; George Witsell, sub-foreman; Henry Smith, sub-foreman; Frank Watkins, recorder; Harry Hopkins, recorder; Capt. H. S. Tabor, Esq., in charge. (Arkansas History Commission.)

CAPTAIN JENKS BROWN, SKIPPER OF THE STEAMBOAT *LITTLE ROCK*, c.1880. (UCA Archives.)

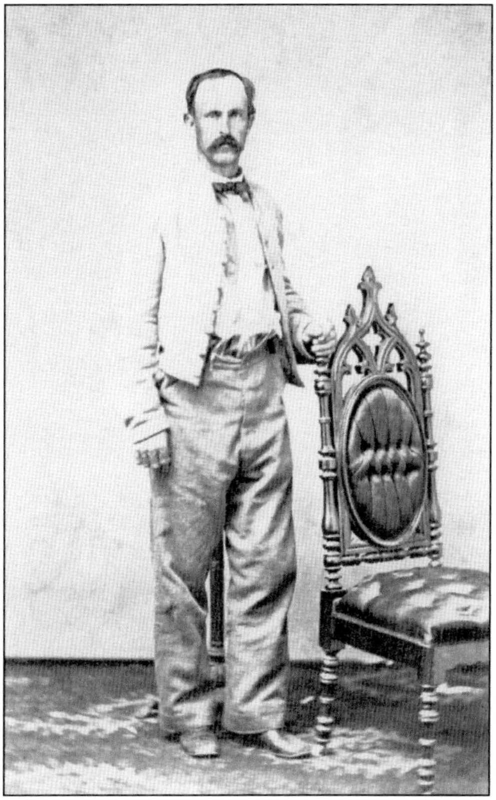

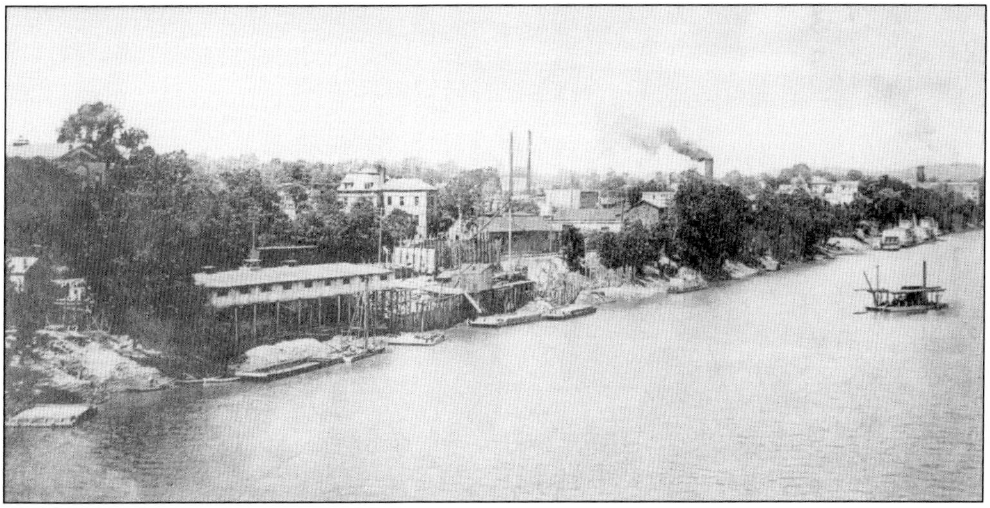

THE WATERFRONT BEHIND THE OLD STATE HOUSE c.1900, TEEMED WITH RIVER TRAFFIC. This was a tough area until the 1880s, with particularly rambunctious areas known as Battle Row, Fighting Alley, and Hell's Half Acre. When the area's most popular saloon and dance hall, the Ocean Wave, burned down in April 1879, the catastrophe destroyed the exuberant vitality of the place. (Arkansas History Commission.)

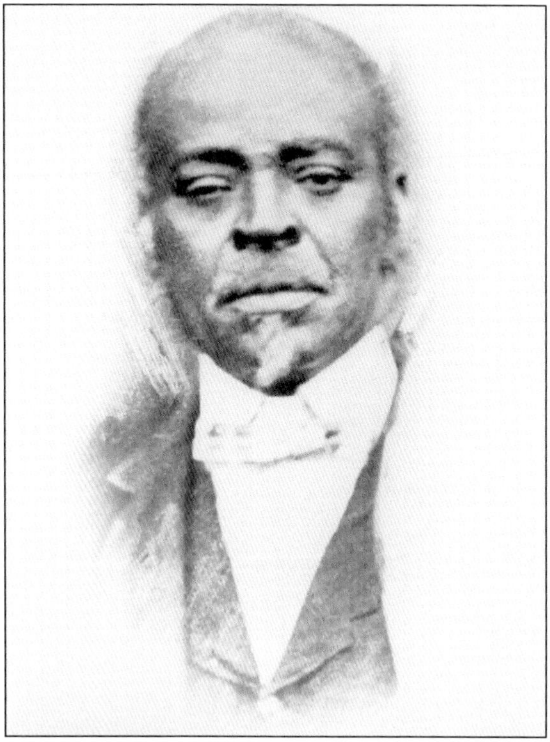

Isaac T. Gillam about 1900. He came to Arkansas as a slave with his mother, enlisting in the 2nd Arkansas Infantry, African Descent, after the Federals captured Little Rock. He returned after the war, married, and became a blacksmith—one of the few skilled trades available to blacks at the time. He eventually served as a state legislator, Little Rock city councilman, and Pulaski County coroner. (UCA Archives.)

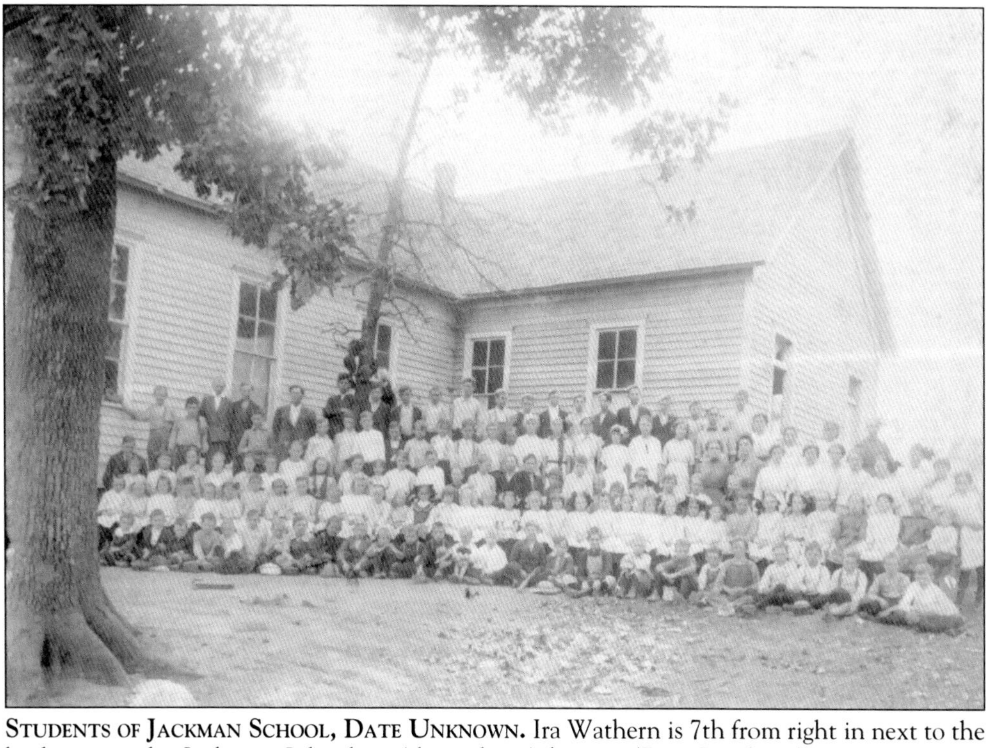

Students of Jackman School, Date Unknown. Ira Wathern is 7th from right in next to the back row at the Jackman School in Alexander, Arkansas. (Doss Reed Collection, Arkansas History Commission.)

George O. Heinrich, Manager of the German Information and Immigration Bureau of Arkansas. Born in Dippoldiswalde, Saxony, on February 11, 1866, Heinrich had a university education in pharmacy and planting. After traveling extensively throughout Europe, Asia, Australia, Africa, and the southern part of North America, Heinrich worked first as a pharmacist and subsequently as a planter and manager of a large plantation until 1907. That was when he became the manager of the GII Bureau, which provided "authentic information" regarding resources available in Arkansas for all home-seekers among the German, Austro-Hungarian, Swiss, Dutch, and Luxembourger immigrants coming to the United States. (UCA Archives.)

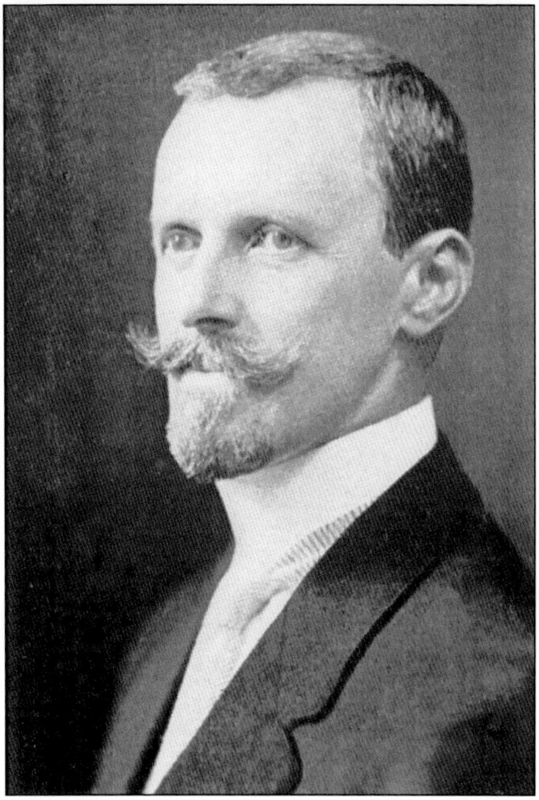

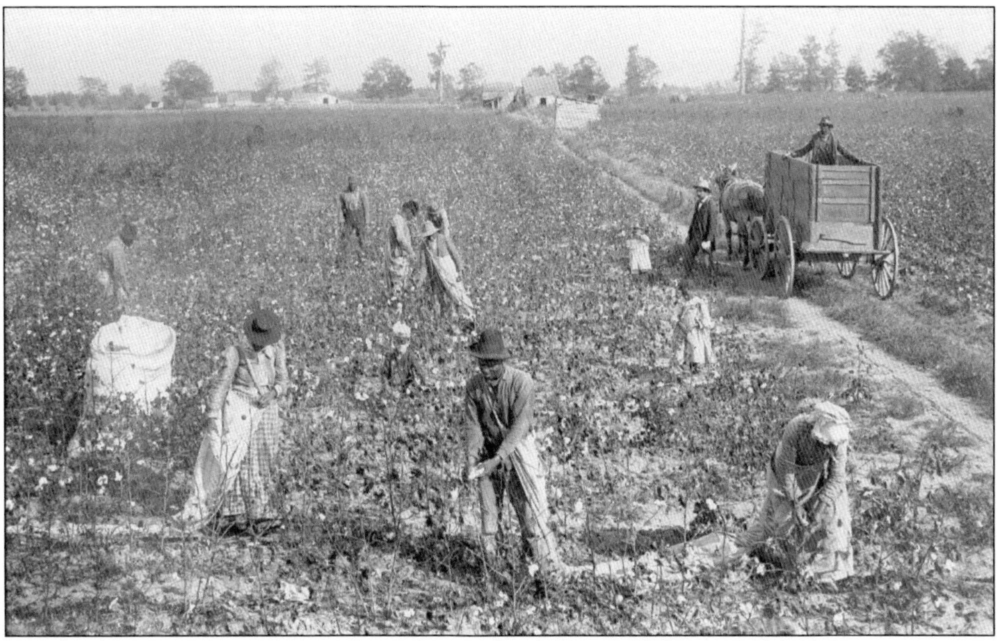

Cotton Picking Near Little Rock c.1880. (Arkansas History Commission.)

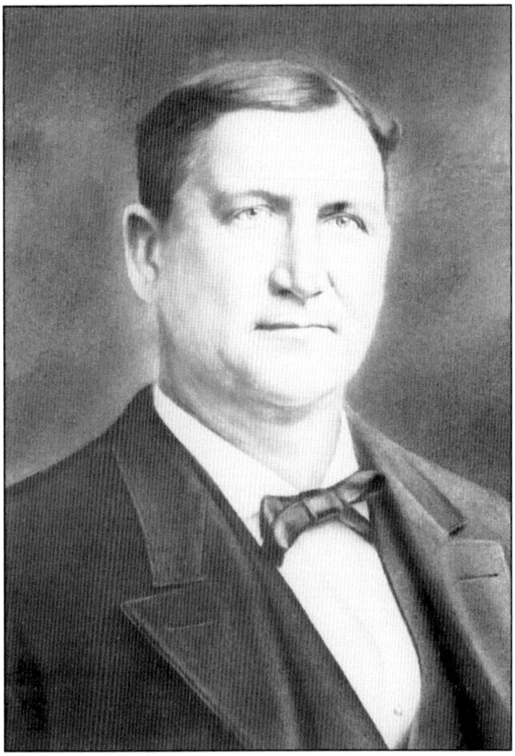

Jeff Davis, Who Served Three Terms as Governor Beginning in 1901. While he is often remembered for reforming the state's disgraceful prison system, he actually achieved those reforms as attorney general before he became governor. A brilliant orator with an uncanny knack at spellbinding his audience, Davis described himself as "a Hard Shell Baptist in religion. I believe in foot-washing, saving your seed potatoes, and paying your honest debts." (Arkansas History Commission.)

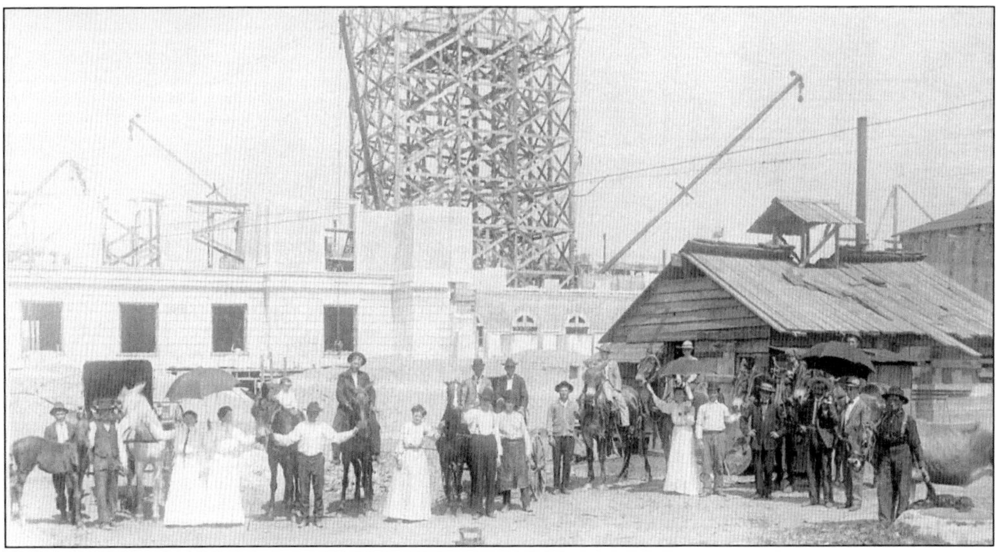

The New State Capitol. After the cornerstone was laid in 1900, work on the new state capitol progressed very slowly and then stopped in 1907. Newly elected governor George W. Donaghey, who was elected in part for promising to complete the building, sent government engineers to inspect the work. This revealed that all the floors would have to be torn out and replaced, and much of the other work would need to be strengthened and fireproofed. The original contractor was fired, and Donaghey appointed a new commission to oversee completion of the project. While the legislature and some state offices moved to the capitol in 1911, the building was not fully completed until 1917. (Arkansas History Commission.)

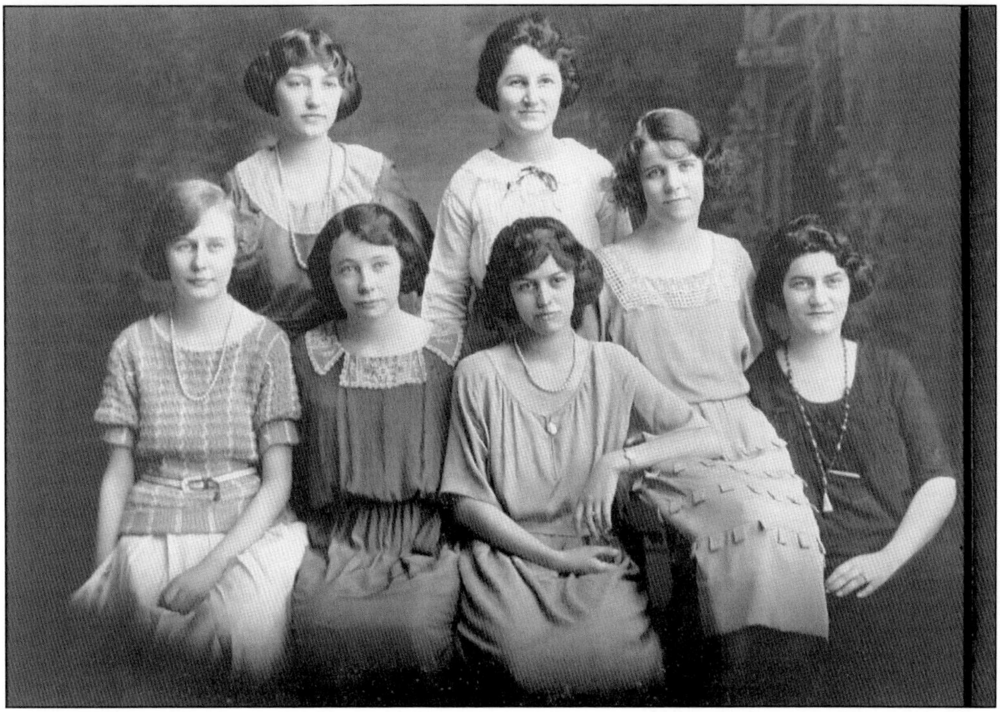

WOMEN WHO WORKED FOR THE C.J. LINCOLN COMPANY, c.1892. C.J. Lincoln was president of the company, Walter Wittenberg was the secretary, and W.R. Eckford was the treasurer. Located at 112 North Main in Little Rock, the company was a wholesale supplier of drugs, liqueurs, tobacco, dental supplies, paints, oils, stationery, and other goods. Its phone number was 112. (Arkansas History Commission.)

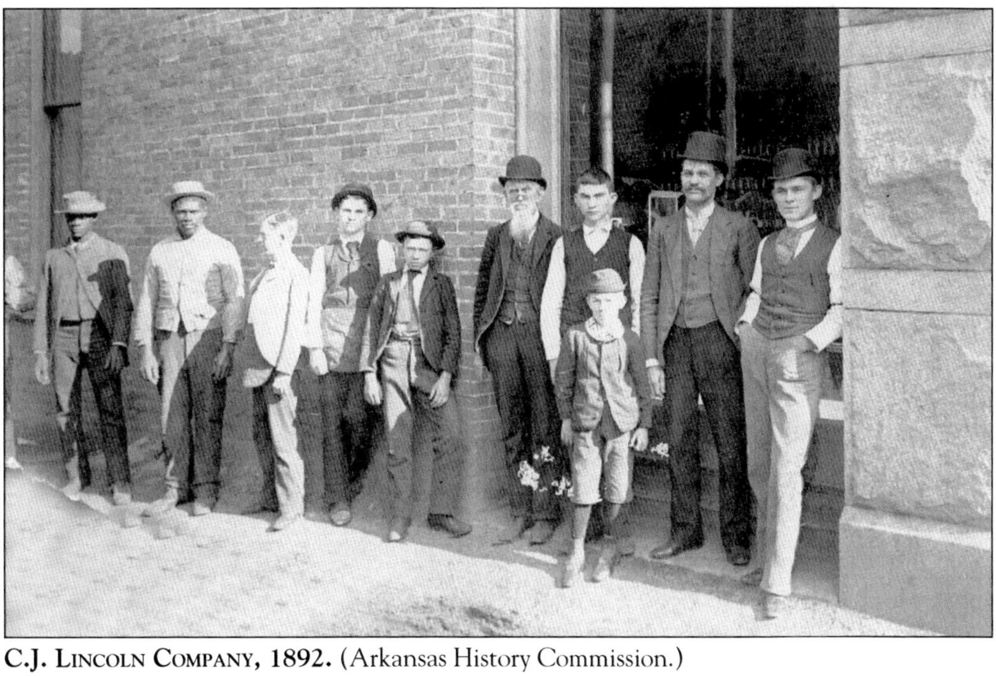

C.J. LINCOLN COMPANY, 1892. (Arkansas History Commission.)

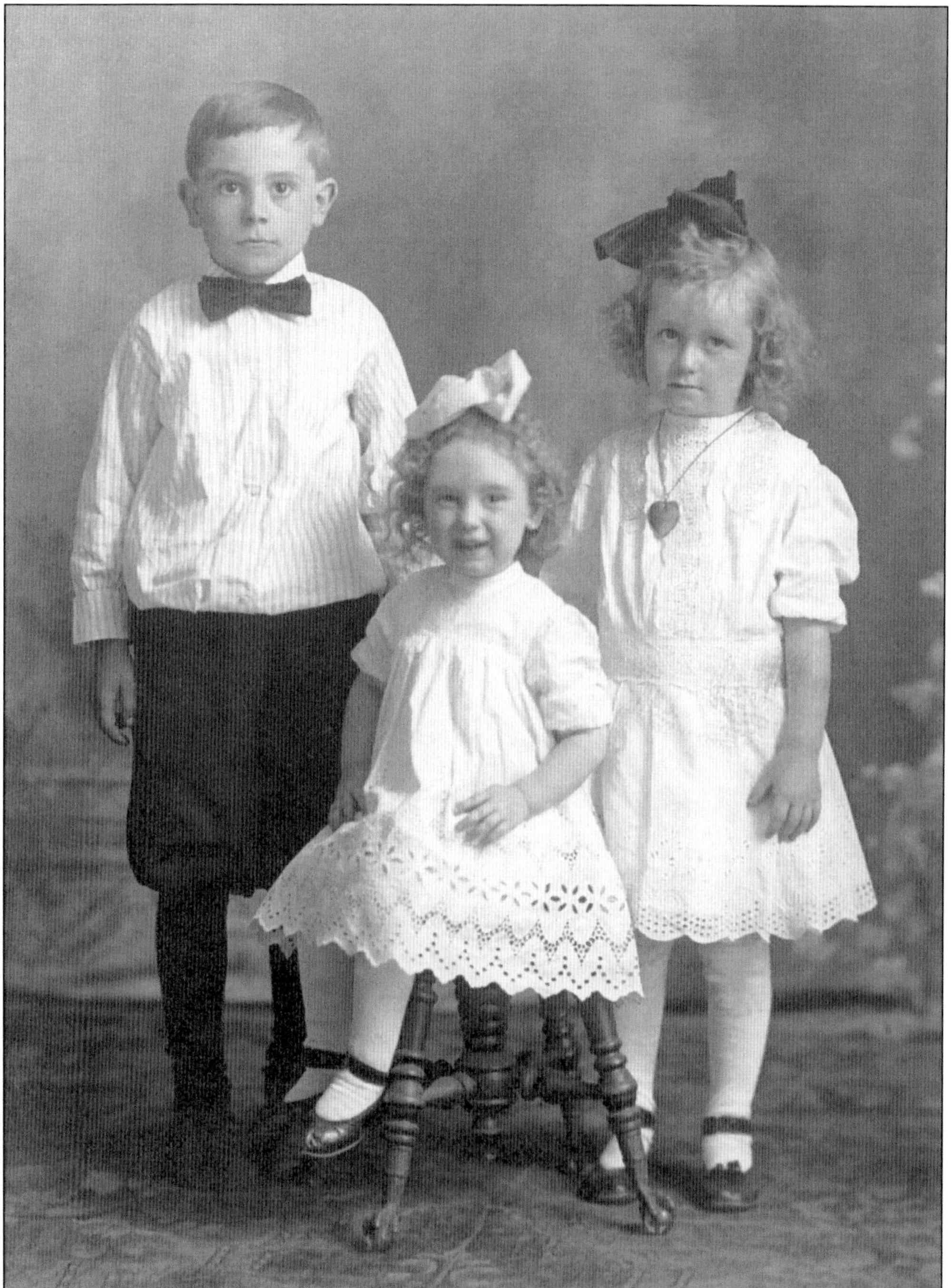

JOHN, LEONA, AND LUCILLE PFAUSER IN 1911. They were the children of Anthony Pfauser and his second wife. This photograph was taken by Kettering of Little Rock. (Arkansas History Commission.)

Five

THE EARLY 1900S

Little Rock had grown a great deal by the dawn of the 20th century. Mule-drawn trolleys that began service in 1876 had long since been replaced by an extensive network of electric trolleys serving the Twin Cities. Telephone service began in 1879, and construction of a public waterworks system dated back to 1884. Four years later, electric streetlights began to replace gaslights. By the 1890s, extensive development was well underway in Pulaski Heights. The first three automobiles appeared in Little Rock around 1902.

Within a dozen years, Arkansas was overrun by more than 5,000 automobiles, much to the consternation of those who still depended upon shoe leather for transportation. The Little Rock Motor Club begged pedestrians to cease their defiant and extremely dangerous "hit me if you dare" attitude. Then the Great War erupted, precipitating major changes in Pulaski County.

When the federal government announced it would create 16 new camps to train draftees to fight, Little Rock leaders organized the Army Post Development Company to entice Washington to build a camp in Pulaski County. They purchased 3,000 acres of land north of Argenta and leased an additional 10,000 acres. Funds contributed by Argenta, Little Rock, and the state government brought the Arkansas bid to $500,000. The effort succeeded and construction of Camp Pike began in 1917. By 1918, more than 100,000 men were stationed at Camp Pike, exceeding the combined populations of Little Rock and North Little Rock (which changed its name from Argenta in 1917). Since the county also swelled with civilian workers and military families, the post had a substantial impact on the local economy.

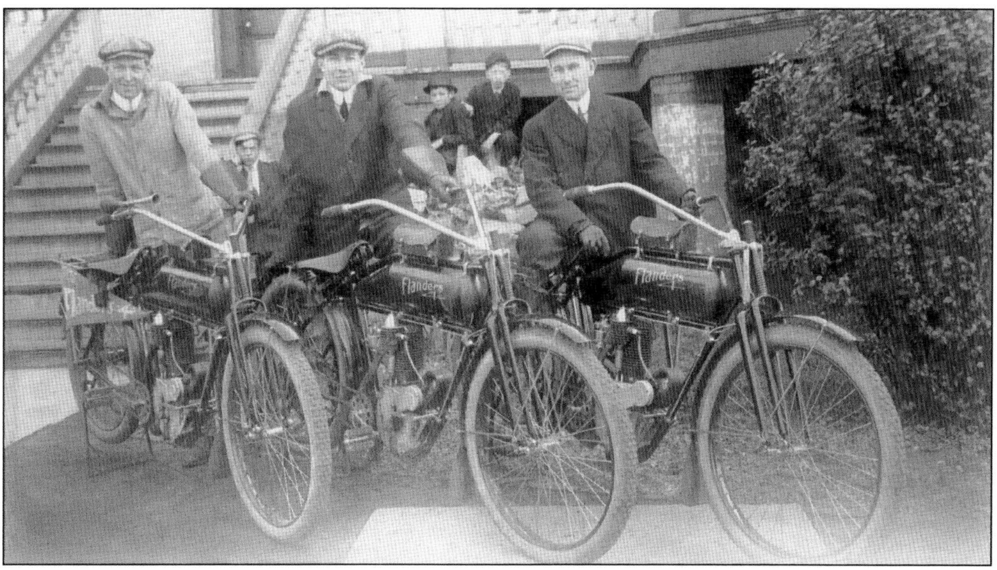

MOTORCYCLE RIDERS IN FRONT OF THE OLD ARSENAL BUILDING AT CITY PARK IN THE SPRING OF 1912. Built in 1836 as part of the Little Rock Arsenal, it was here in 1880 that General Douglas MacArthur was born. While Little Rock was gracious enough to rename City Park in honor of the general, MacArthur ungraciously disavowed any link to Arkansas. (Arkansas History Commission.)

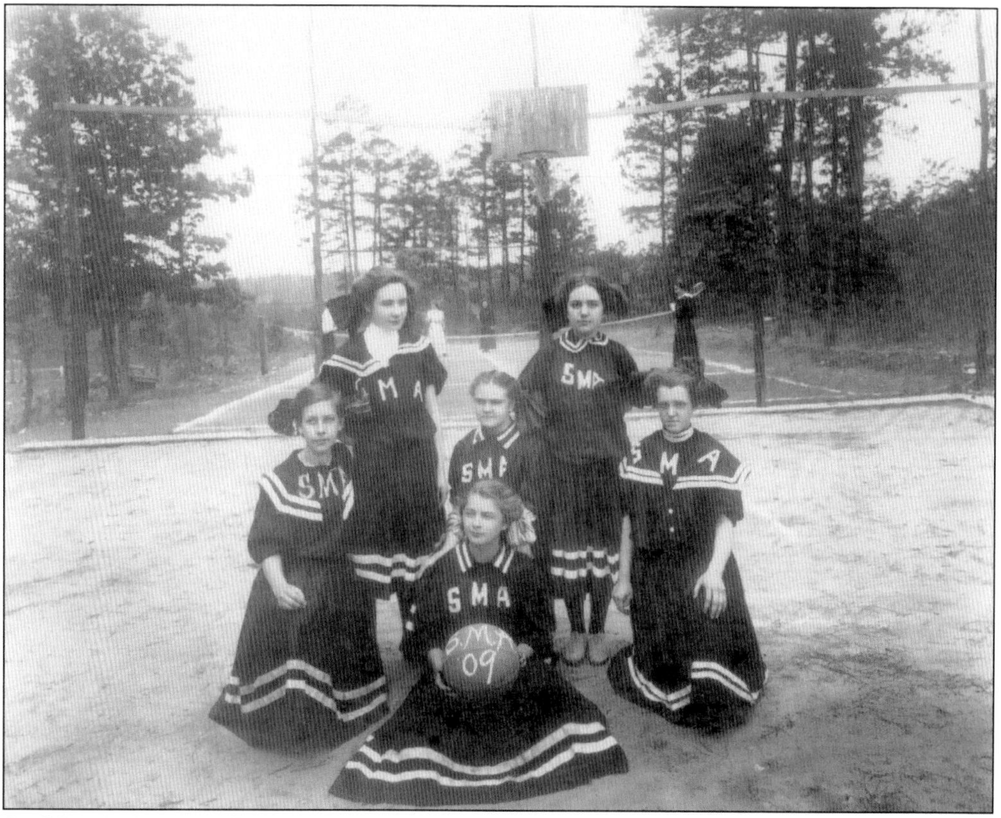

ST. MARY'S ACADEMY BASKETBALL TEAM, C.1909. Located on Kavanaugh Boulevard, St. Mary's was established in 1908 as a Catholic school for girls from kindergarten through high school. The school was run by the Sisters of Mercy. (Arkansas History Commission.)

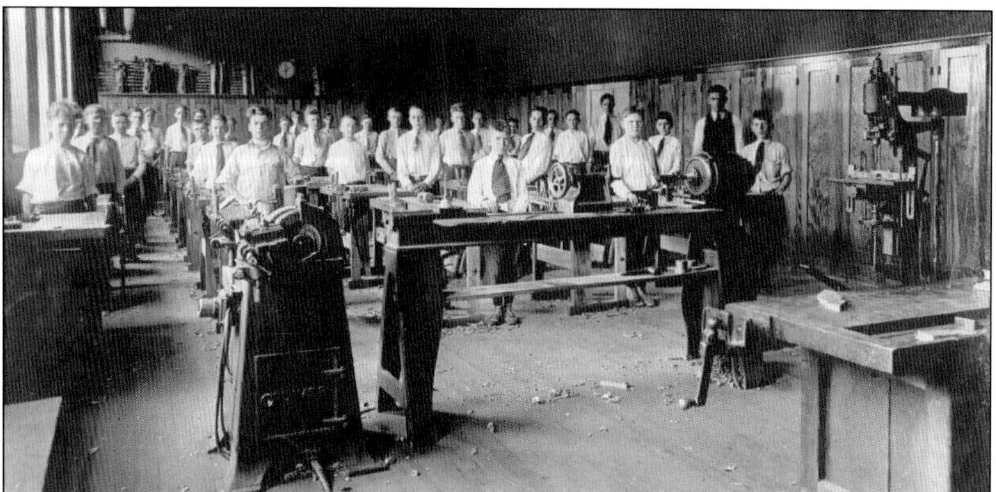

AN INDUSTRIAL ARTS CLASS AT WEST SIDE JUNIOR HIGH SCHOOL IN LITTLE ROCK, 1919. (Arkansas History Commission.)

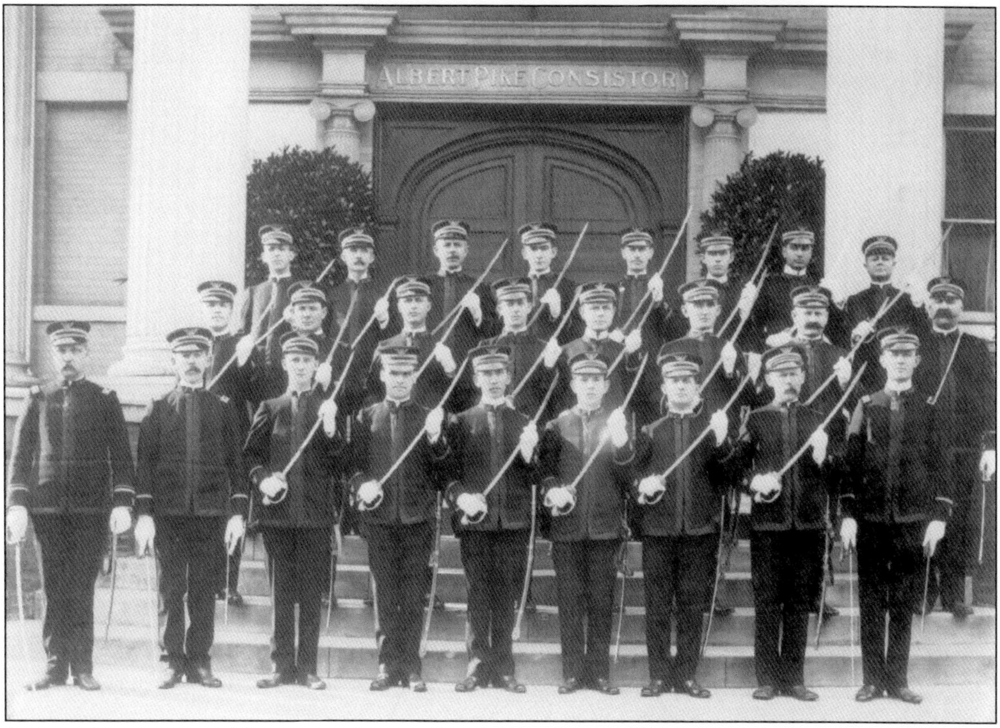

GROUP STANDING IN FRONT OF ALBERT PIKE CONSISTORY (SCOTTISH RITE MASONIC LODGE). Built on Scott Street between 7th and 8th streets, the temple was completed in 1924. The block-long facade featured an impressive row of 19 Iconic columns. The Masons have been active throughout Arkansas since the antebellum era. (Arkansas History Commission.)

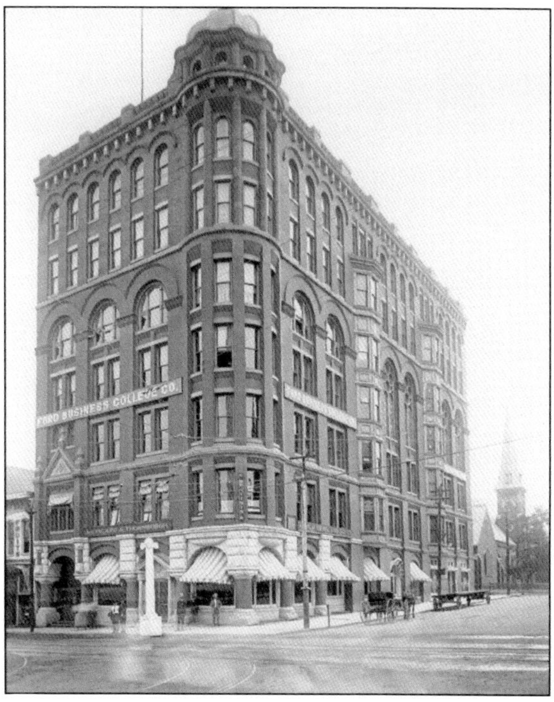

MASONIC TEMPLE IN LITTLE ROCK, c.1915. Tenants of the building included the Ford Business College Co., Dr. M.C. Karr, the American National Insurance Company, and Drs. Picard and Thrornburgh, who were dentists. The Masonic emblem appears over the door on the left side of the building. (Arkansas History Commission.)

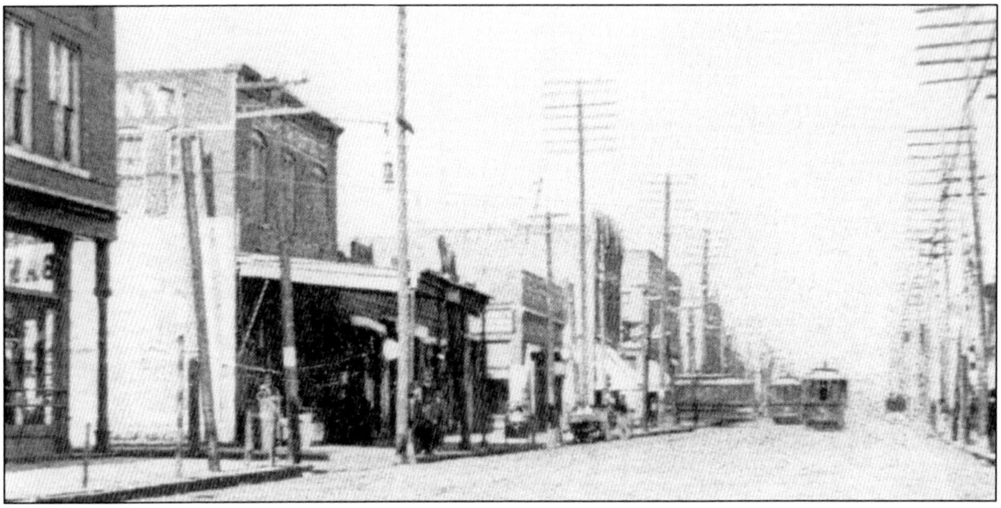

INTERCITY TERMINAL RAILWAY, ARGENTA. Three streetcars are pictured about 1910, along with both sides of an Intercity ticket. (Arkansas History Commission.)

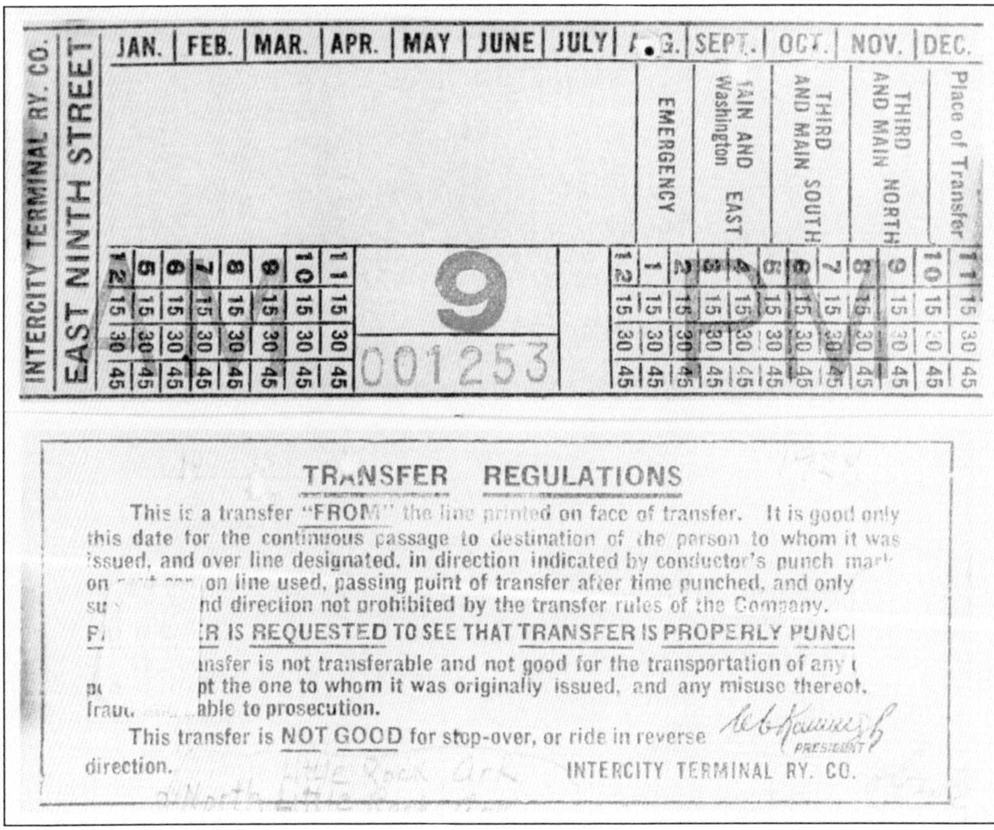

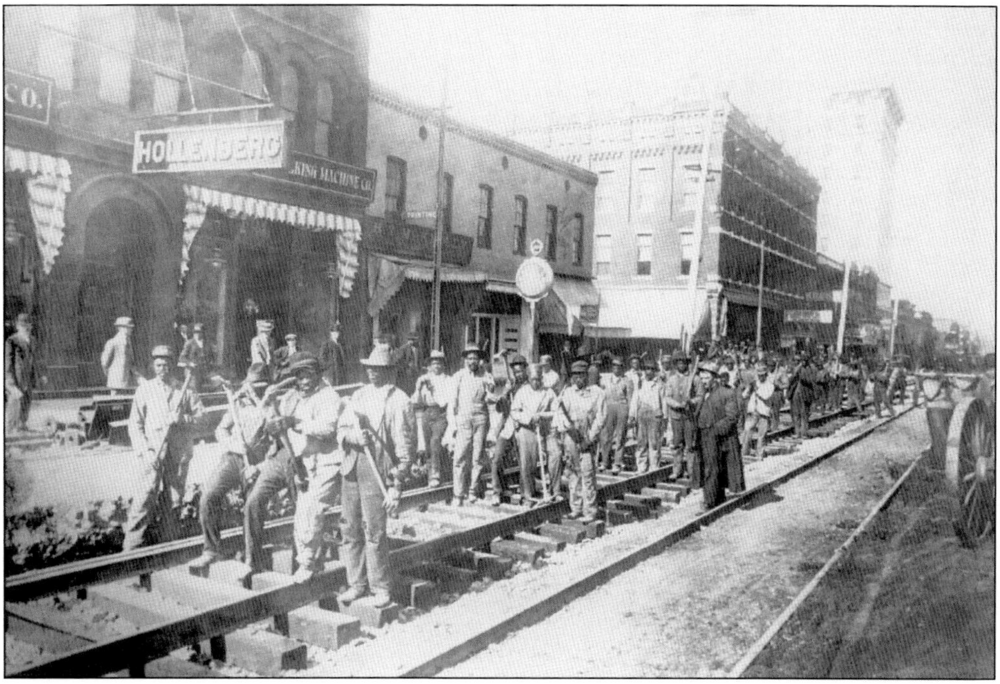

Streetcar Track. The track was being laid by workers in the 600 block of Main Street in Little Rock in 1910. (Arkansas History Commission.)

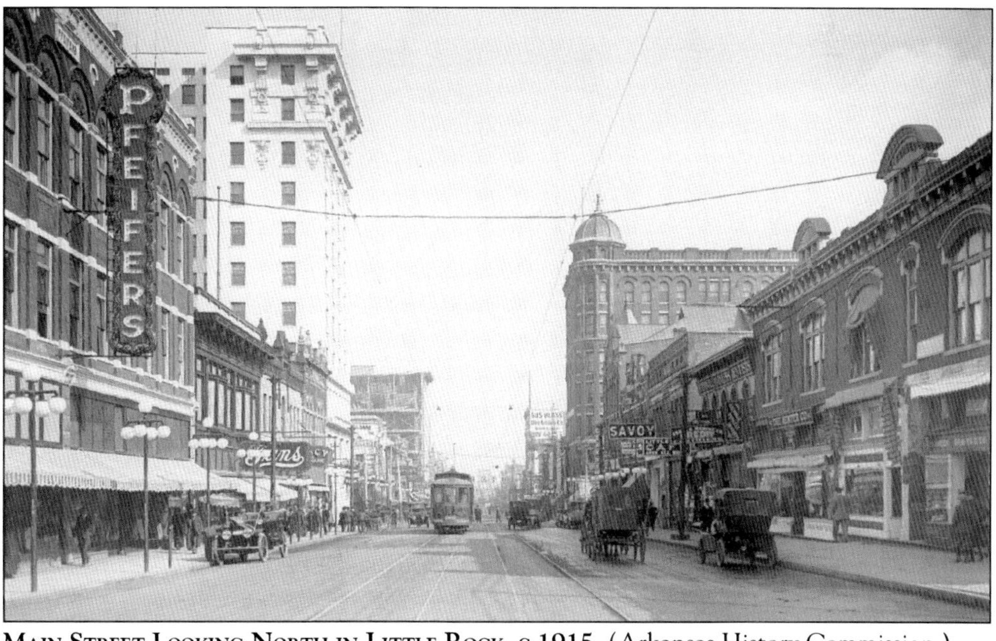

Main Street Looking North in Little Rock, c.1915. (Arkansas History Commission.)

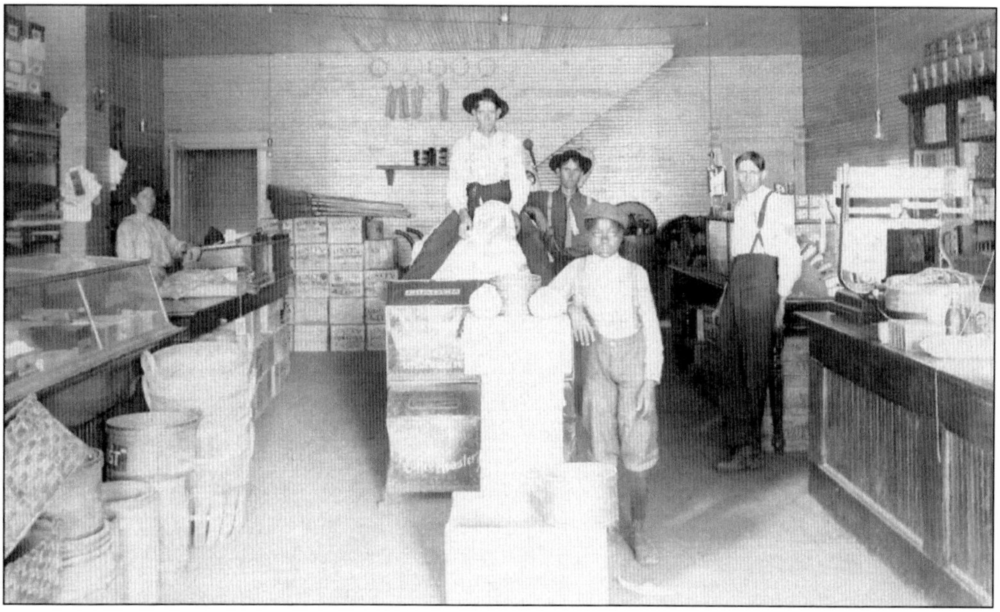

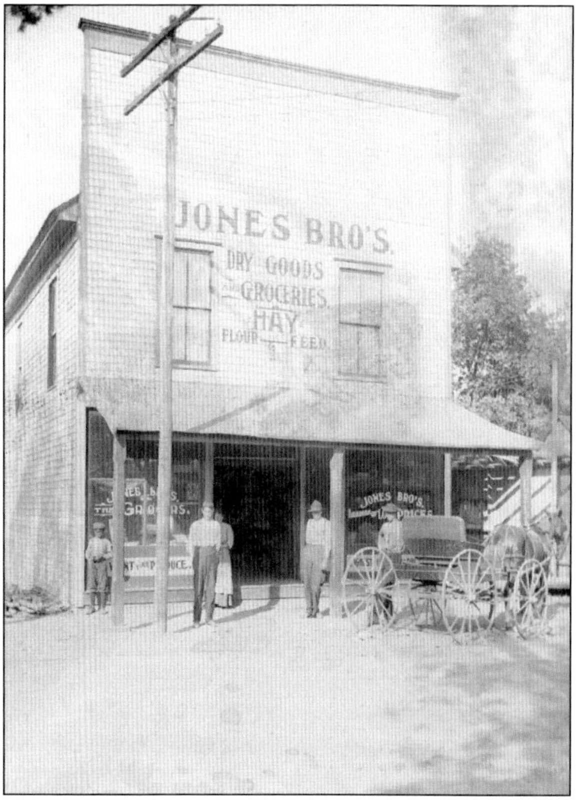

JONES BROTHERS GROCERY. The store was located at 1924 Wright Avenue in Little Rock about 1908. (Arkansas History Commission.)

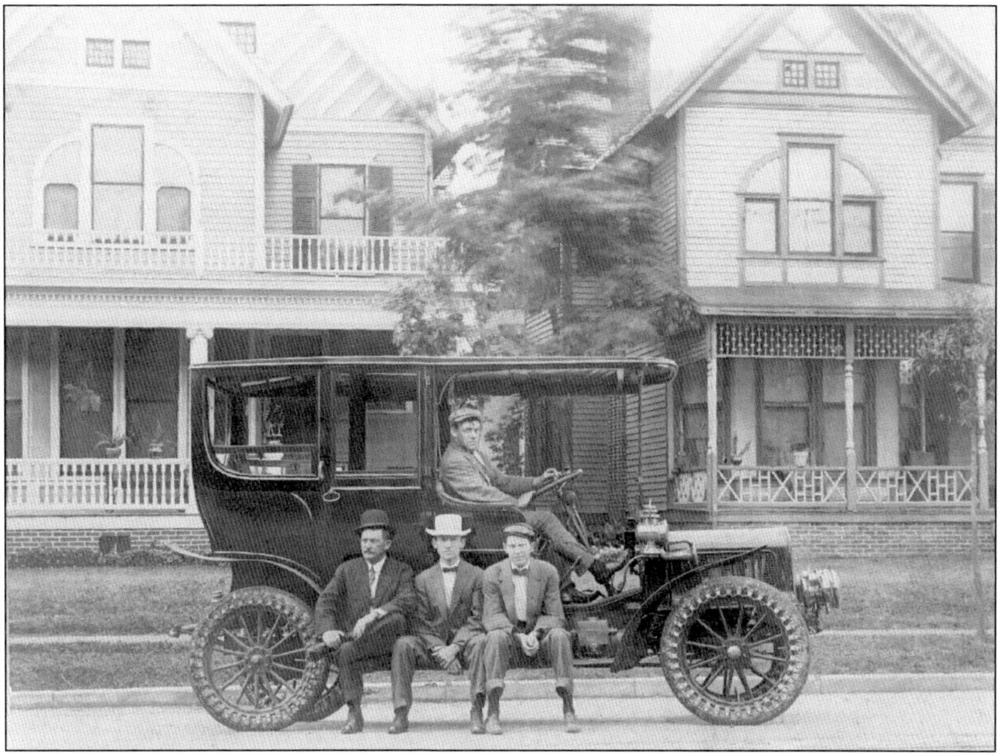

Early Little Rock Scene, c.1910. (Arkansas History Commission.)

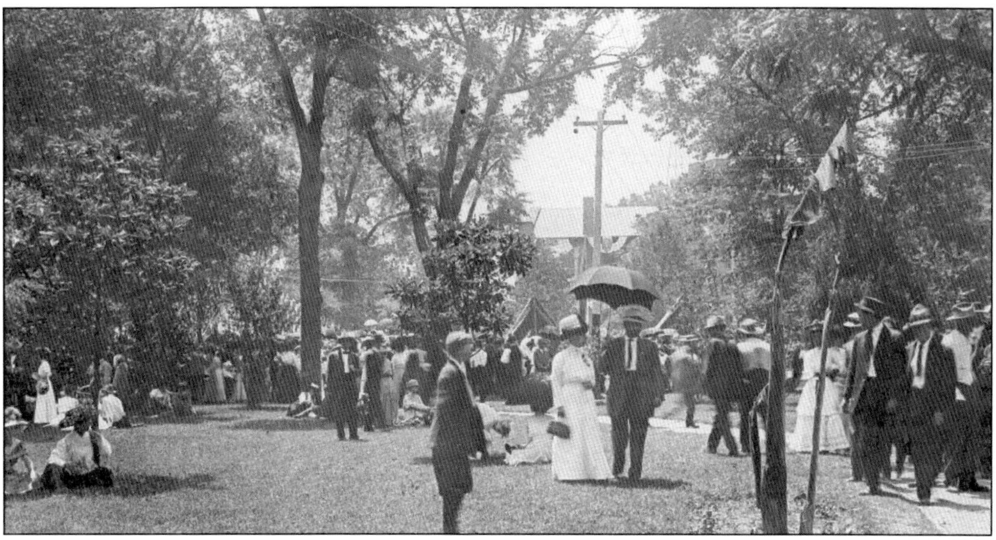

Reunion of Confederate Veterans in 1911. Organized by the Union of Confederate Veterans, which had more than 1,500 local chapters, the 21st national reunion was held at Camp Shaver in City Park, which is now called MacArthur Park. For three days, Little Rock's population of 45,941 swelled to 140,000 people. The federal government even pitched in, providing 1,333 tents from Little Rock's Fort Logan Roots. The annual reunions began at New Orleans in 1889. (Arkansas History Commission.)

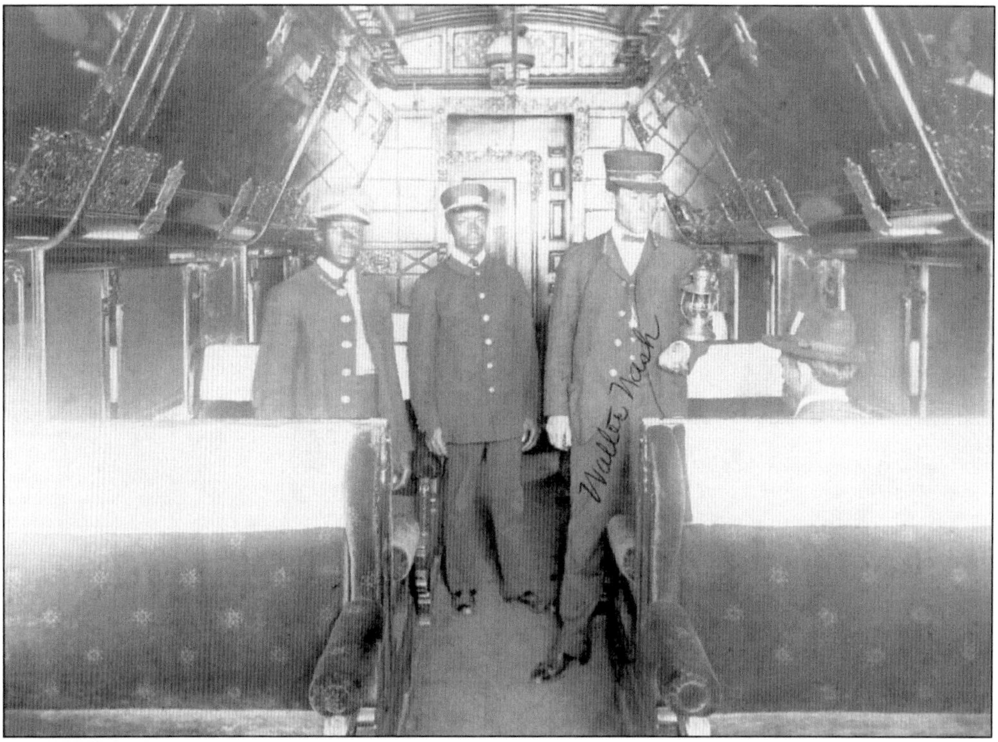

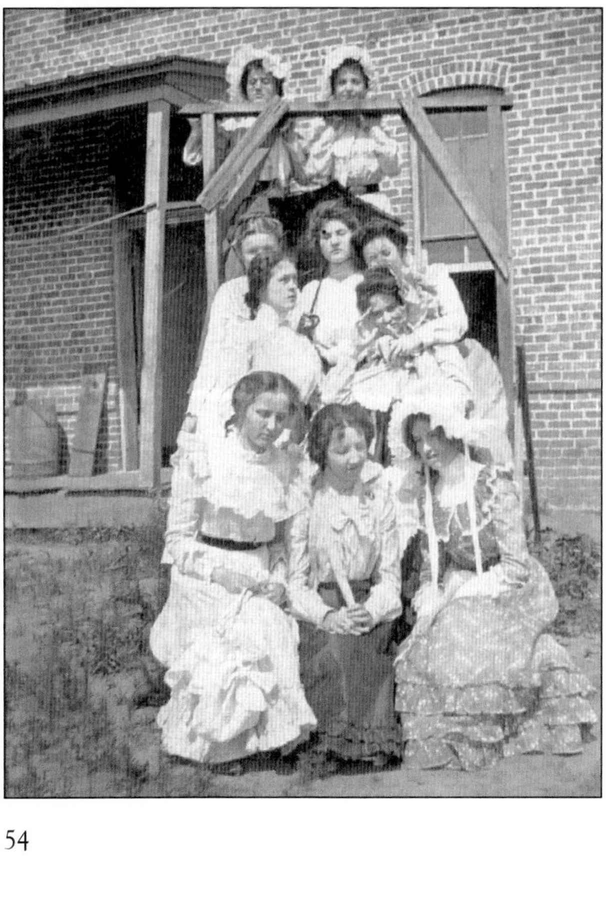

Interior of Railroad Car on the Rock Island Railroad about 1909. Walter Nash is the conductor. (Arkansas History Commission.)

Maddox Seminary Students about 1902 or 1903. Lillian Lester Burton is pictured on the front right. She was the daughter-in-law of John Benjamin Burton. (Arkansas History Commission.)

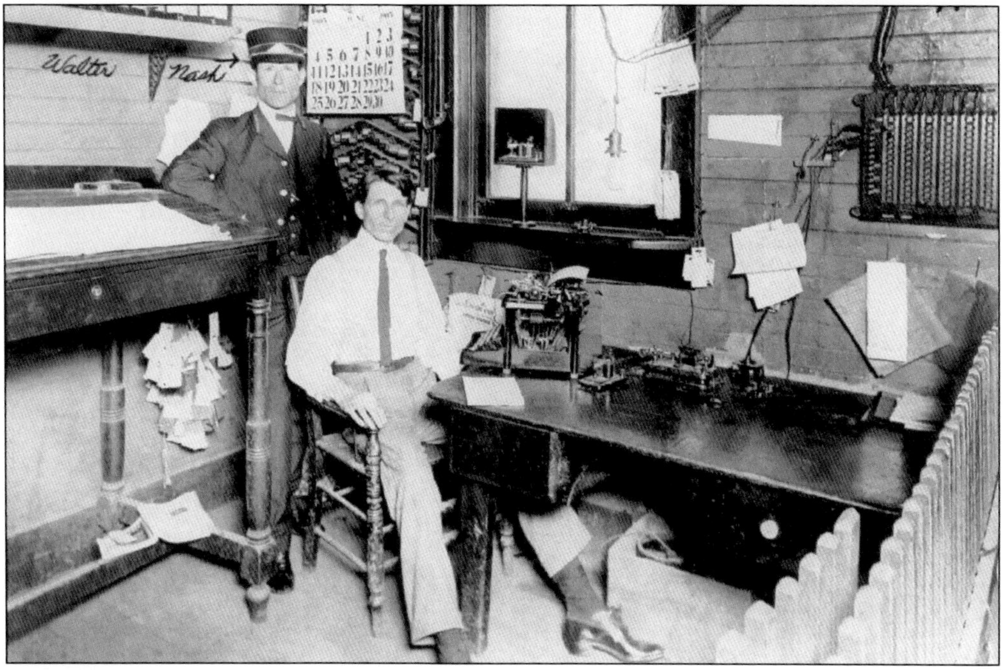

ROCK ISLAND DEPOT ON THE LINE TO LITTLE ROCK ABOUT 1909. Conductor Walter Nash is standing. (Arkansas History Commission.)

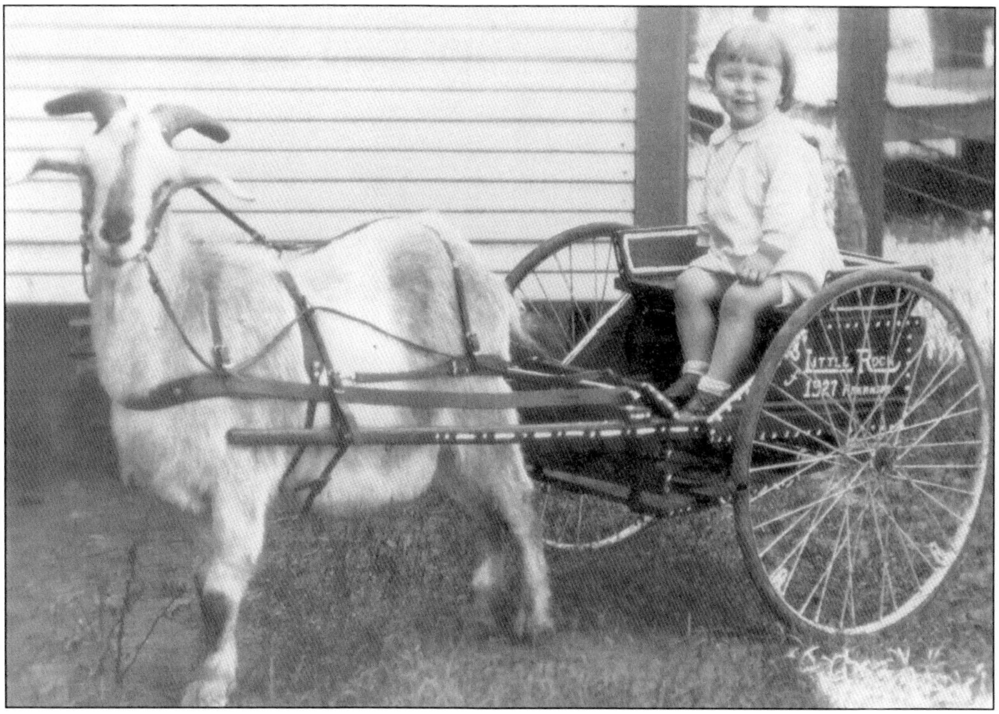

CHILD IN GOAT CART, 1927. (Arkansas History Commission.)

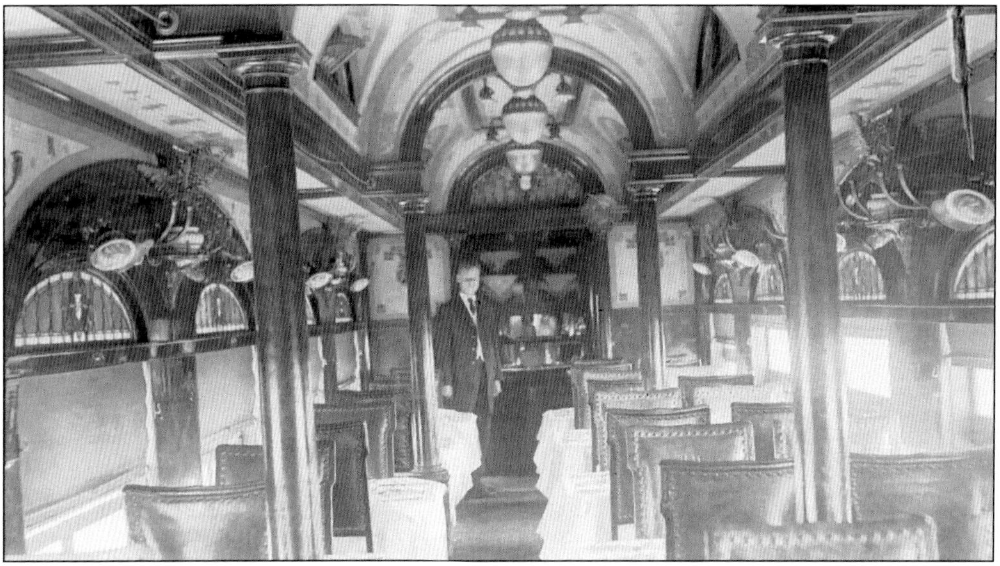

The 1910 Election Campaign. G.W. Donaghey and his friend William Jennings Bryan traveled throughout Arkansas to drum up support for a proposed Amendment 10 to the Arkansas constitution, which would permit ballot initiatives and referendums. Arkansas newspapers and lawyers bitterly opposed this amendment. Bryan traveled 1,750 miles on a special train paid for by Donaghey himself, Bryan making 55 speeches in just 5 days. The Amendment passed with a 71 percent majority. The top photograph shows Donaghey inside the train's dining car, while the bottom photograph shows Donaghey and Bryan in a car with Judge Hays and Tom Terral. (Arkansas History Commission.)

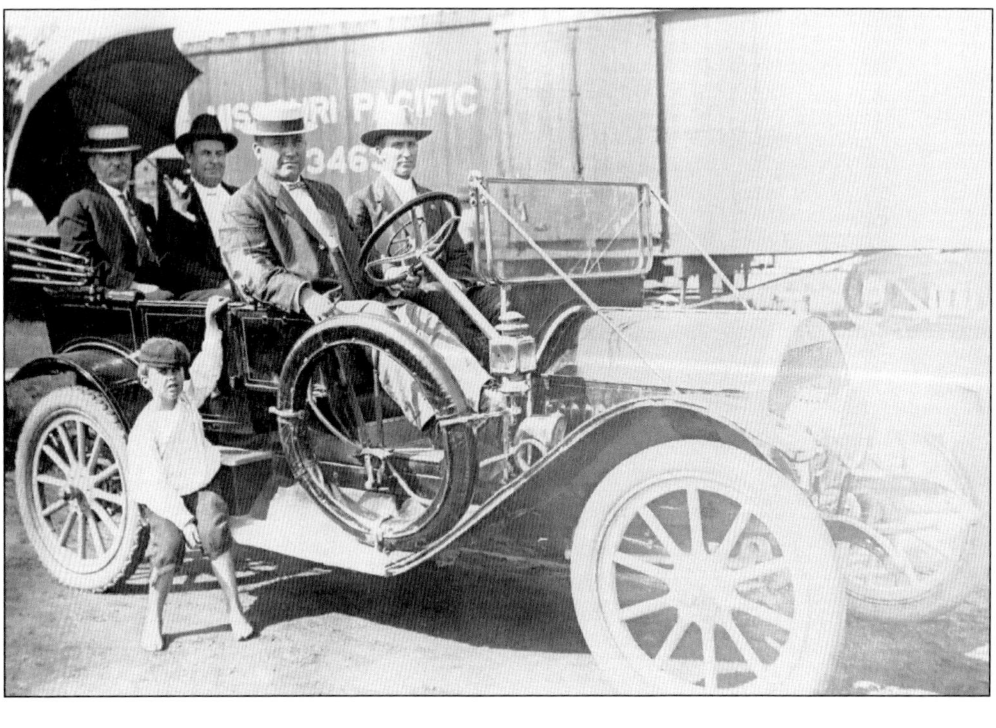

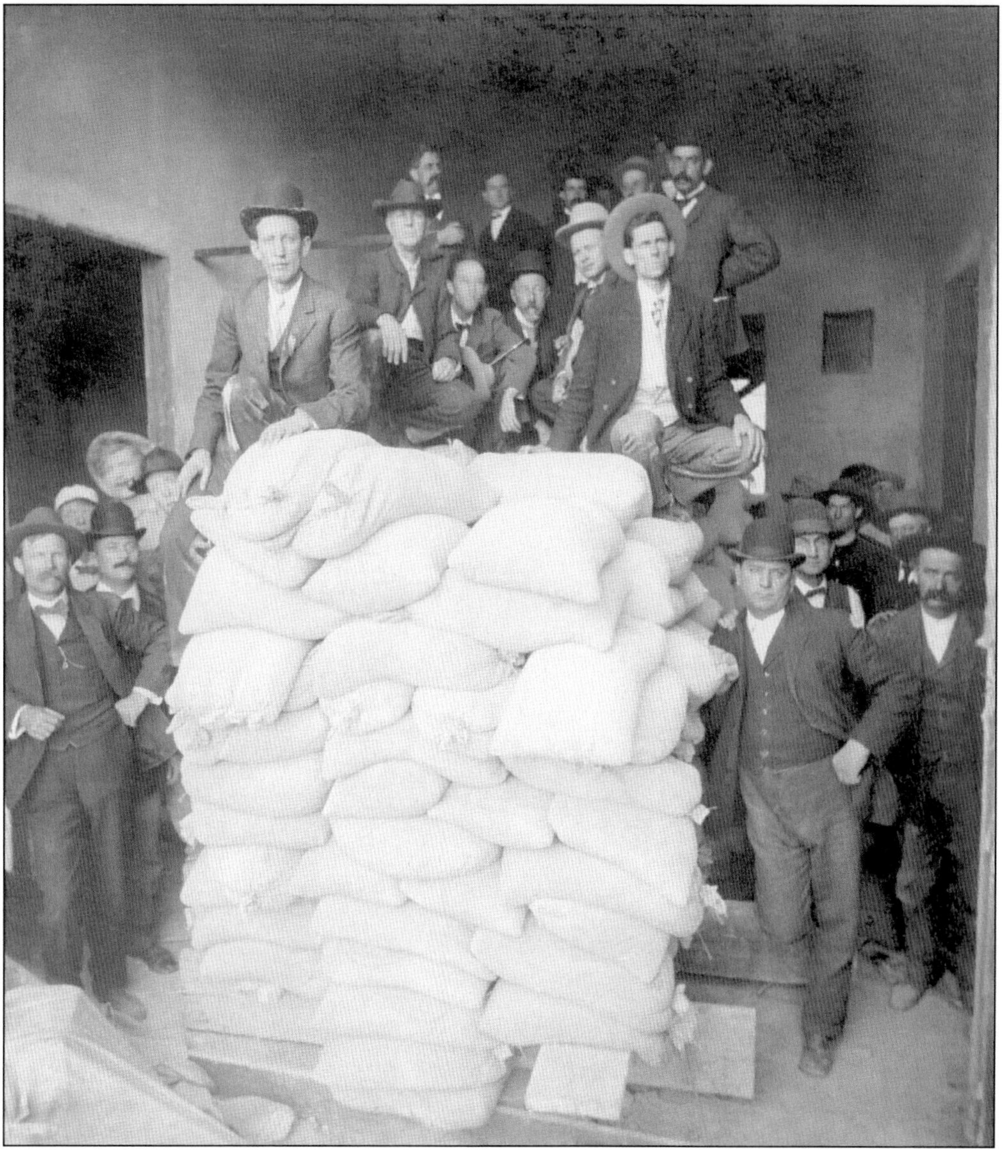

Testing the New Capitol. Testing a section of the first floor of the new Capitol in 1907 was conducted by engineering expert G.B. Strickler. This floor required a test load of 200 pounds to the square foot. Strickler's test load of 270 pounds to the square foot produced no perceptible deflection. Sidney Hunt, Chairman of the House Committee; R.W. McFarlane, Member of the Capitol Commission; and G. B. Strickler, the engineering expert, are among those in the photograph. (Caldwell and Drake photo, Arkansas History Commission.)

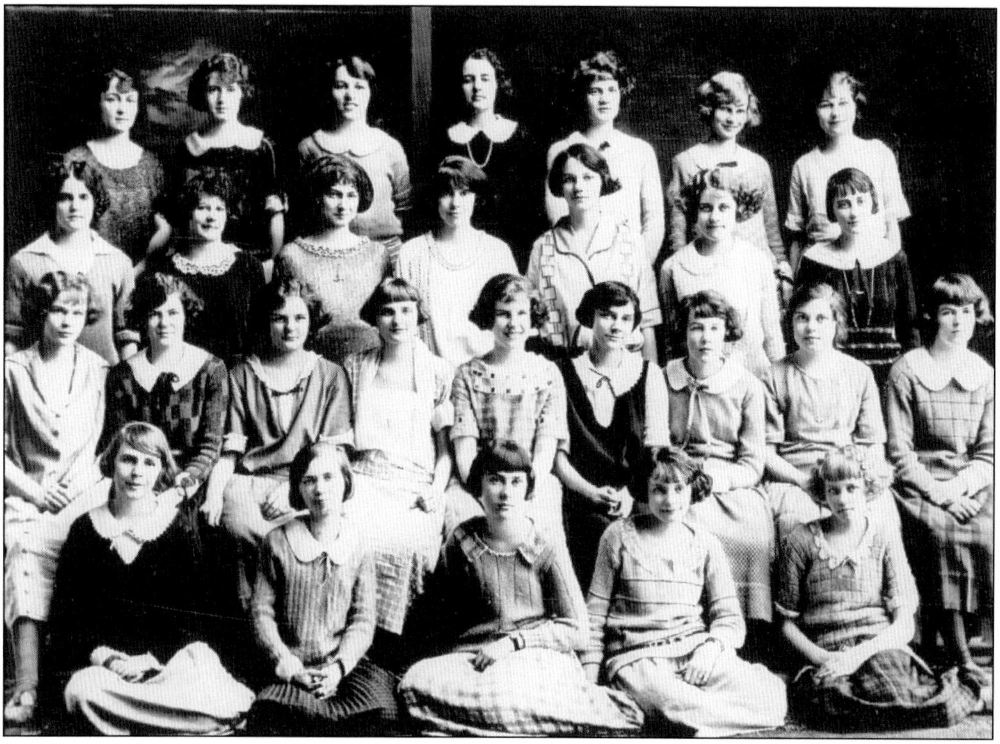

Little Rock High School, c.1918. Sibyl Branner is in the second row on the right end of Miss Hill's class, Room 21. (Arkansas History Commission.)

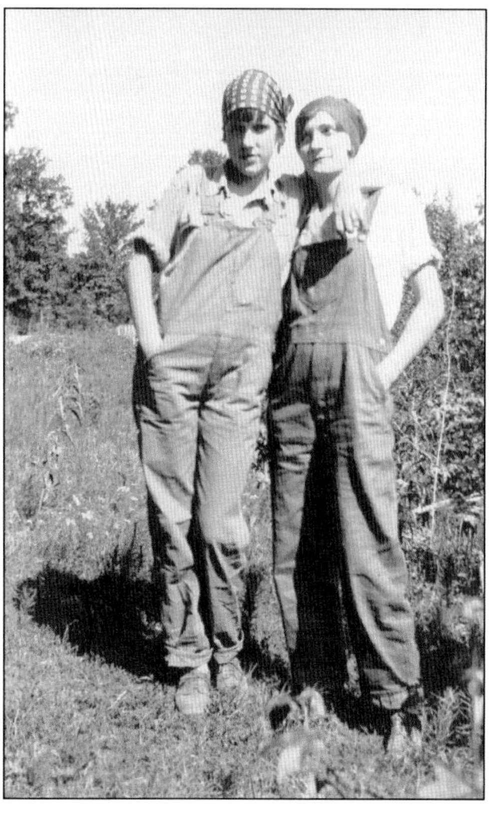

Nellie Wage and Fruza Ford in Little Rock in 1927. (Arkansas History Commission.)

S.S. and Allie Taylor Currie. They were married in Little Rock in 1922, and she died in 1933. (Arkansas History Commission.)

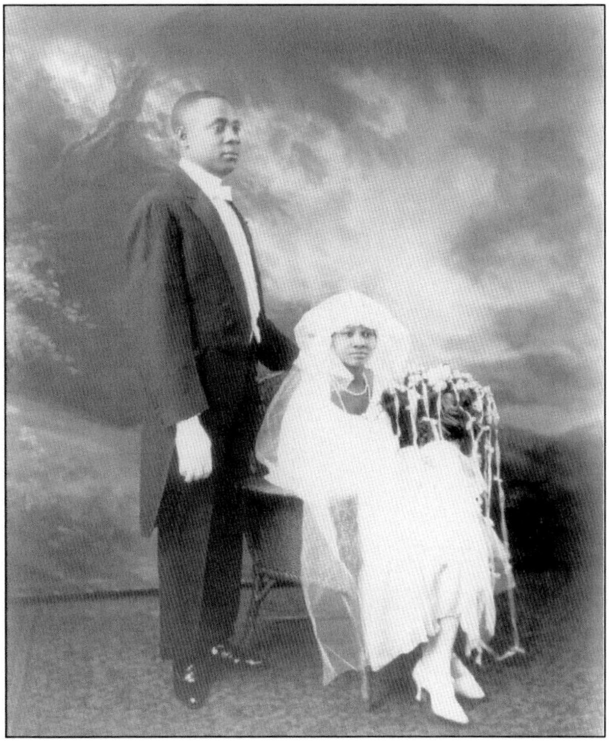

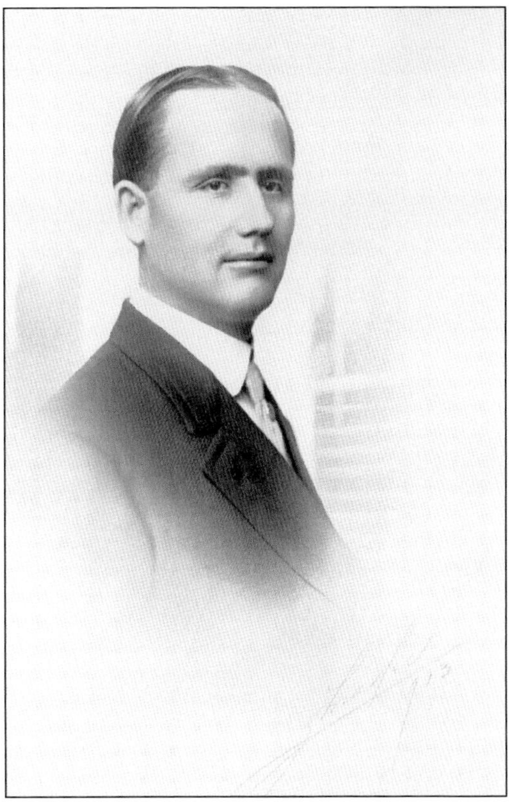

Tom J. Terral, Arkansas Secretary of State, Photographed in 1913. Terral subsequently served as the governor of Arkansas from 1925 to 1927. A contemporary described him as "a big, bumbling likable person, young and vigorous," but also observed that Terral's "education lagged far behind his aspirations." (UCA Archives.)

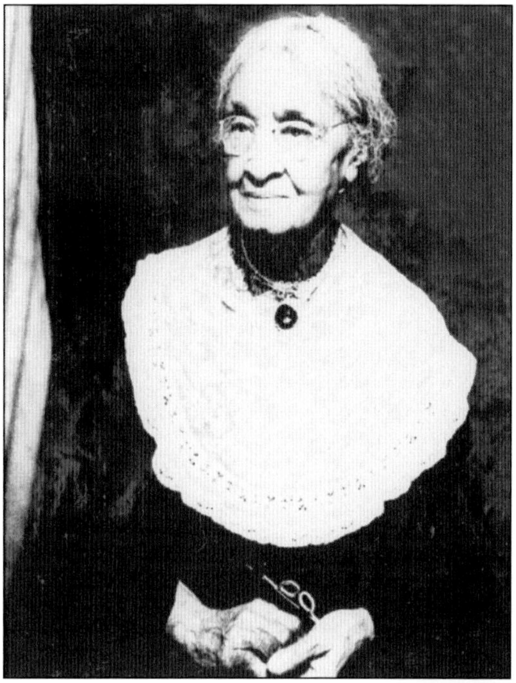

CHARLOTTE STEPHENS, A LITTLE ROCK EDUCATOR C. 1925. (UCA Archives.)

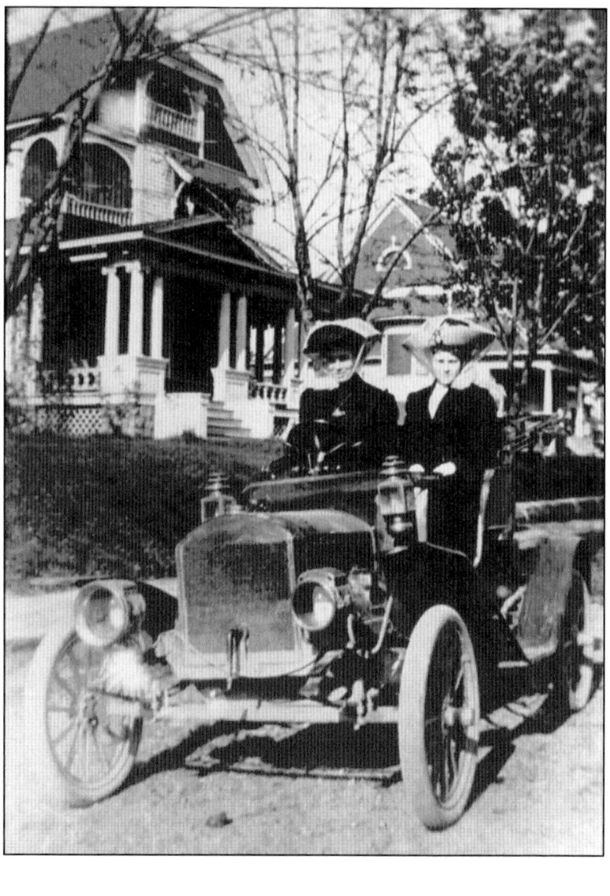

TWO WOMEN OF THE WALLACE FAMILY, C.1910. They are pictured in front of their house in the First Ward. (Arkansas History Commission.)

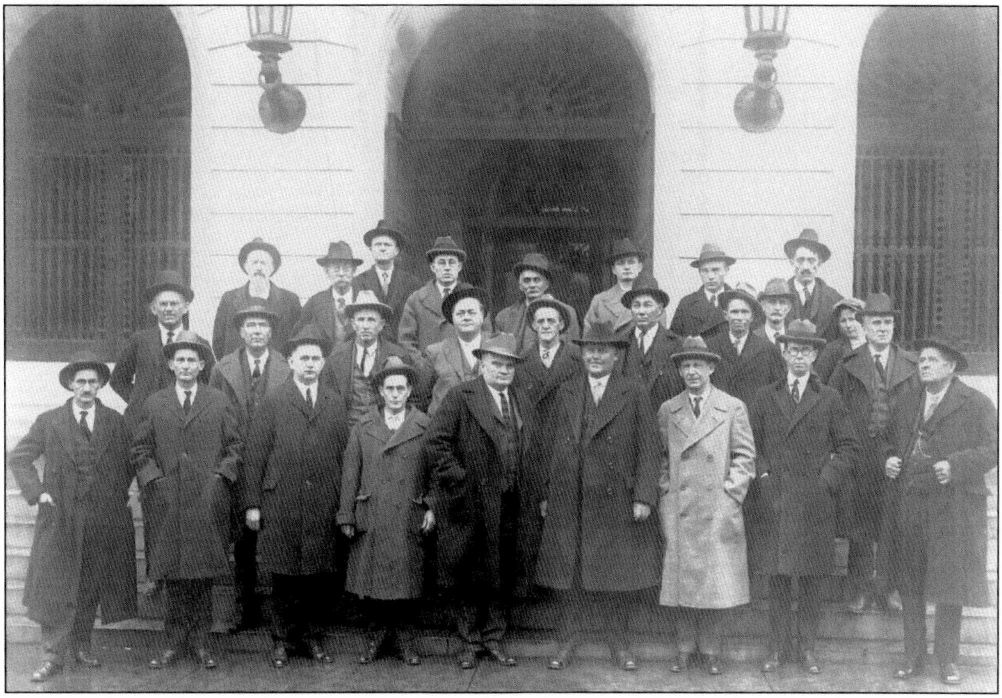

ARKANSAS COUNTIES SHERIFFS ASSOCIATION MEETING IN LITTLE ROCK ABOUT 1926. (Arkansas History Commission.)

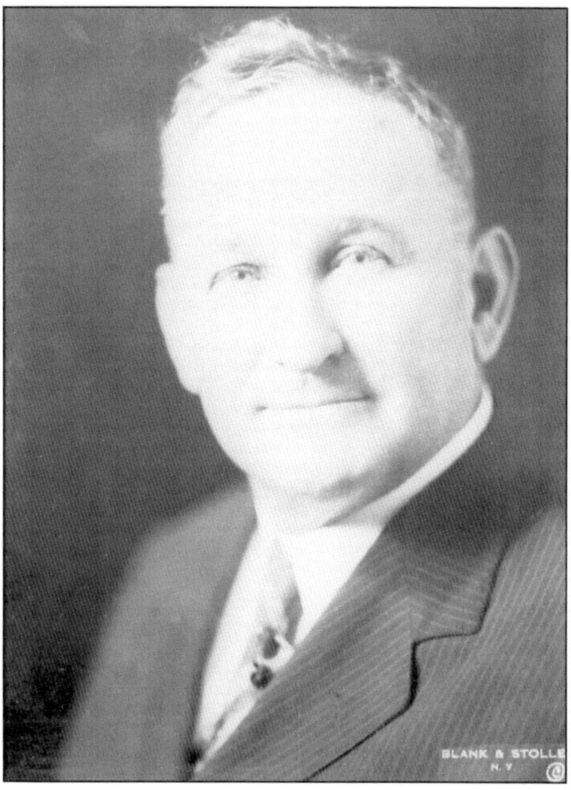

JOSEPH T. ROBINSON. Known simply as "Joe T" to his constituents, he was elected Arkansas governor and then served as a U.S. senator until the day he died. Robinson is remembered fondly as a big man with a powerful voice who championed causes like providing relief to poverty-stricken farmers during the Great Depression, and fighting against religious prejudice. During his 35-year political career, Joe T did a lot of good for a lot of folks. (Arkansas History Commission.)

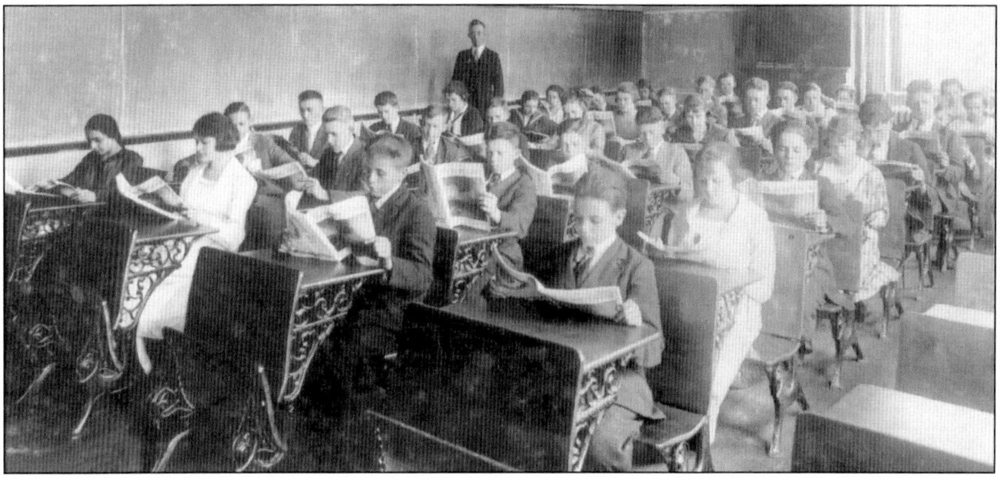

LITTLE ROCK HIGH SCHOOL HISTORY CLASS IN 1919. Future movie actor and producer Dick Powell was a student in this class; the teacher was J.H. Atkinson. Pictured on the first row from wall, front to rear, are: Marie Austin, John Autry, Raymond Beem, James McCormick, Agnes Brizzollara, Valeria Brown, Marion Alcorn, Charles Shinault, and Lilia Redmond. Second row from wall, front to rear: Mona Collins, Horace Cox, Randall Dixon, Fred Gilman, Lucia Fly, Thelma Henson, Richard Curzon, George Fish, Henry Moorehead. Third row from wall, front to rear: Richard Powell, John Lofton, Robert Yusby, Joe Mann, Frances Massey, Oswald Manis, Ellis Pool, Nelle Taylor, Eugene Woods. Fourth row from wall, front to rear: Elmer Newton, Mary Nell Pourell, Winston Howlan, Kathlene Powers, Herbert Rule, Henry Spitzberg, Frank Thompson, and Juanita Watson. (Arkansas History Commission.)

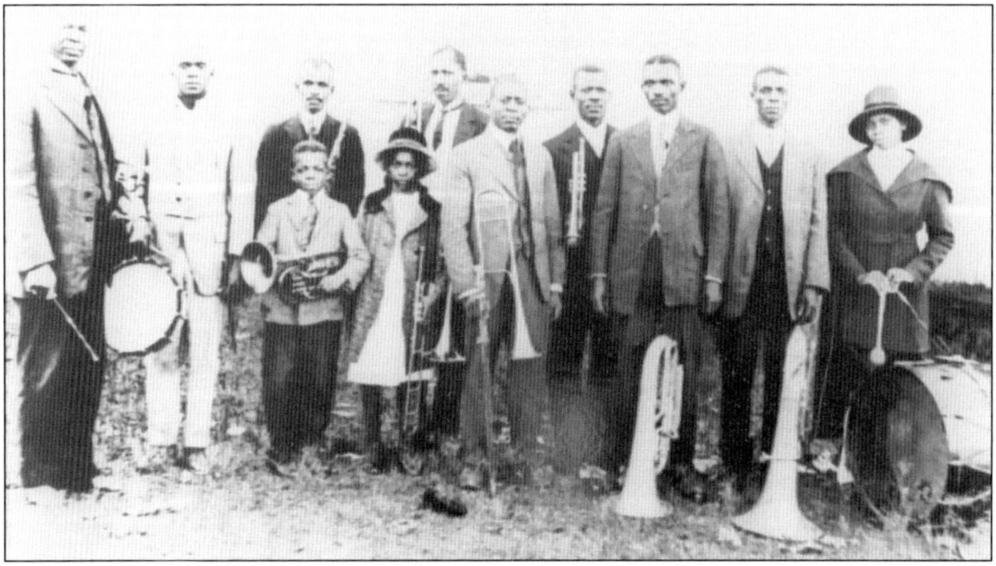

ARGENTA COMMUNITY BAND ABOUT 1920. (UCA Archives.)

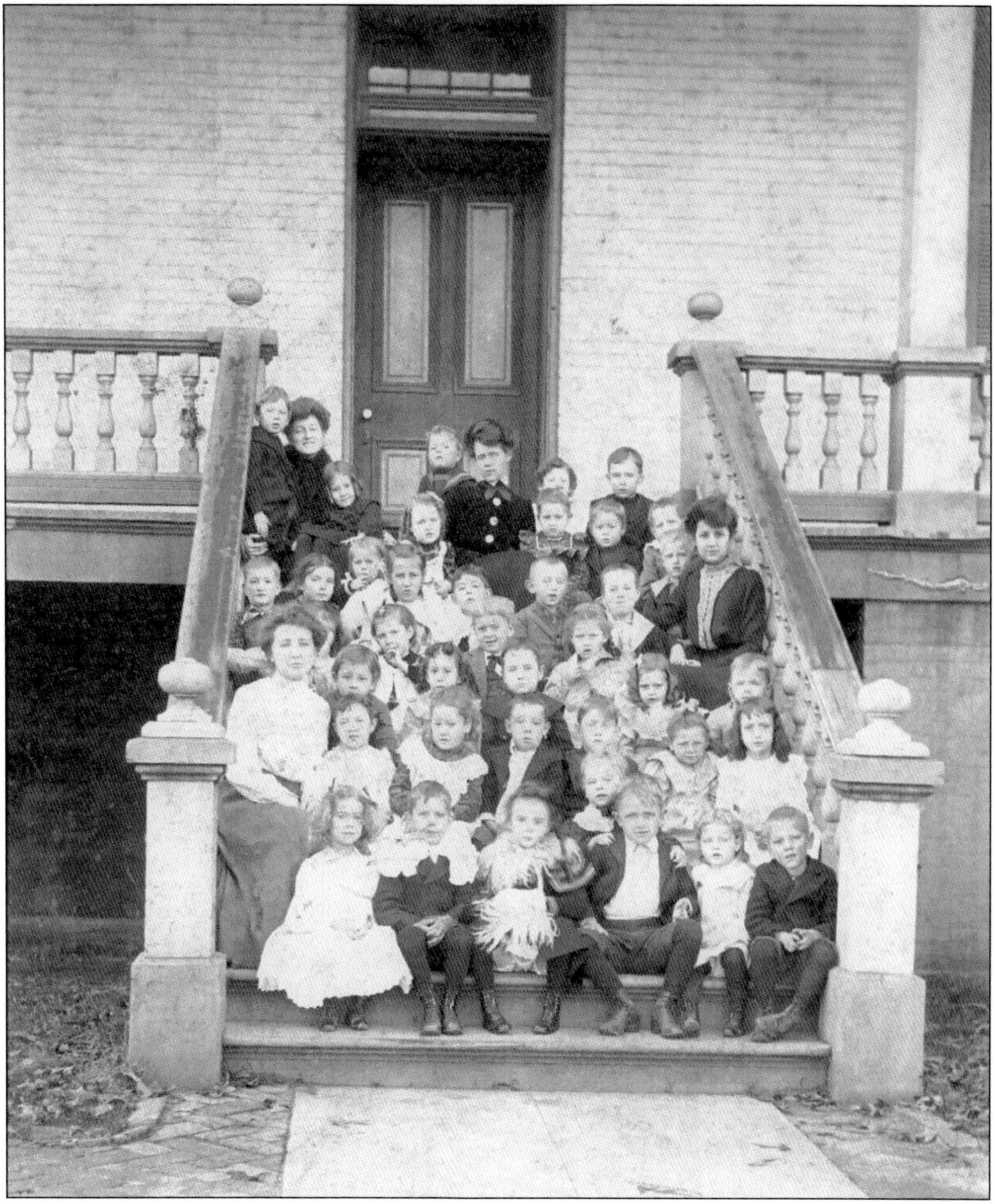

Sunday School Class at the Tower Building in MacArthur Park. This photograph was taken in December 1902. The names include (to the best of our deciphering the handwriting on the print): Richard Warner, Miss S? Chusky, Austin Taylor, Marie Murray, Bettie Ward, Margaret Heilstedt, Alfred Bracy, Ruth Prather, Marie Hafer, Herbert Tennebaum, Jakie Besser, Helen Ruebal, Frankie West, Bentley Badgett, Paralee Koonce, Ruth Bellew, Chester Woodruff, Louis Goldberg, Ned Sayle, Lucile Walters, Steve Hall, Evelyn Hempstead, Willie Davis, Hazel Larry, Gordon Chapline, Letia Wagner, Willie Davis, Billie Byrd, Laura Hipolite, Roger Bailey, Florence Irvin, Clifton Chism, Miss Lucie Leymer, Lillie May Johnson, Zadia Witlock, Fannie Huiet, Campbell Marshall, Marie Boyles, Ruth Johnson, Robertelle Hunter, Arthur Jones, Katherine ?, and Charlie Taylor. (Arkansas History Commission.)

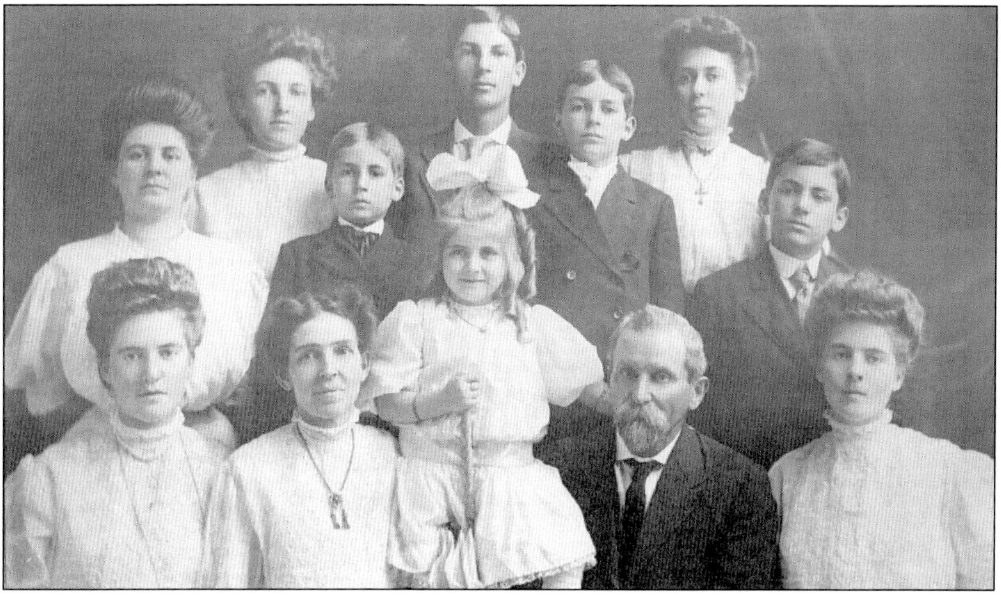

The Joe Belcher Family of Pulaski County, Photographed about 1907. Pictured from left to right are: (front row) Elizabeth (Mrs. Eugene) Swift, Mrs. Joe N. Belcher (nee, Sallie Booker Rison), Sarah Bibb (Mrs. Byron W. House), Josiah Nichol Belcher, Estelle (Mrs. Robert T.) Balch; (second row) Louise (Mrs. George F.) McFadden, Anderson Mills, Robert Ambrose, June C. Belcher; (top row) Marguerita Fones (Mrs. Thomas L. Hill), Joe Booker, Virginia Rison (Mrs. Edward C. Brock). (Arkansas History Commission.)

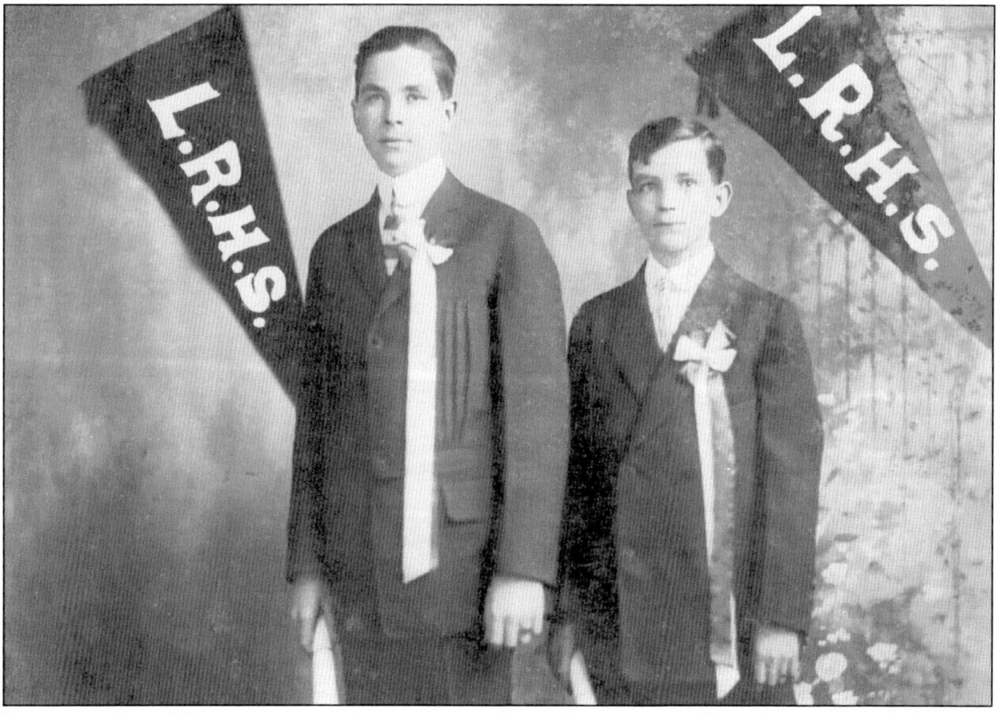

Rex and Ray Wehrfritz on Graduation Day, June 1917. Rex later opened the Rex Clothing Store at 304 E. Washington in North Little Rock. (Arkansas History Commission.)

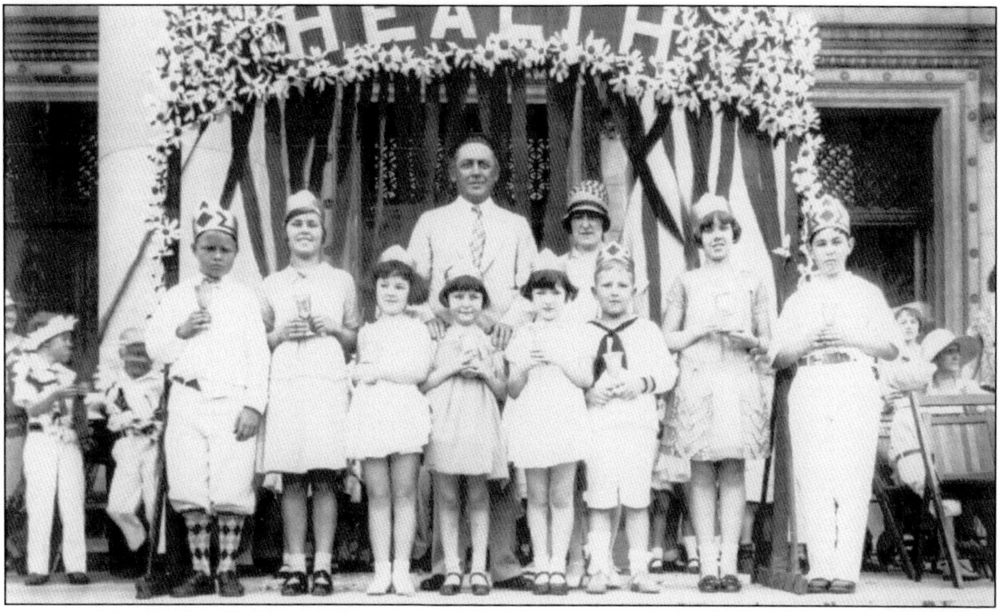

The 1928 Health Winners Selected From all the Grade Schools in Little Rock. Pictured from left to right are Jack Buck ?, L. Gertrude Vinton White (owner of the photograph), Jane Hurst, Rosemary Marshall, Sallie Gracie, Billie Frouke, Lois Brillhart Keith, and Albert Rosenbaum. Gertrude Vinton and Lois Brillhart tied for first place in the upper grades. (Arkansas History Commission.)

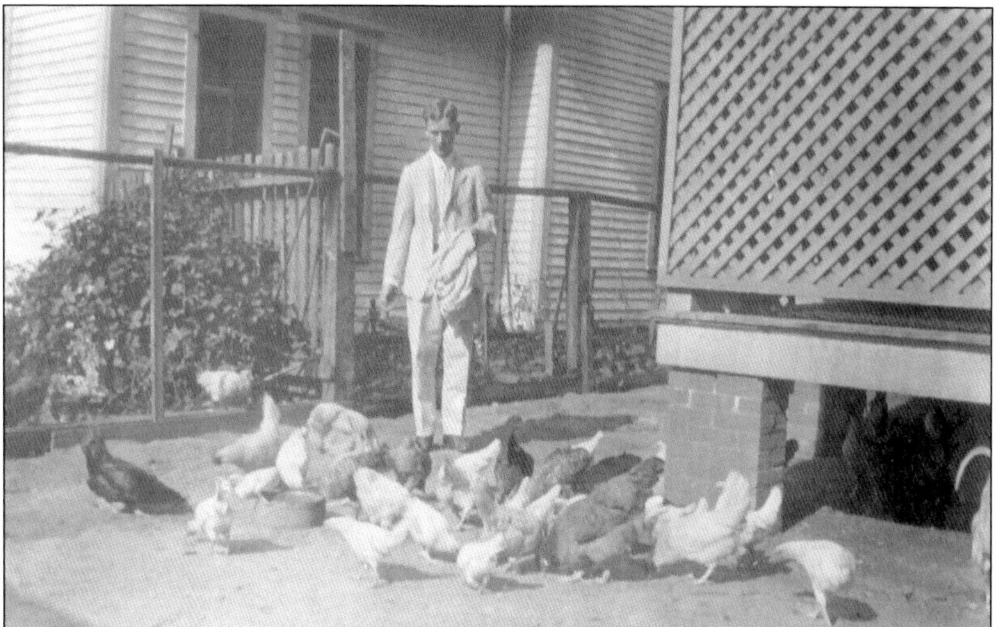

Allen T. Brillhart Feeding His Chickens. This scene is in his backyard at 1420 Park Lane in Little Rock about 1916, the year when Lois Brillhart Keith was born in this house. Twelve years after this photograph was taken, young Louis Brillhart would tie for first place in a city-wide health contest held for school children. (Arkansas History Commission.)

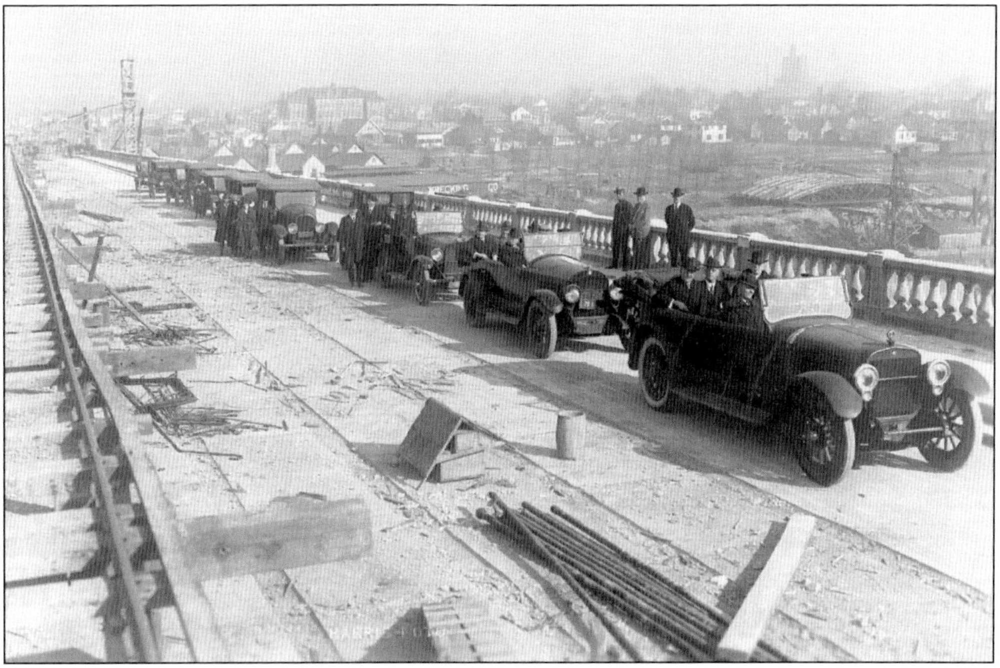

The First Traffic to Cross the Broadway Bridge. Traffic began on December 25, 1922, even before construction was completed, providing an important link between Little Rock and North Little Rock (which had changed its name from Argenta five years earlier). (Arkansas History Commission.)

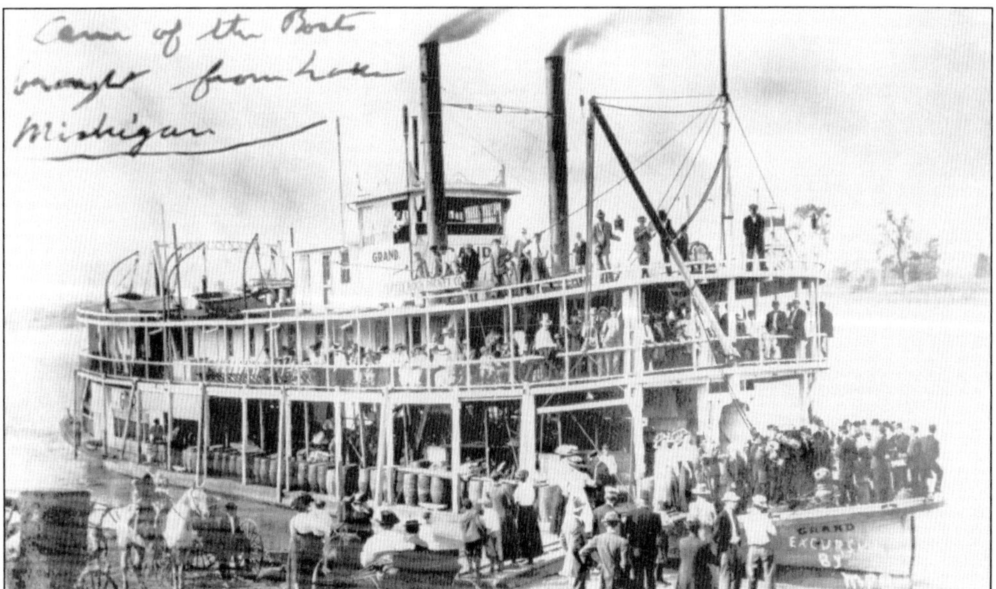

Excursion Boat on Arkansas River, about 1920. Called the *Grand*, the boat was brought to Arkansas from Lake Michigan by the Little Rock Packet Company. (Arkansas History Commission.)

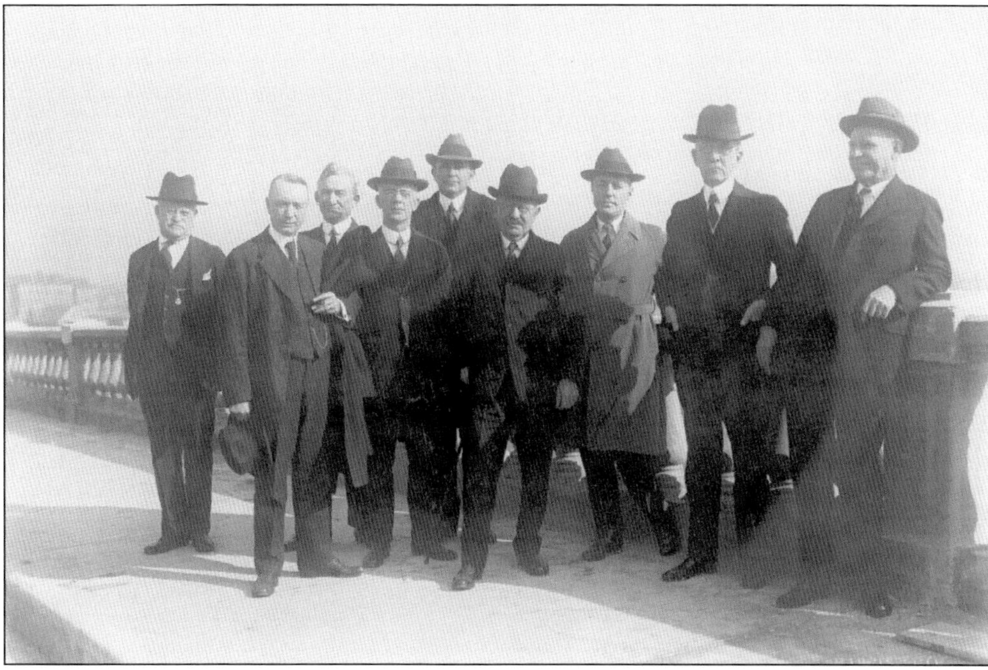

Bridge Commissioners. They were among the first traffic to cross the Broadway Bridge on December 25, 1922. Bridge commissioners (from left to right) include: Ress P. Horrocks, secretary; Fred W. Alsopp; George Vaughn, Assistant Attorney; Moorehead Wright; Justin Matthews; Herman Kahn; Joseph M. Stanley; Judge John M. Moore, Attorney; and G.W. Donaghey. (Arkansas History Commission.)

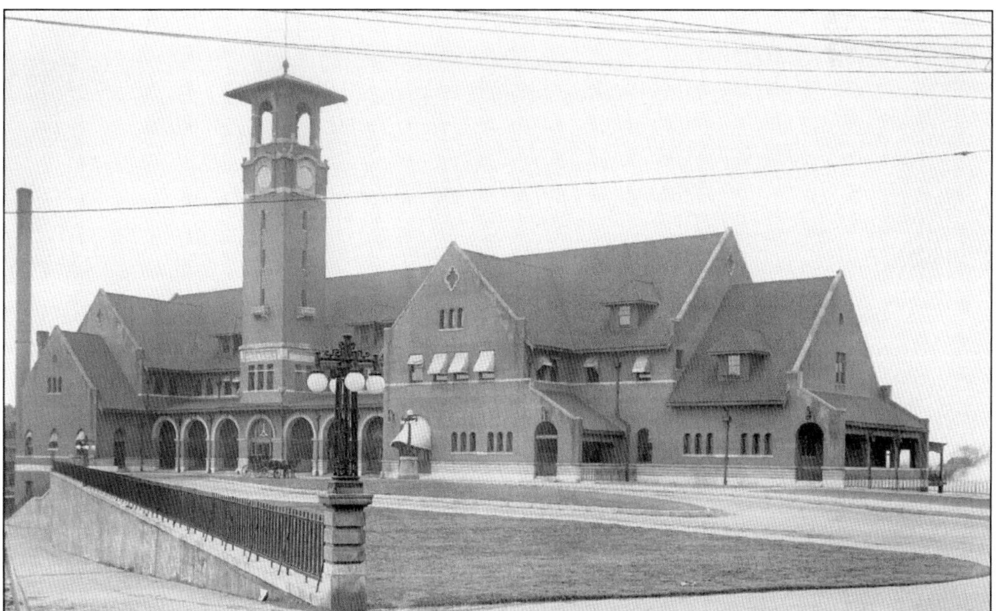

Union Railroad Station in Little Rock. (Arkansas History Commission.)

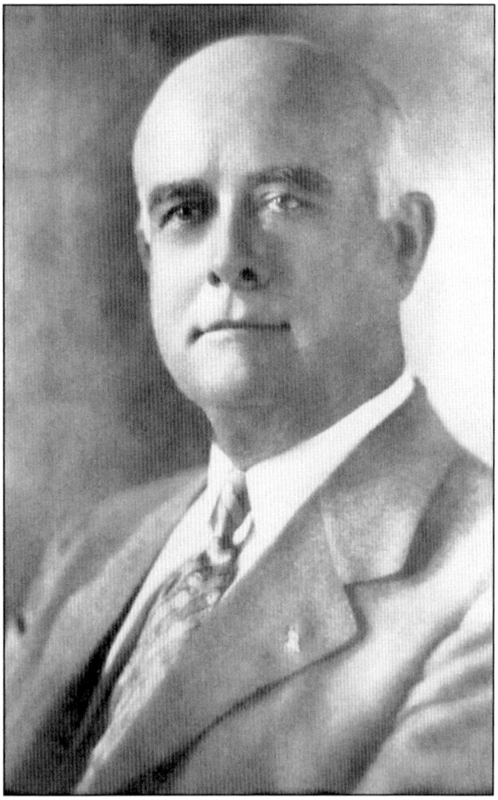

James Peter Faucette, Photographed about 1910. Faucette was the first mayor of Argenta, which was known as the toughest town in the state. Trains brought civilian patrons to the saloons, gambling houses, and bordellos of Argenta. The U.S. Army declared Argenta off limits to military personnel, a sure sign that Argenta was the Fun City of Arkansas. (UCA Archives.)

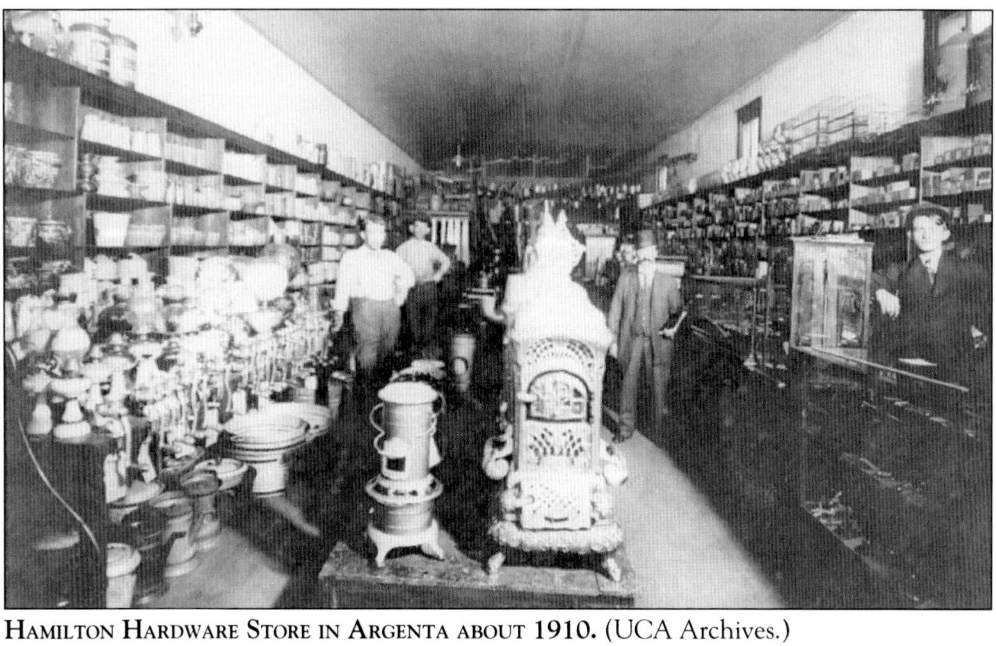

Hamilton Hardware Store in Argenta about 1910. (UCA Archives.)

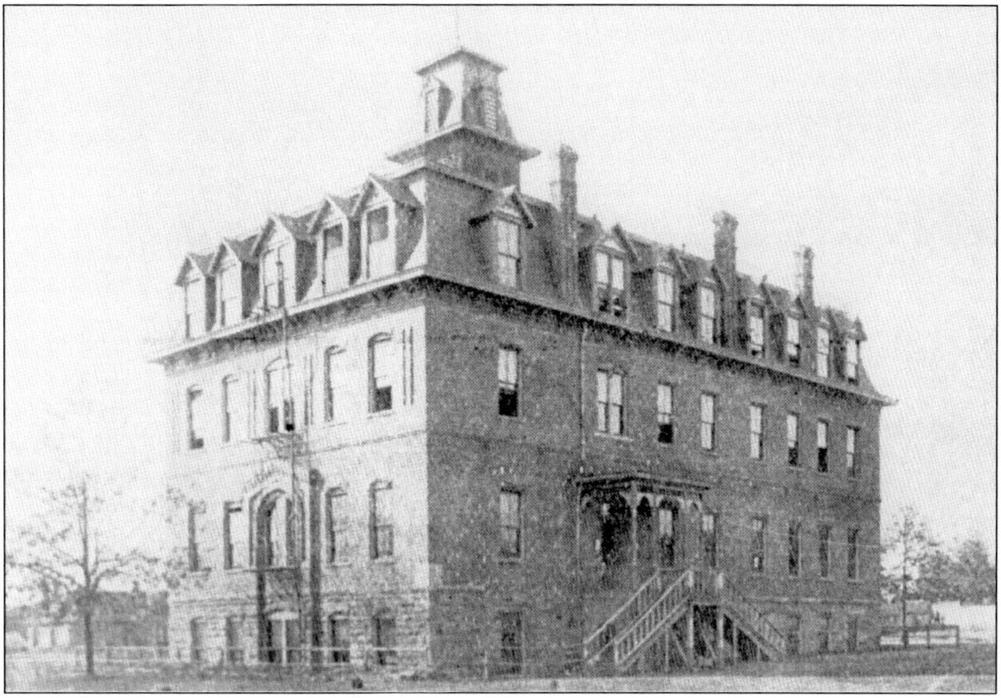

THE ARKANSAS BAPTIST COLLEGE IN 1910. Called the Baptist Institute when it was created in 1884 to train black teachers in Arkansas, the institute changed its name to Arkansas Baptist College in 1885. (Arkansas History Commission.)

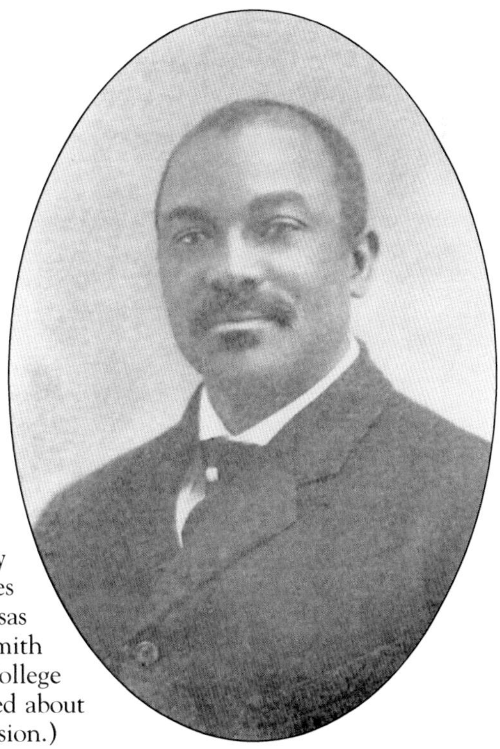

PROFESSOR JOSEPH A. BOOKER AM, DD. He served as the president of Arkansas Baptist College, which was one of three traditionally black, so-called denominational private colleges in Little Rock. Prior to World War II, Arkansas Baptist College, together with Philander Smith College (a Methodist school) and Shorter College (an African Methodist Episcopal school) served about 600 black students. (Arkansas History Commission.)

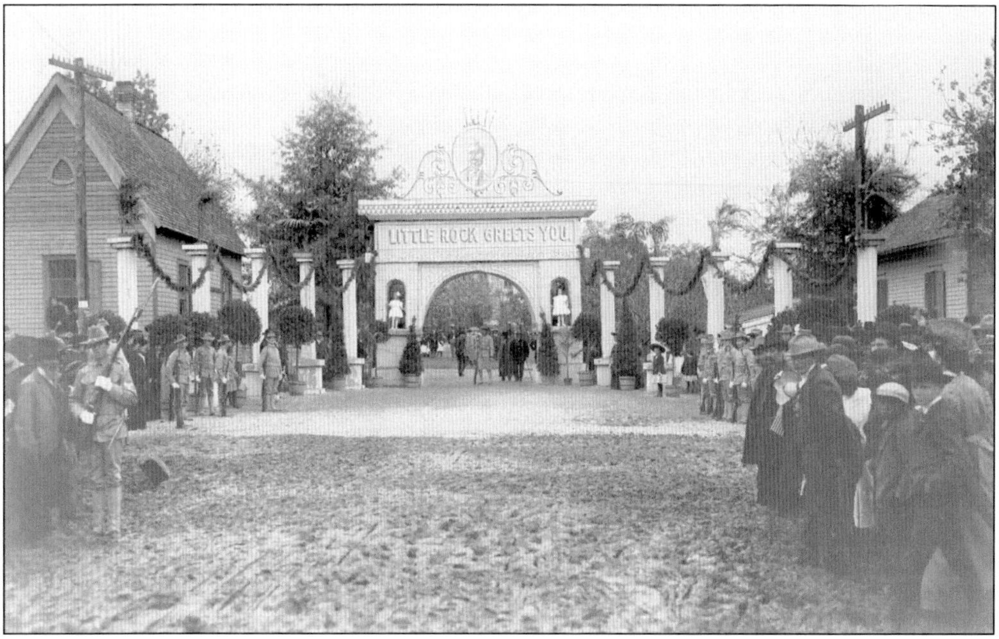

Little Rock Greets You! These people were preparing for the arrival of President Theodore Roosevelt at the 10th Street entrance to City Park in Little Rock, when they were photographed on October 25, 1905. (Arkansas History Commission.)

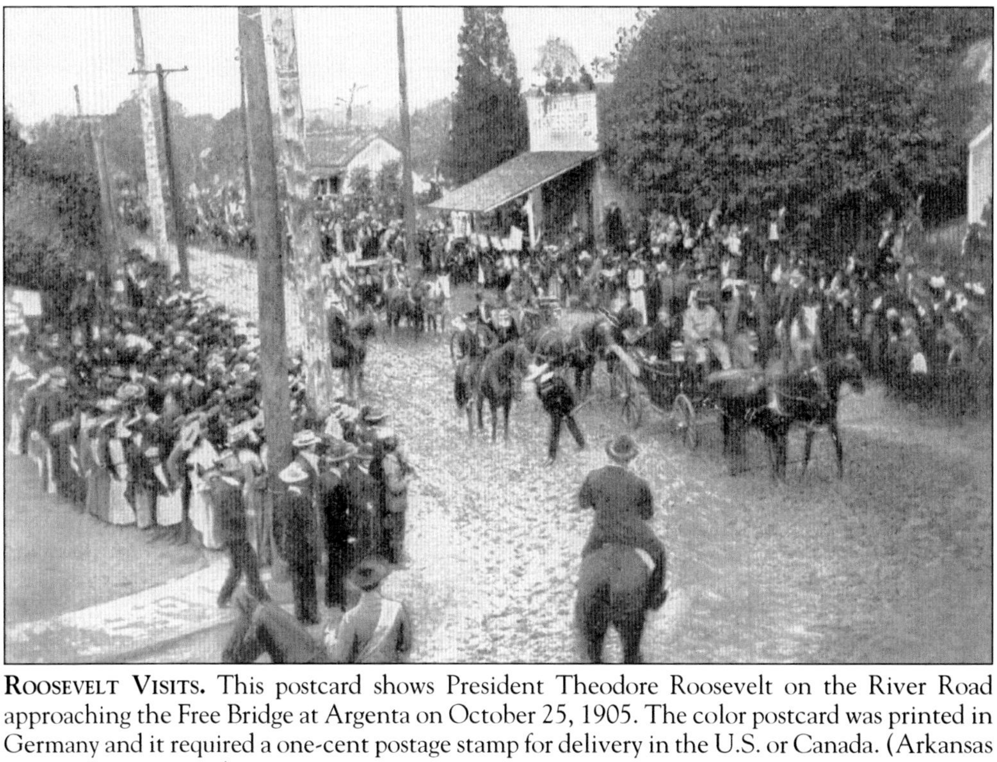

Roosevelt Visits. This postcard shows President Theodore Roosevelt on the River Road approaching the Free Bridge at Argenta on October 25, 1905. The color postcard was printed in Germany and it required a one-cent postage stamp for delivery in the U.S. or Canada. (Arkansas History Commission.)

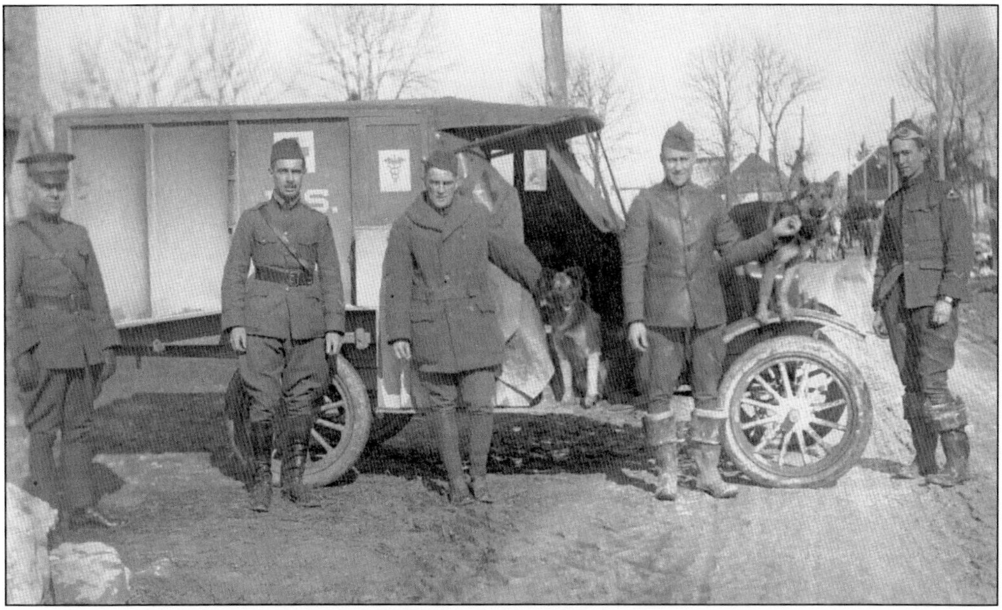

AMBULANCE CREW WITH RESCUE DOGS AT CAMP PIKE DURING WORLD WAR I. Captain Thornburg commanded the Medical Corps at Camp Pike. New troops arriving at the post were restricted to barracks for a ten-day quarantine period to protect the residents of Pulaski County against the spread of contagious diseases. (Arkansas History Commission.)

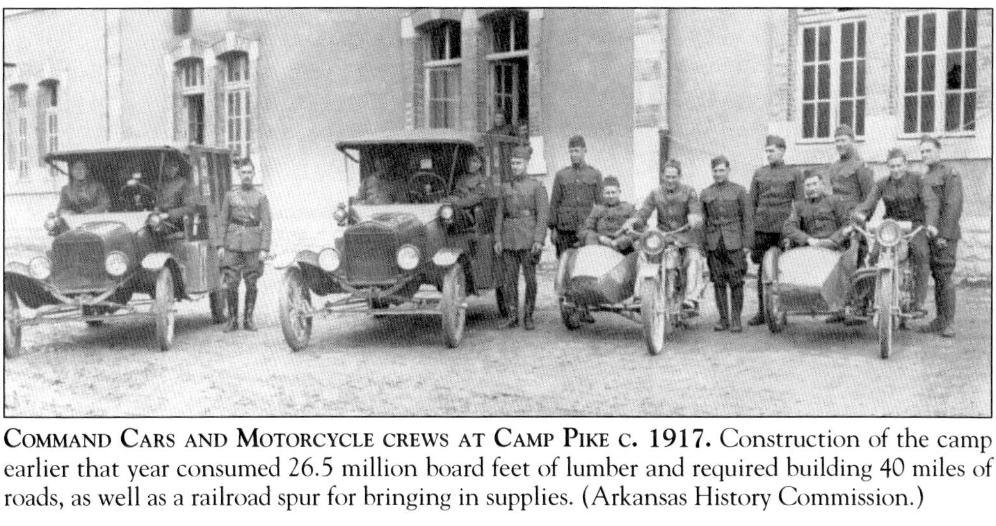

COMMAND CARS AND MOTORCYCLE CREWS AT CAMP PIKE C. 1917. Construction of the camp earlier that year consumed 26.5 million board feet of lumber and required building 40 miles of roads, as well as a railroad spur for bringing in supplies. (Arkansas History Commission.)

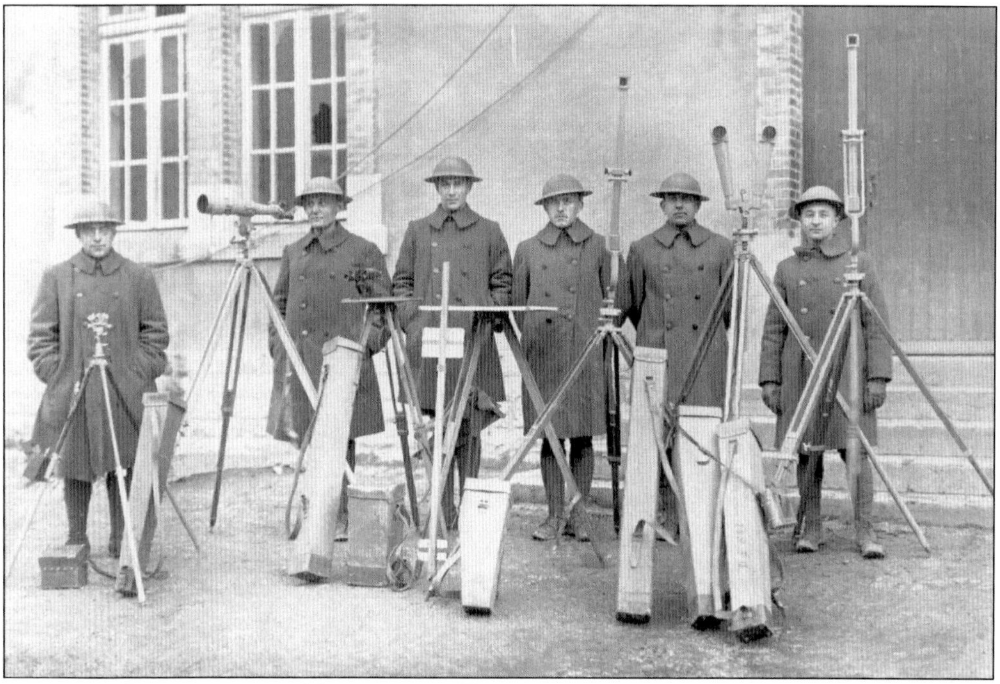

ARTILLERY OBSERVERS WITH TOOLS OF THE TRADE AT CAMP PIKE, C.1918. This photograph is from the Drew S. Williams Collection. (Arkansas History Commission.)

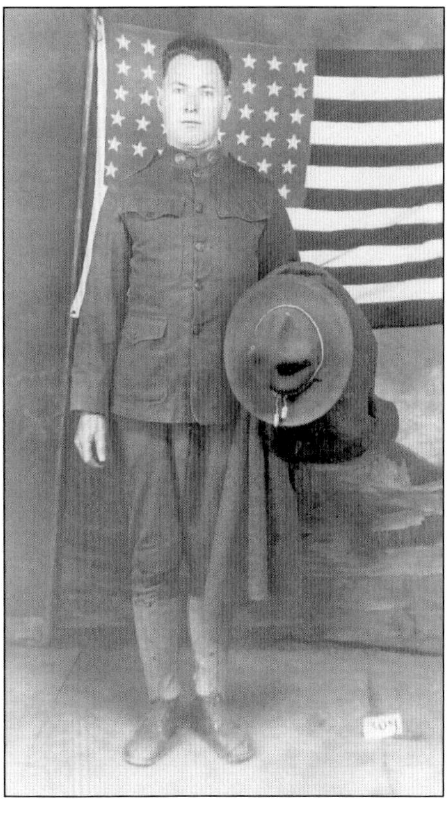

CLARENCE FERGUSON OF COMPANY A, 1ST REGIMENT, AT CAMP PIKE IN 1918. (Arkansas History Commission.)

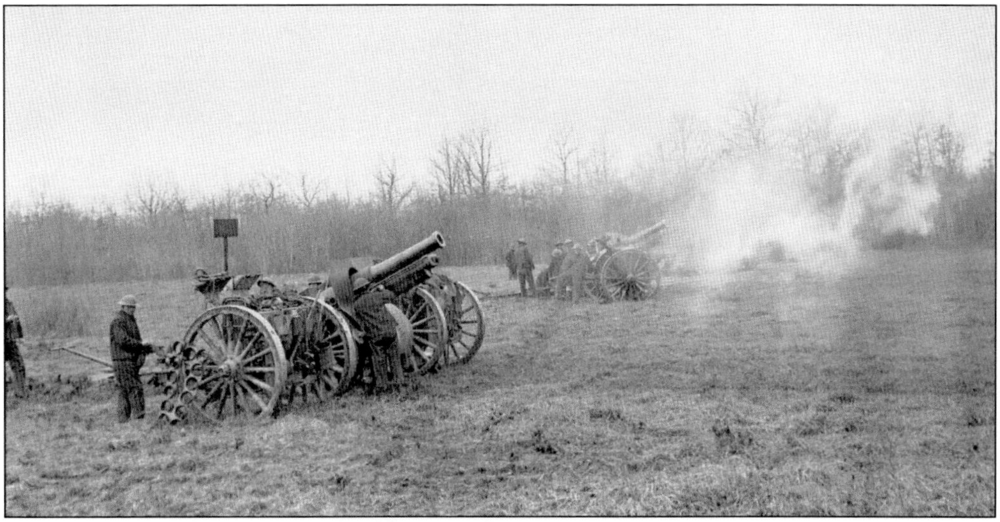

FIELD ARTILLERY FIRING AT CAMP PIKE IN 1918. When the federal government announced it would create 32 camps to train draftees to fight in World War I, local leaders raised $300,000 to buy and lease land north of Argenta in an effort to get a camp built in the county. Additional funds contributed by Argenta, Little Rock, and the state government sweetened the bid. The effort was successful and construction of the facility began on June 26, 1917. (Arkansas History Commission.)

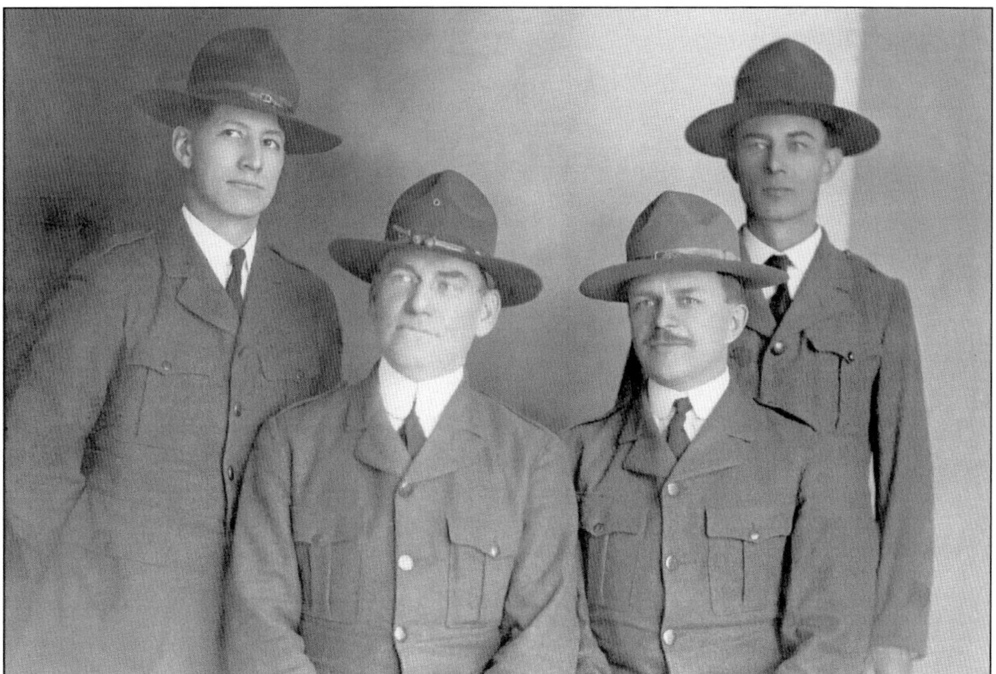

THE HEADQUARTERS STAFF OF 7TH COMPANY AT CAMP PIKE, SPRING 1918. Pictured are: Hagenbuck, athletic officer; Appleget, educational officer; Kurtyhall, camp secretary; Mitchell, religious officer. (Arkansas History Commission.)

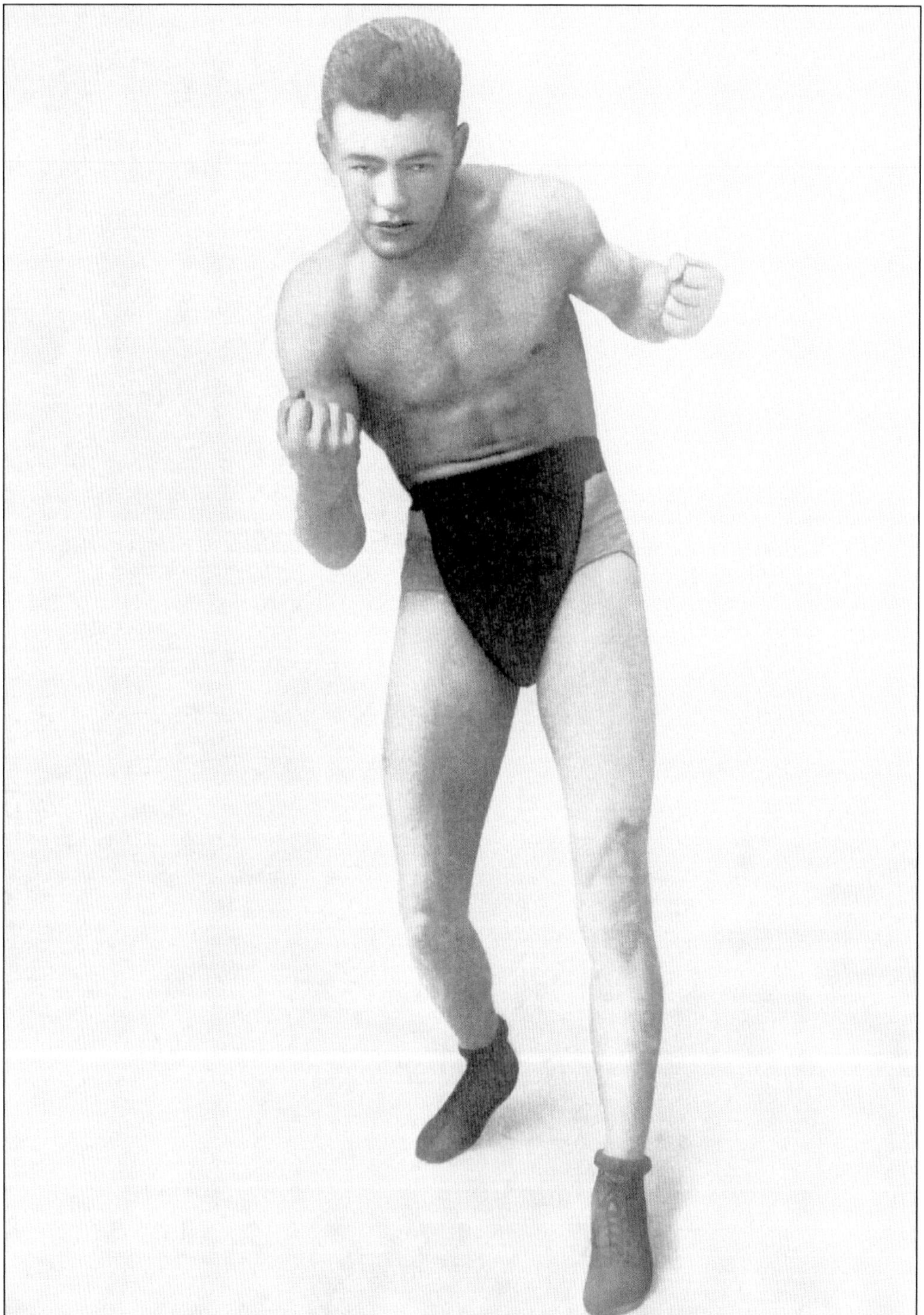

Bobby Waugh, Pugilist *Par Excellence*. Waugh was an "aggressive lightweight who has fought some clever battles in the West," according to Supplement No. 1910 to the *National Police Gazette*, dated Saturday March 21, 1914. (UALR Library Archives.)

Six

THE THIRTIES AND FORTIES

By the end of the Great Depression, the long-standing rivalry between Little Rock and North Little Rock was much more subdued than several decades earlier, when the residents of Little Rock were encouraged to dump unwanted dogs and puppies on the north side of the river. After several years of this biological warfare, North Little Rock became so overrun with feral canines that the community acquired the nickname "Dogtown." After the Twin Cities collaborated on wooing the establishment of Camp Pike into the county, community rivalry gradually became largely limited to an annual football game between the high schools on either side of the river. But one wag running for alderman in North Little Rock nevertheless campaigned on the platform that Pulaski County needed a flood control project, which was based upon widening the Arkansas River by seven miles on the southern side.

After the end of World War I, Camp Pike remained one of the few cantonment camps that was not sold off to the public. The post was used to train the Arkansas National Guard, and the facility was also used for annual meetings of farm organizations. Camp Pike was renamed Camp Robinson in 1937 to honor U.S. Sen. Joseph Taylor Robinson of Arkansas (1872-1937). When World War II erupted, the federal government enlarged the camp to 48,188 acres and used the post for basic training, reaching a peak strength of about 60,000 men. A prisoner of war camp was also established on the grounds to house captured members of the German Afrika Korps.

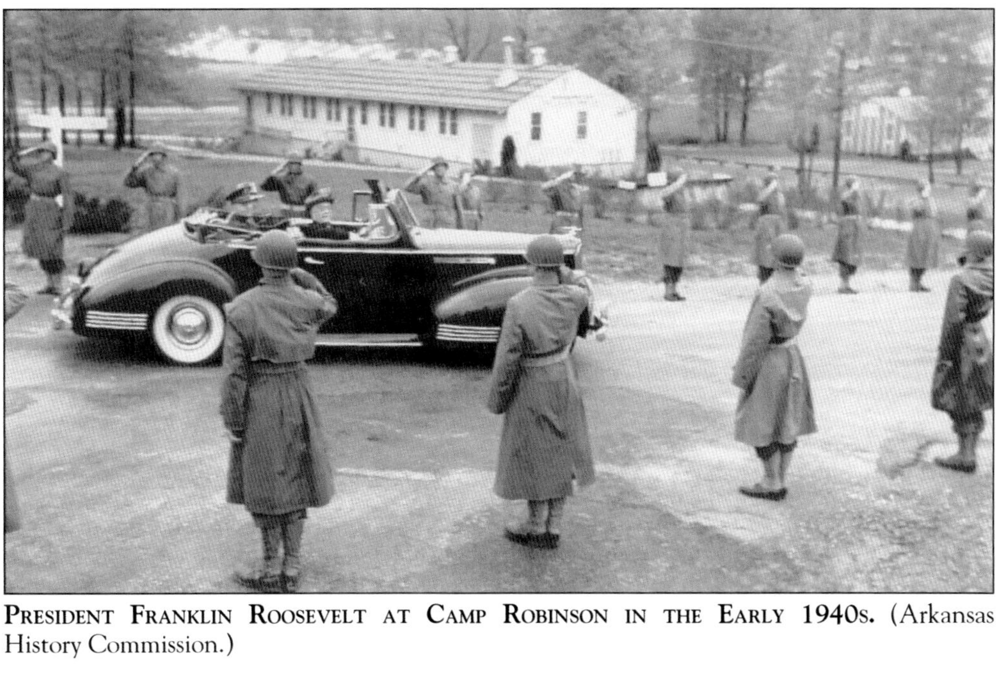

PRESIDENT FRANKLIN ROOSEVELT AT CAMP ROBINSON IN THE EARLY 1940S. (Arkansas History Commission.)

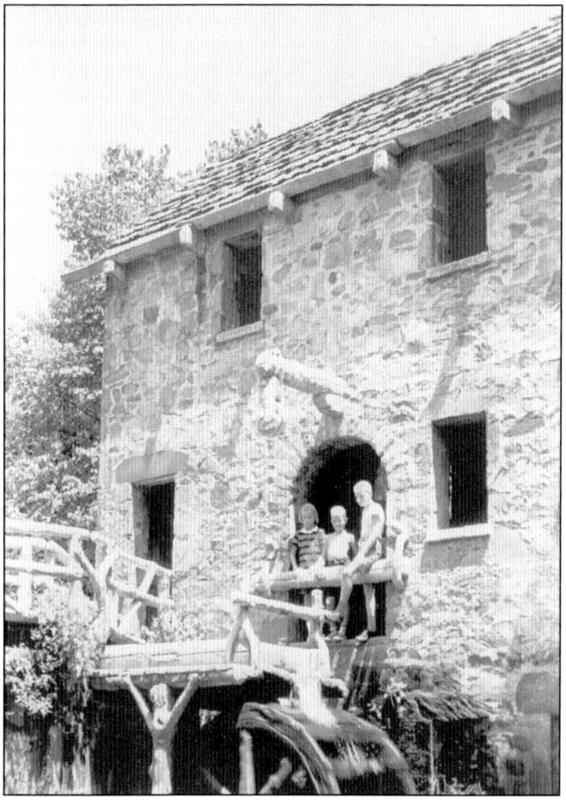

Two Views of the Old Mill at Pugh's Mill Park. Built in 1933 at Lakewood in North Little Rock, the Old Mill is an authentically designed replica of a mill from about 1828. Fabricated entirely of concrete to give a carefully planned look of neglect, the Old Mill was used for the opening scene in the film classic "Gone With the Wind." These photographs were taken by Capt. F.G. Hall, U.S. Army. (Arkansas History Commission.)

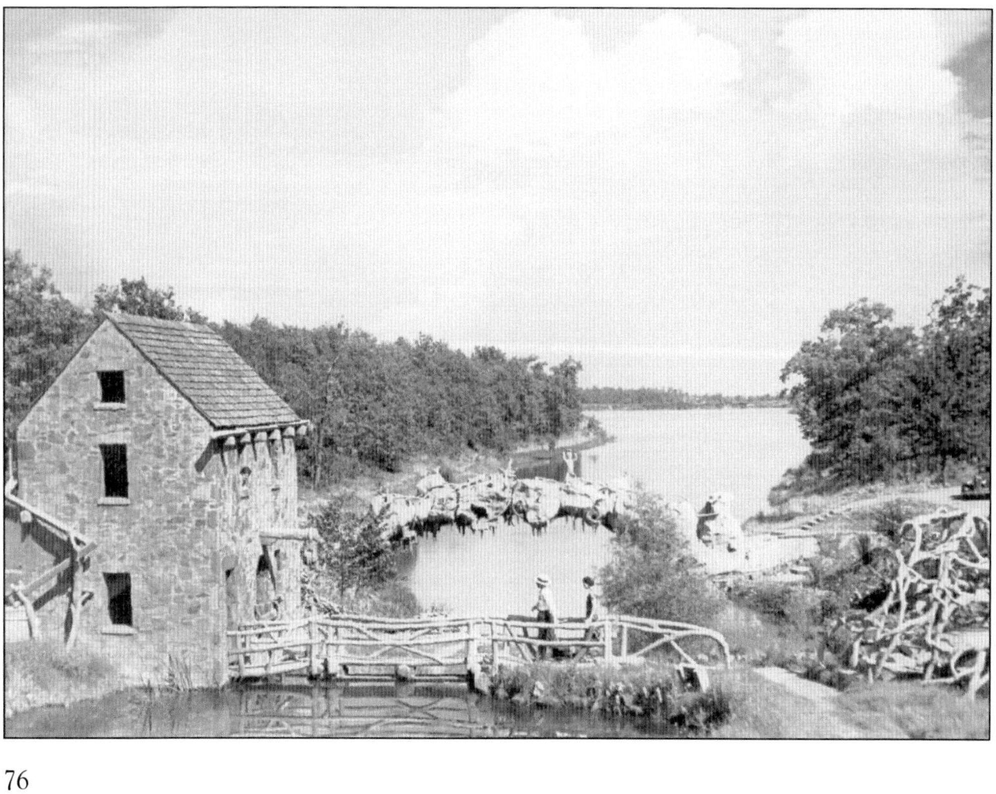

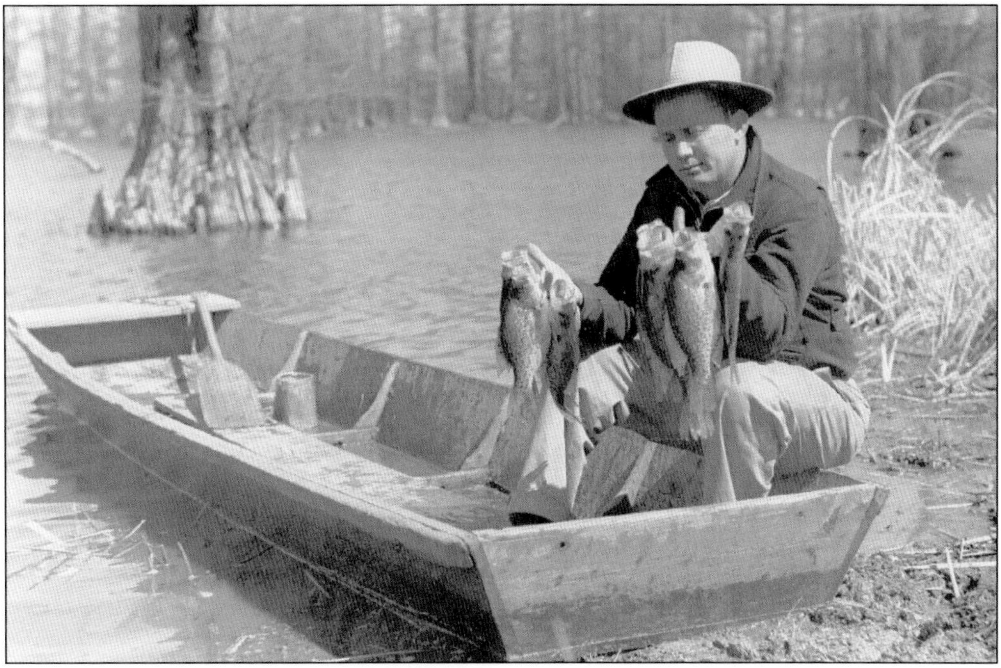

Living the Good Life. Fishing could really improve the quality of life during the desperately hard times of the Great Depression. This fisherman was photographed on Hill Lake near Little Rock in the 1930s. (WPA photo, Arkansas History Commission.)

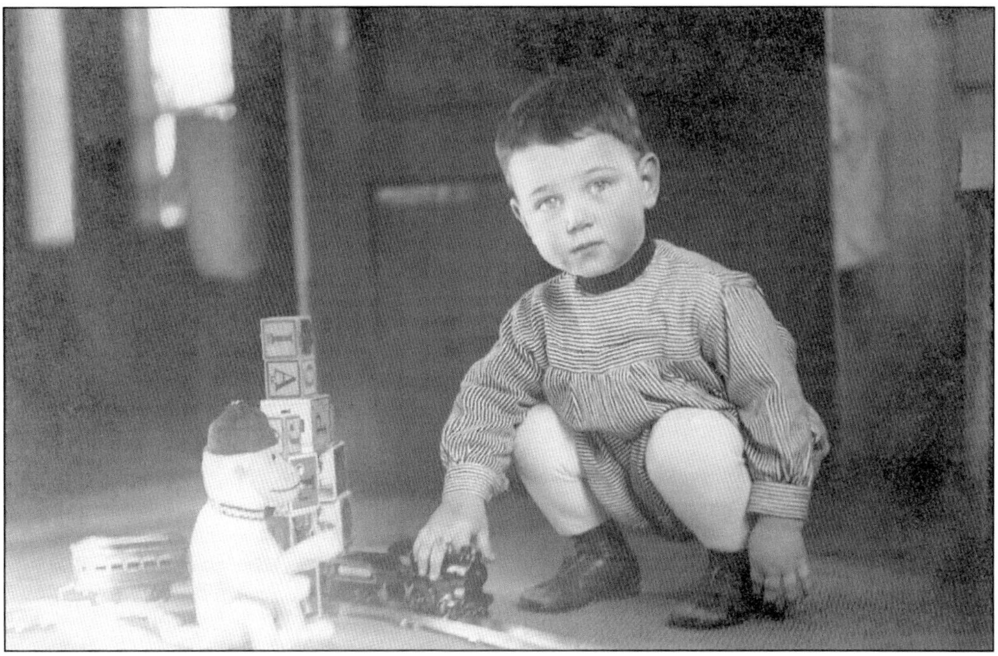

Allan Dunlap Richardson. He was photographed at "age 2 and three months." (Lenora Scott England Collection; Arkansas History Commission)

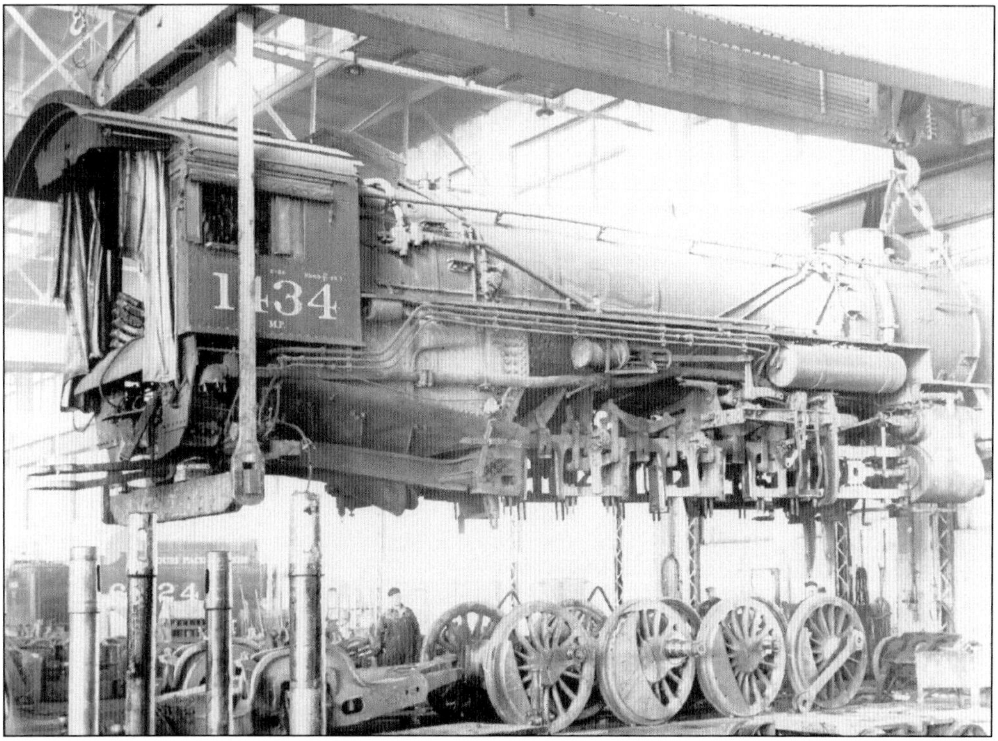

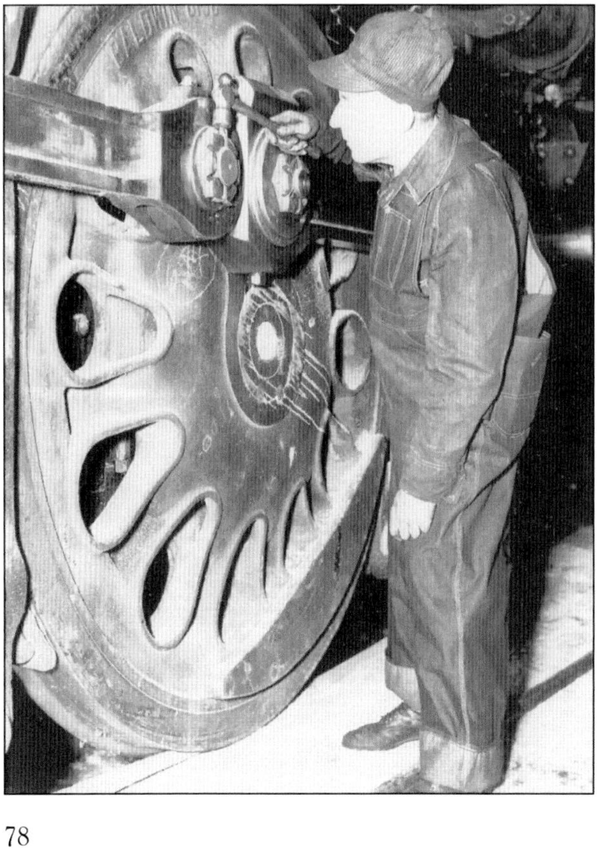

DEWHEELING A LOCOMOTIVE AT THE MISSOURI PACIFIC SHOPS IN NORTH LITTLE ROCK. (Arkansas History Commission.)

MACHINIST WORKS ON DRIVE SIDE RODS OF LOCOMOTIVE AT THE MISSOURI PACIFIC SHOPS IN NORTH LITTLE ROCK. (Arkansas History Commission.)

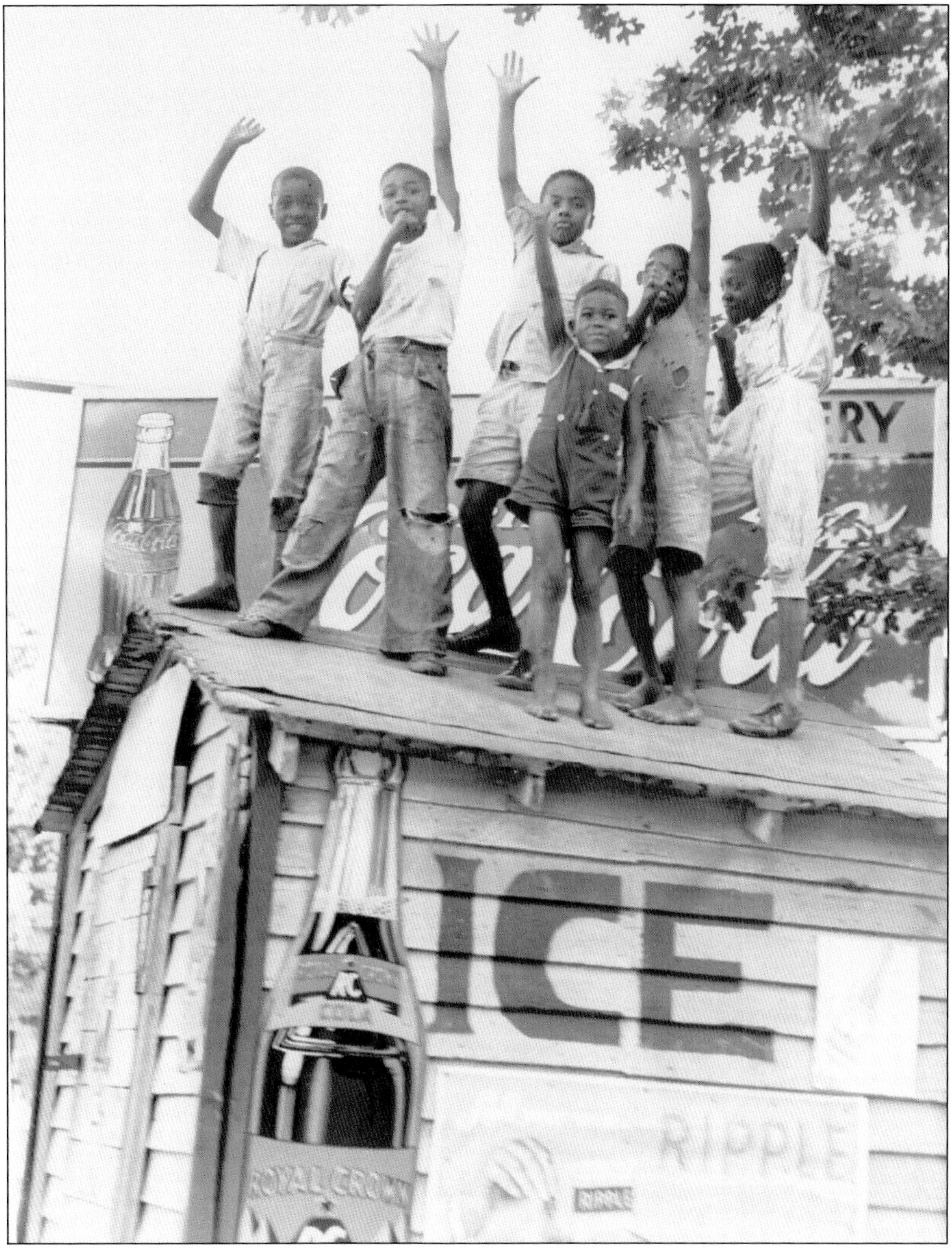

Boys Playing on a Coca-Cola Stand. This photograph was taken in Little Rock about 1938. (Arkansas History Commission.)

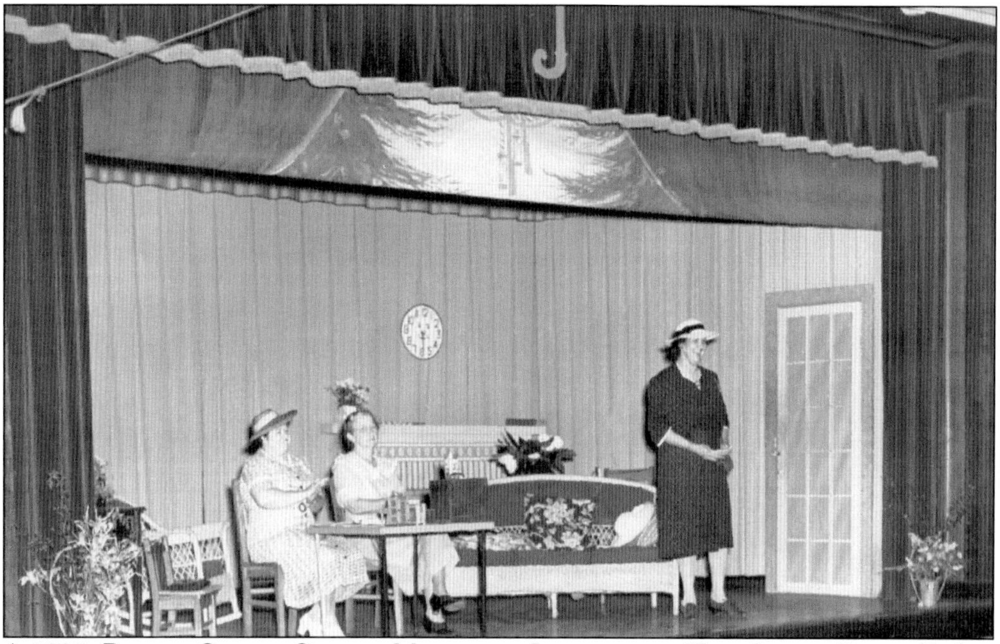

A 1930s Pulaski County Council Meeting at Jacksonville High School Pictured below is a group portrait of the council members. (WPA Photo, Arkansas History Commission.)

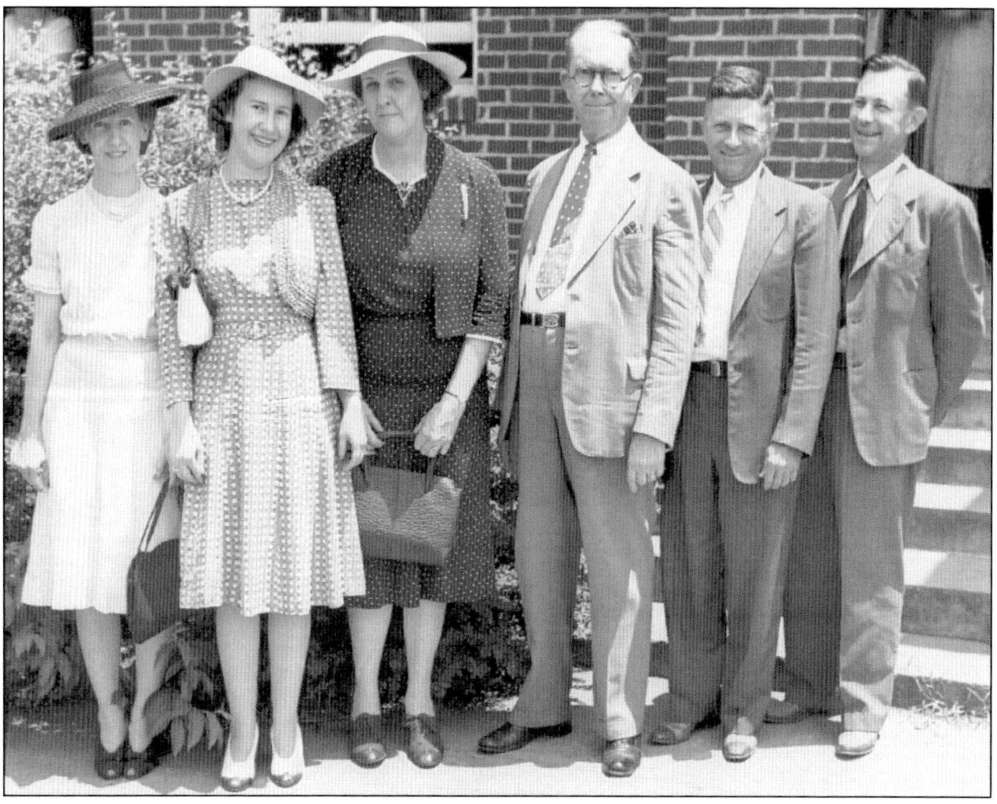

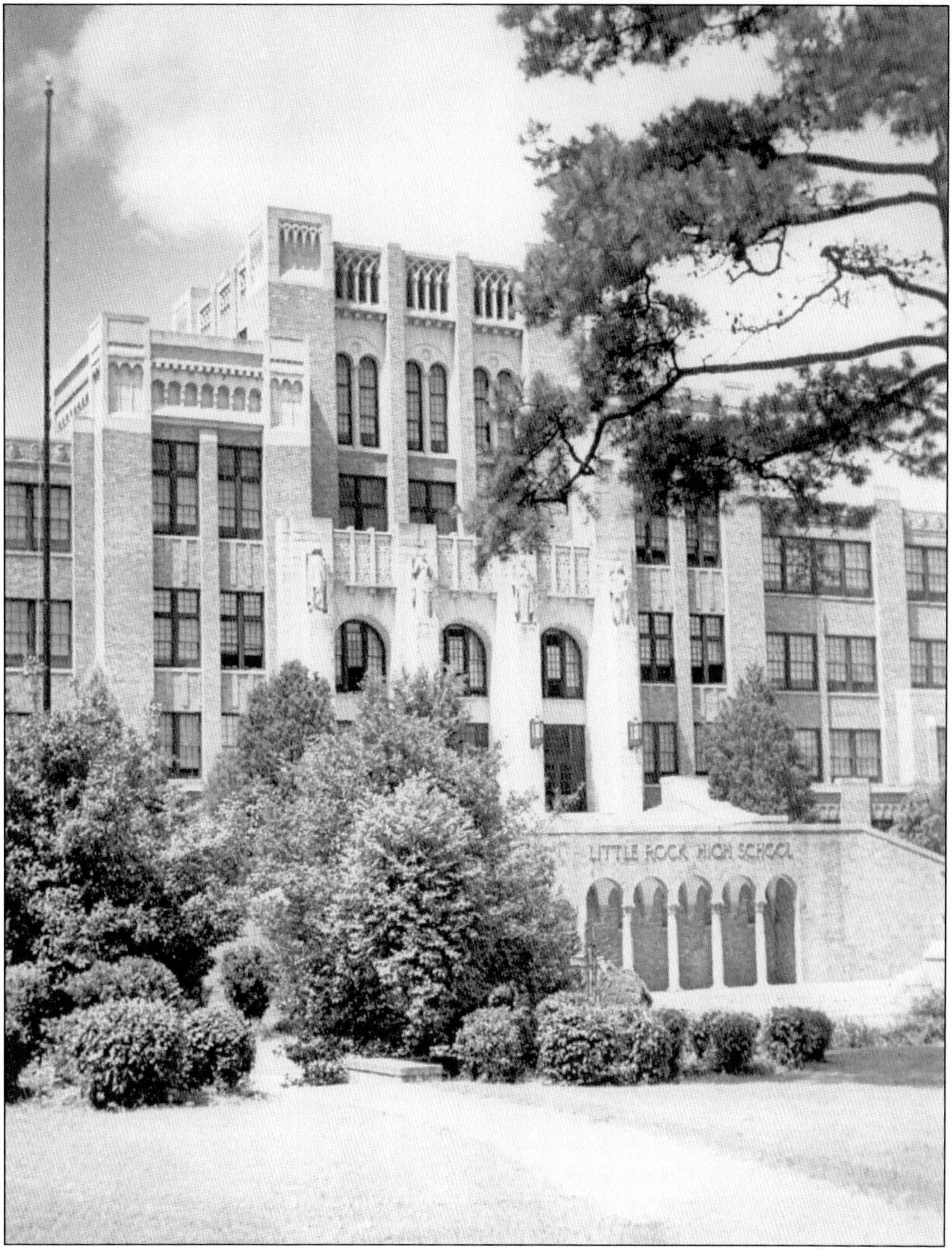

LITTLE ROCK HIGH SCHOOL IN THE 1930S. This photograph was taken by a photographer of the Works Progress Administration (WPA), which was a federal program during the Great Depression designed to provide work for as many people as possible. These work programs got unemployed workers off relief and put money back into the moribund economy. The goal was to hire as many people as possible to perform useful services, so many diverse projects were funded. (Arkansas History Commission.)

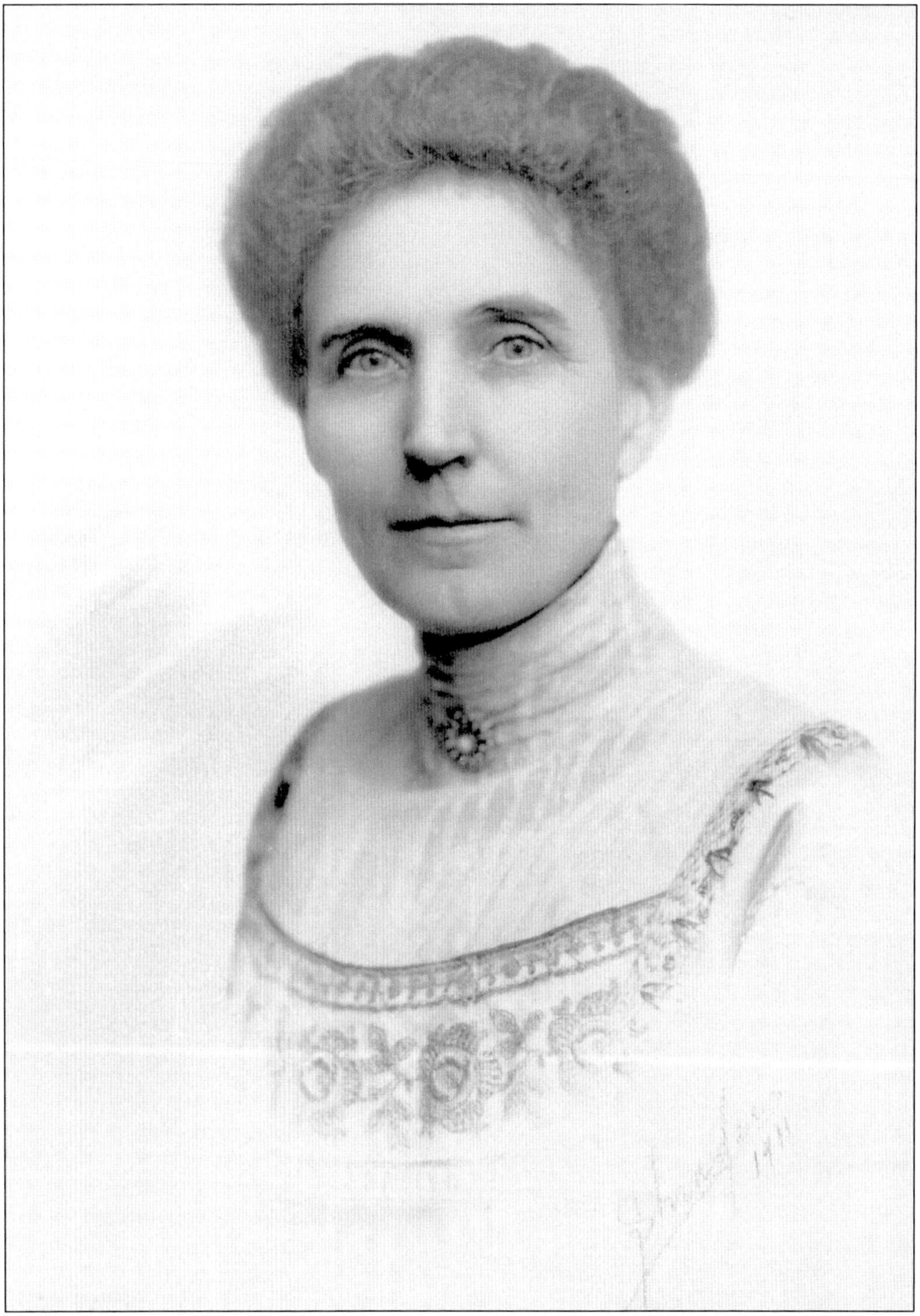

Louvenia Wallace Donaghey, Wife of Governor George W. Donaghey. They met at a Christmas party in 1879, when George was working as a carpenter in Conway. After a four year courtship, they were married in 1883. This photo was taken by Shrader Photography in 1910. (UCA Archives.)

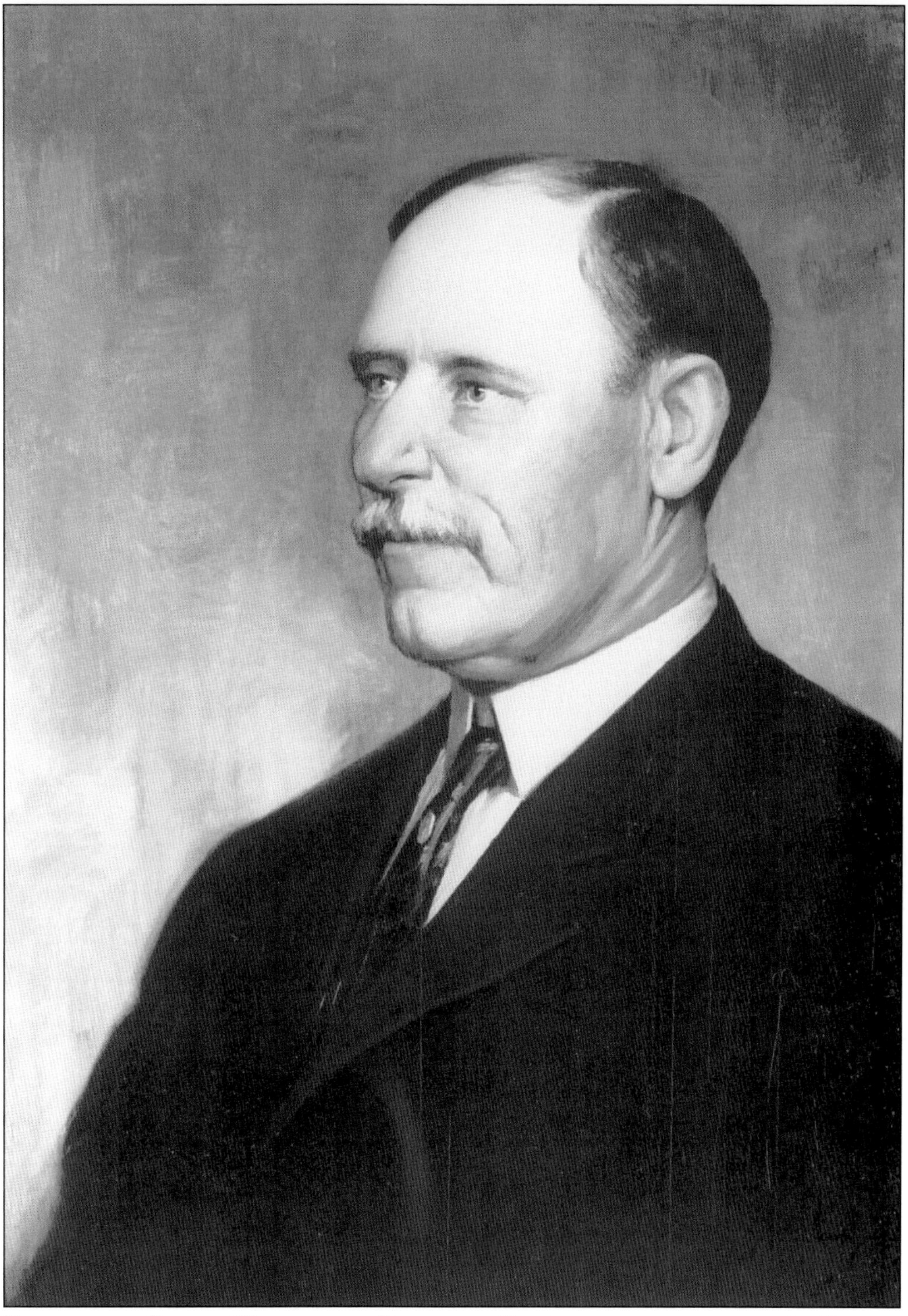

PORTRAIT OF GEORGE WASHINGTON DONAGHEY. Starting out as a carpenter in Conway, Donaghey became arguably one of the best and most influential governors and philanthropists in Arkansas history. (Arkansas History Commission.)

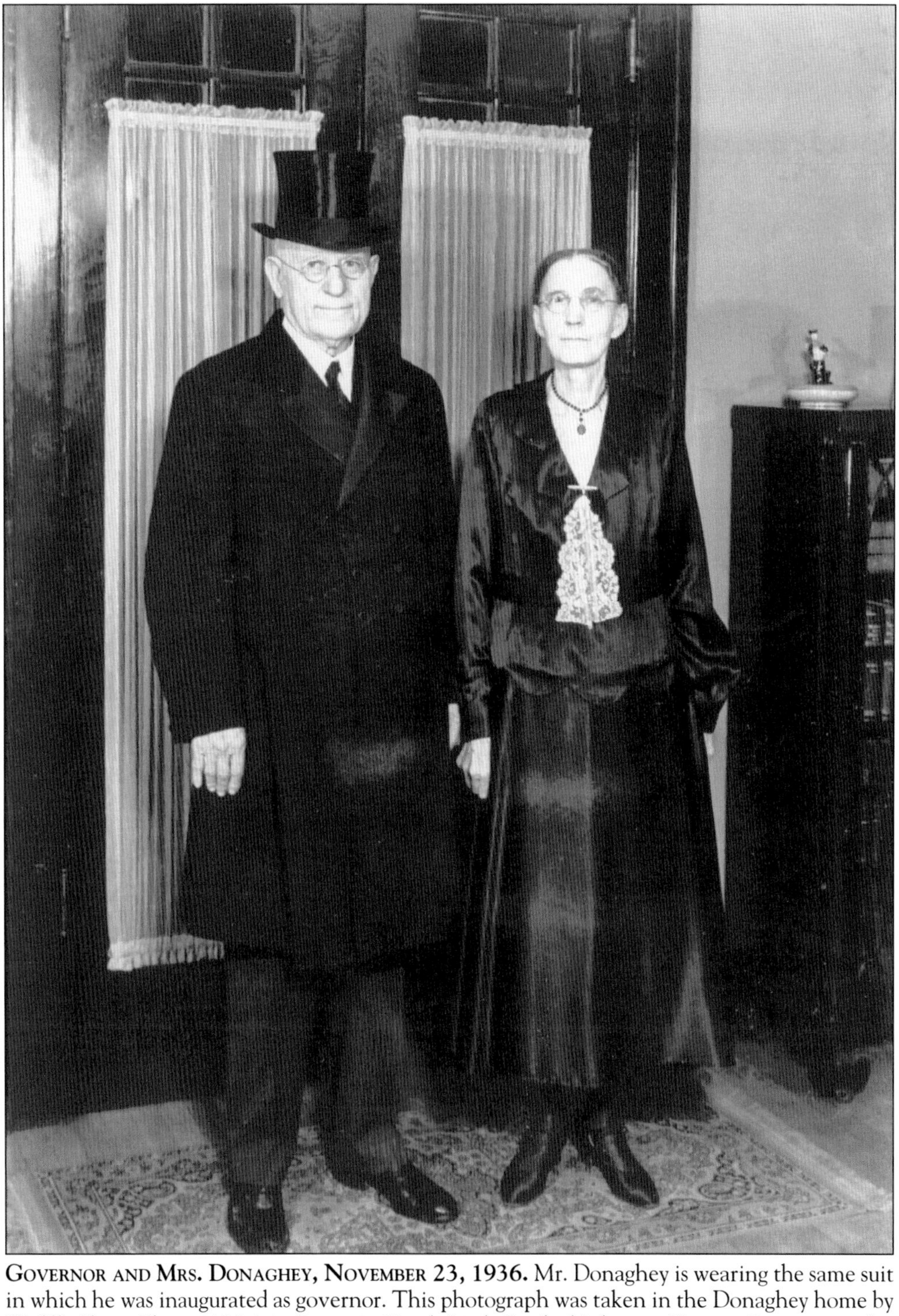

GOVERNOR AND MRS. DONAGHEY, NOVEMBER 23, 1936. Mr. Donaghey is wearing the same suit in which he was inaugurated as governor. This photograph was taken in the Donaghey home by Wolff's Photo Shop, 419 Main Street in North Little Rock. (Arkansas History Commission.)

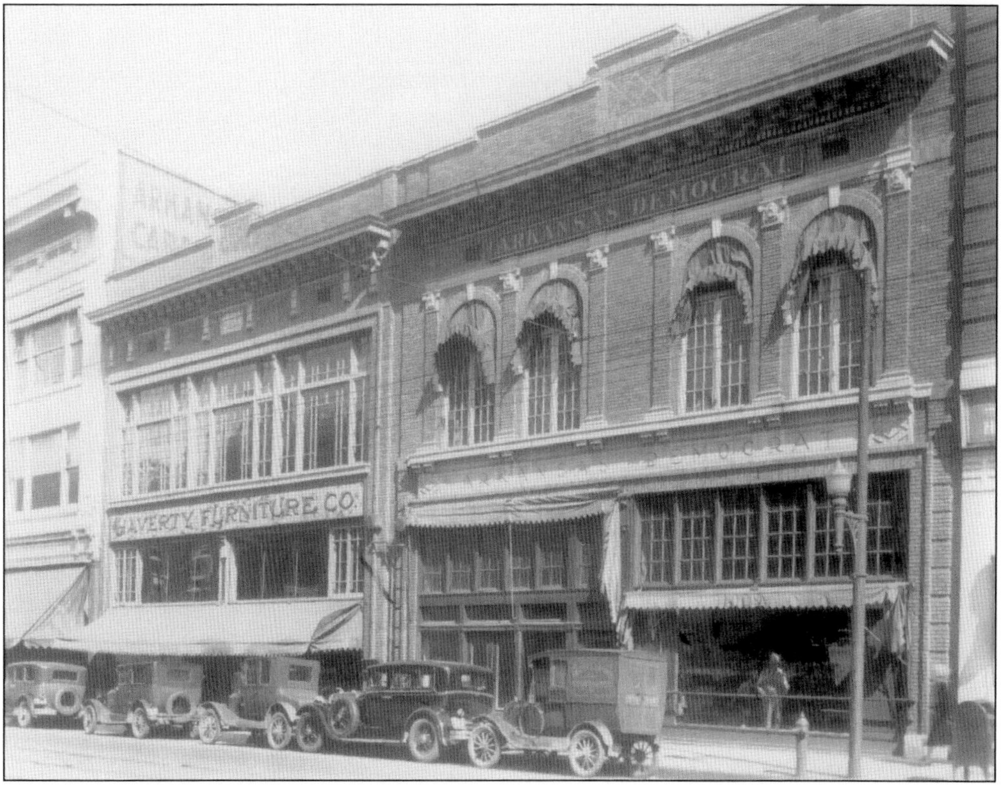

ARKANSAS DEMOCRAT, 609-15 MAIN STREET, C.1930. Haverty Furniture can be seen next door to the newspaper office. (Arkansas History Commission.)

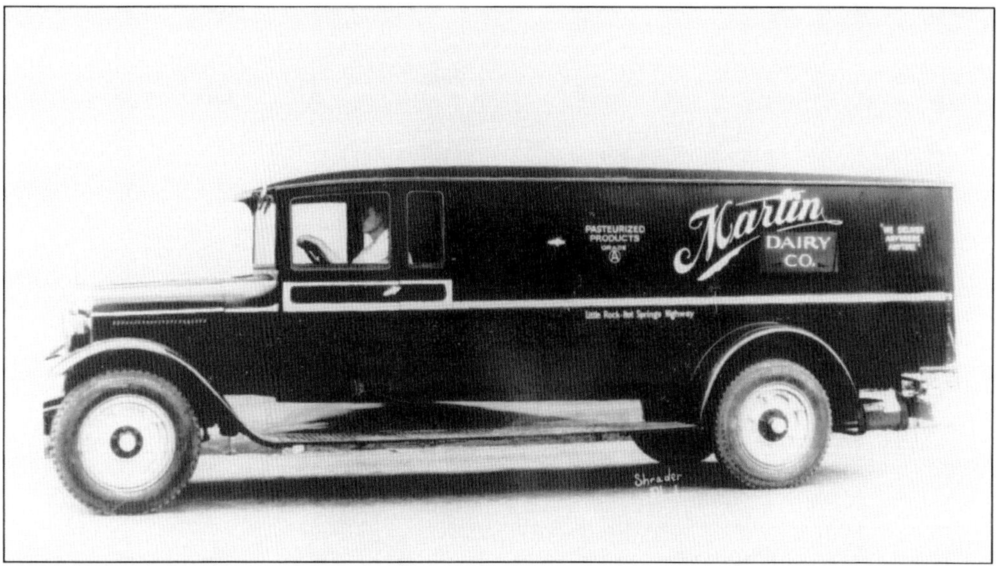

THE MARTIN DAIRY DELIVERY TRUCK IN LITTLE ROCK ABOUT 1935. (UCA Archives.)

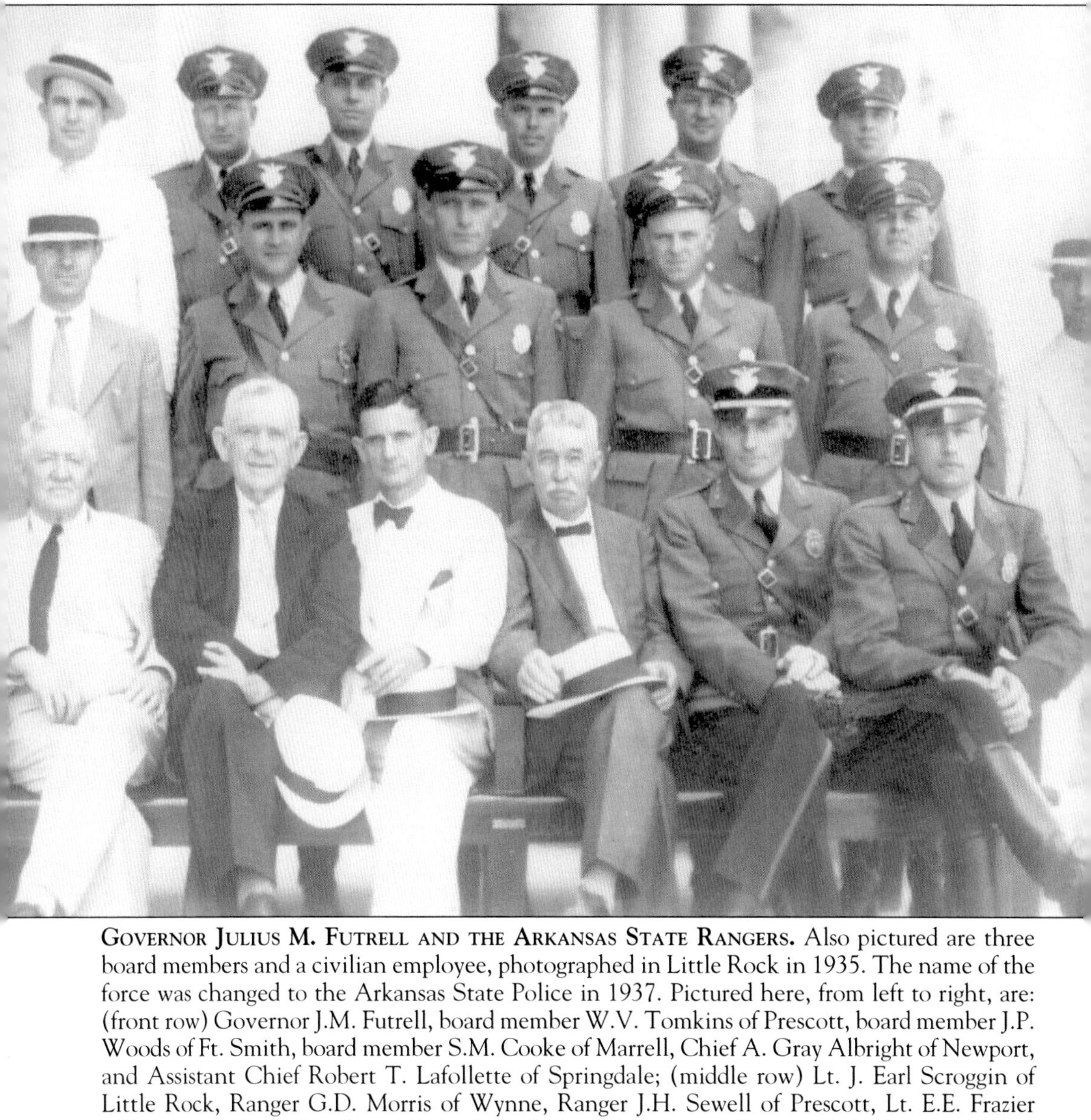

Governor Julius M. Futrell and the Arkansas State Rangers. Also pictured are three board members and a civilian employee, photographed in Little Rock in 1935. The name of the force was changed to the Arkansas State Police in 1937. Pictured here, from left to right, are: (front row) Governor J.M. Futrell, board member W.V. Tomkins of Prescott, board member J.P. Woods of Ft. Smith, board member S.M. Cooke of Marrell, Chief A. Gray Albright of Newport, and Assistant Chief Robert T. Lafollette of Springdale; (middle row) Lt. J. Earl Scroggin of Little Rock, Ranger G.D. Morris of Wynne, Ranger J.H. Sewell of Prescott, Lt. E.E. Frazier of Hardy, and Leon Gershner of North Little Rock; (back row) Ranger Neil Shannon of Pine Bluff, Capt. Cliff Atkinson of Morrilton, Ranger John Hendricks of Ft. Smith, Ranger J.P. "Frip" Hill of El Dorado, Ranger Gene "Buck" Mooney of Mountain Home, and Ranger J. Ed Clark of Little Rock. J.E. Scroggin set up the state's fingerprint files, and Leon Gershner was a civilian employee of the Rangers when this photograph was taken, but he joined the force the year after it became known as the Arkansas State Police. (UCA Archives.)

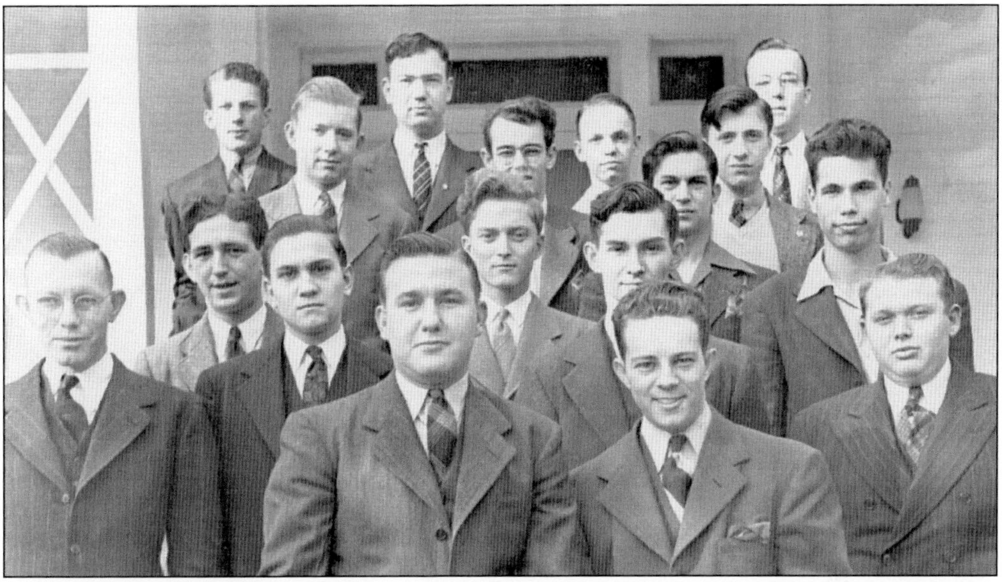

DELTA KAPPA FRATERNITY AT LITTLE ROCK JUNIOR COLLEGE ABOUT 1940. The college was founded in 1927, employing 8 instructors who taught about 100 students. The school became accredited in 1929 and continued to hold classes in Little Rock's public school buildings. (Arkansas History Commission.)

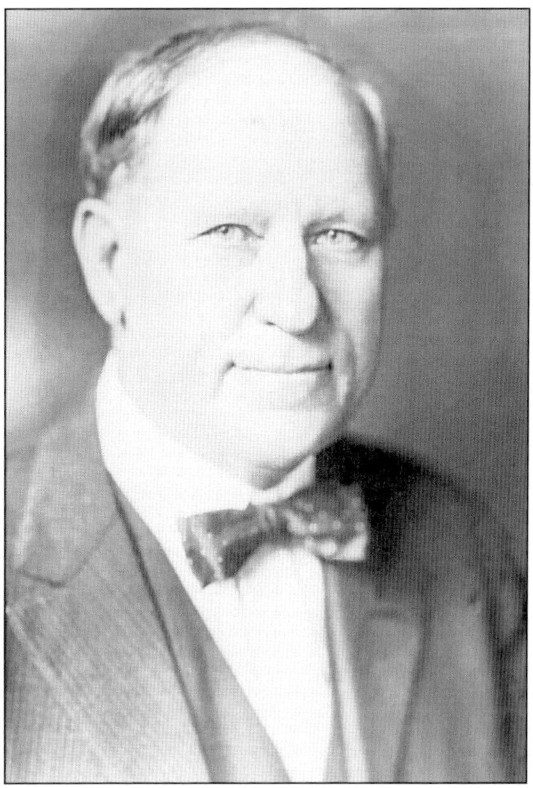

UALR BENEFACTOR. George Washington Donaghey, former governor of Arkansas, gave a generous endowment to help establish the Little Rock Junior College. This endowment continues to provide funding to LRJC's successor, the University of Arkansas at Little Rock (UALR). (UALR Library Archives.)

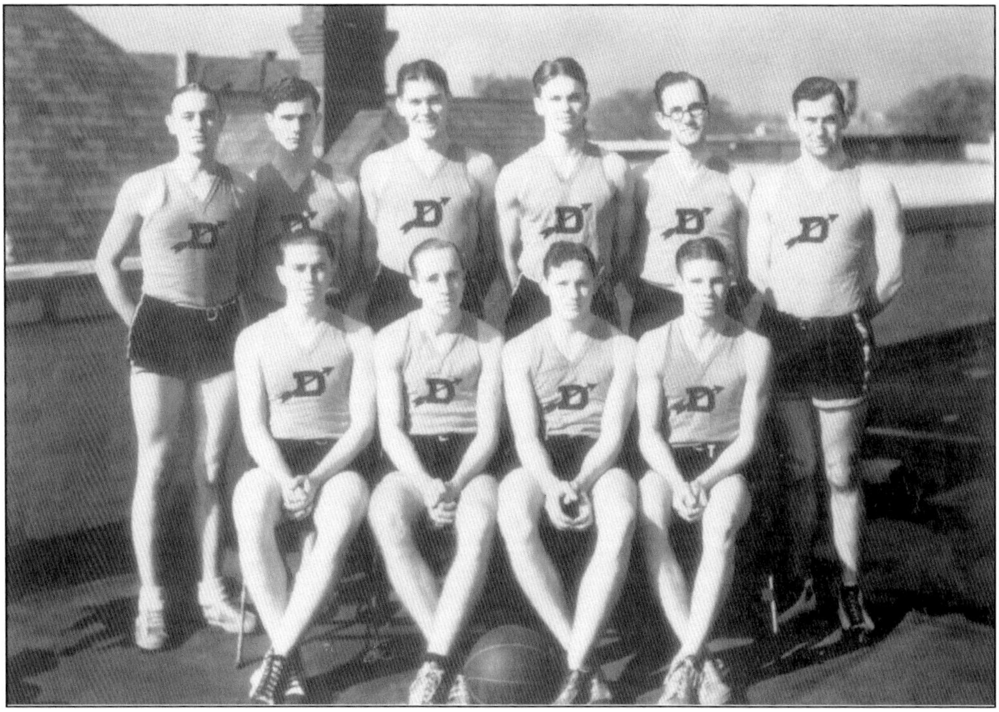

Draughon's Basketball Team in 1929 or 1930. This photograph was taken by R.D. Wolfe, who was a commercial and press photographer with a studio located at the Federal Bank Building in Little Rock. (Arkansas History Commission.)

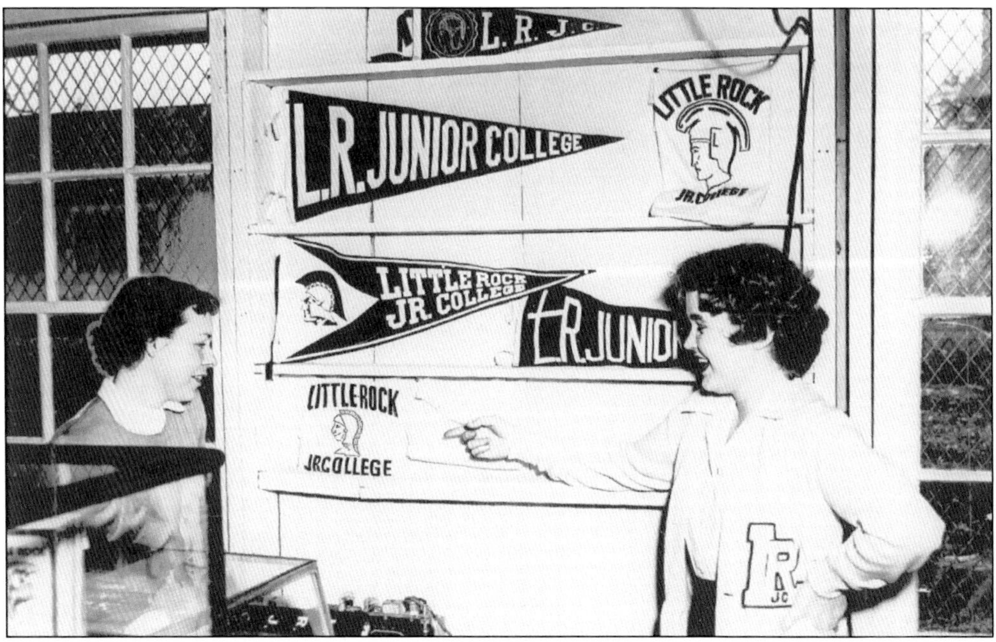

Two students Admiring Pennants at Little Rock Junior College in 1949. (UALR Library Archives.)

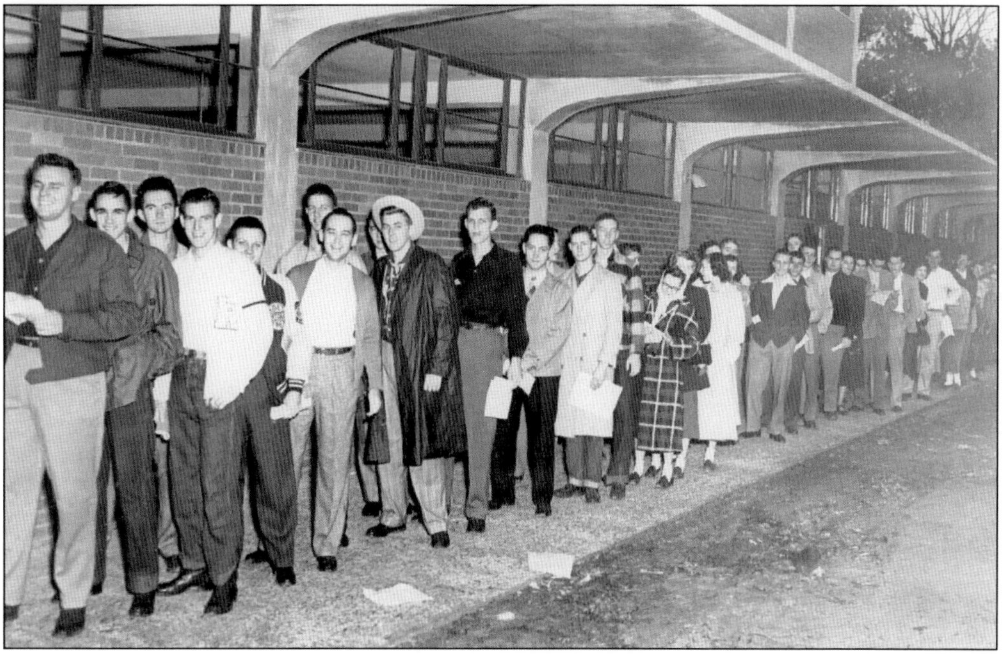

Students Lined up to Register at Little Rock Junior College in 1949. (UALR Library Archives.)

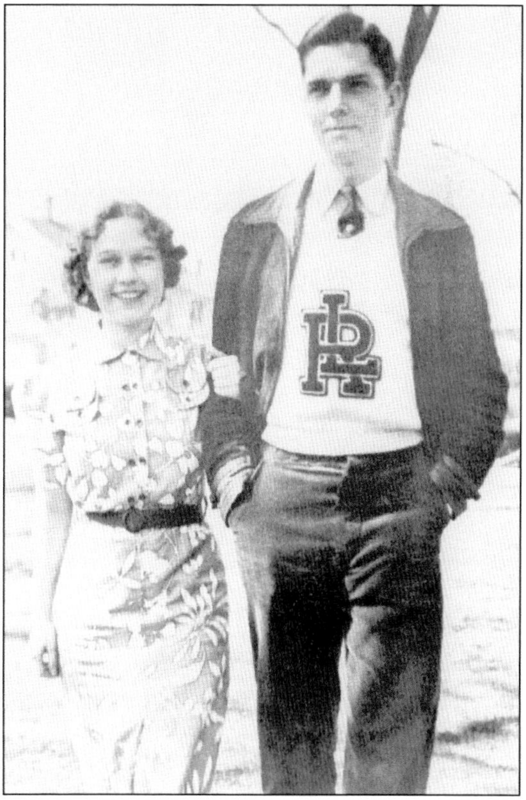

Robert Gannaway and Amanda Dunaway. They were the popularly elected king and queen of Little Rock Junior College in 1938. (UALR Library Archives.)

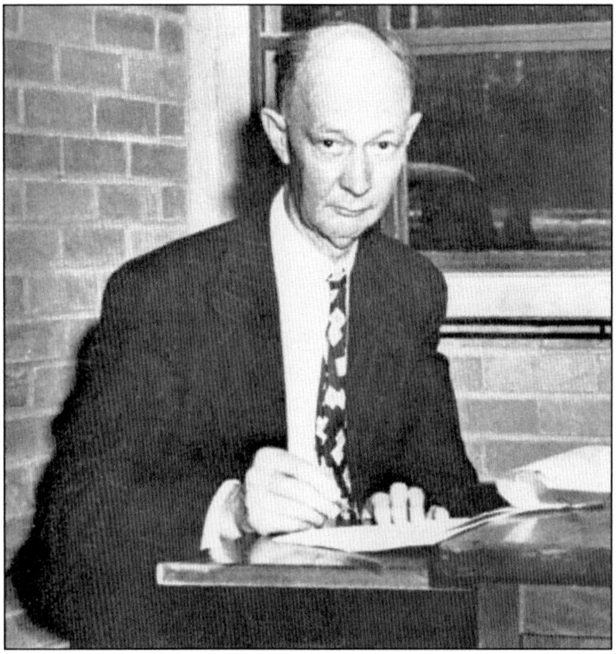

John A. Larson, Founder of Little Rock Junior College. He served as president of LRJC from 1929 until his death in 1949. (UALR Library Archives.)

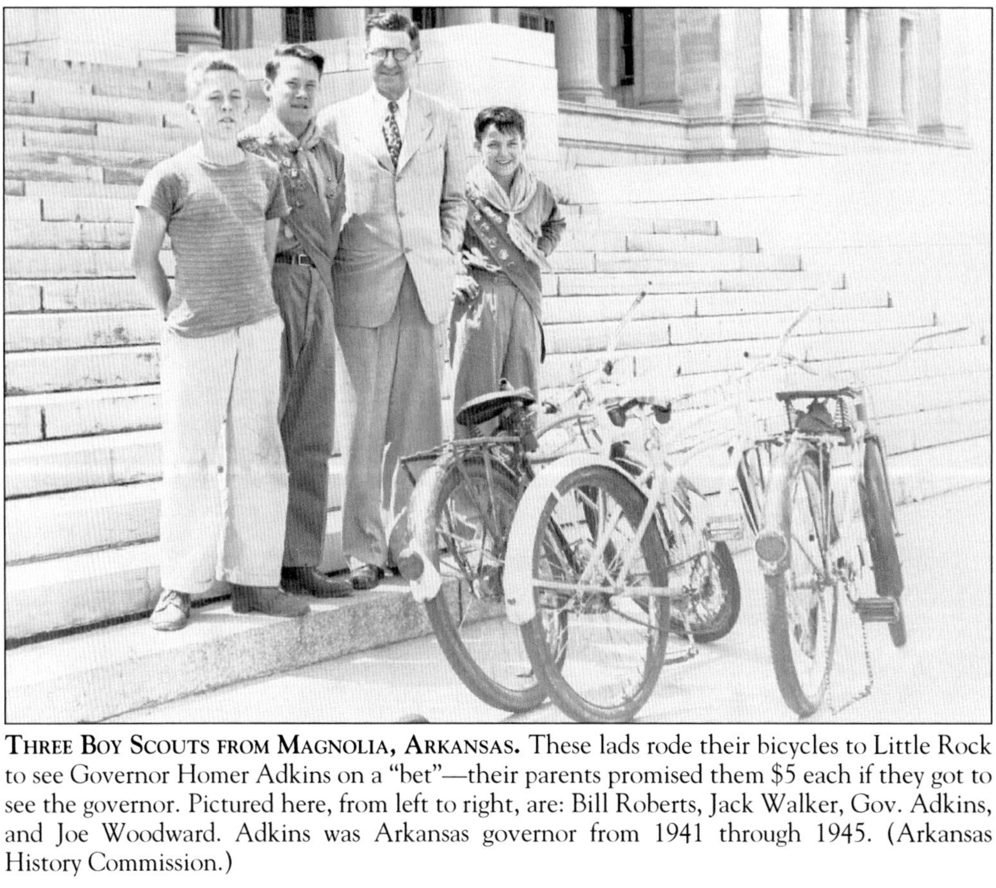

Three Boy Scouts from Magnolia, Arkansas. These lads rode their bicycles to Little Rock to see Governor Homer Adkins on a "bet"—their parents promised them $5 each if they got to see the governor. Pictured here, from left to right, are: Bill Roberts, Jack Walker, Gov. Adkins, and Joe Woodward. Adkins was Arkansas governor from 1941 through 1945. (Arkansas History Commission.)

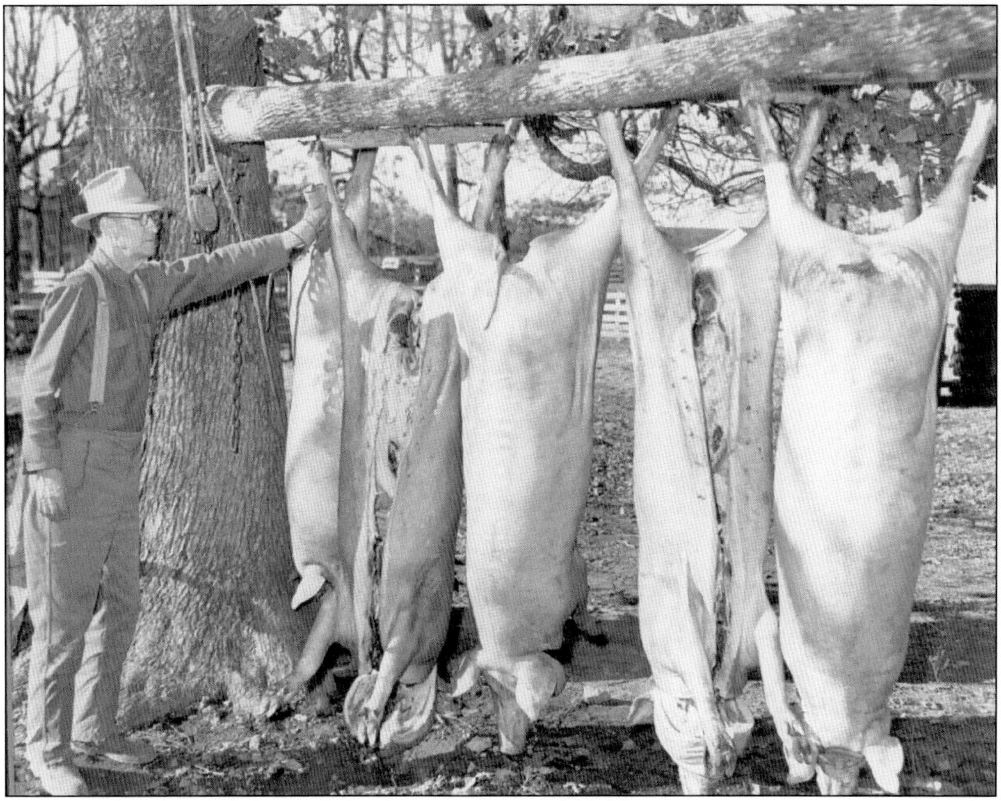

HOMER M. ADKINS BUTCHERING HOGS AND PLOUGHING A FIELD ON HIS "SLEEPY HOLLOW FARM" IN THE 1940S. A trusted local lieutenant of U.S. Senator Joe T. Robinson, Adkins became the heir apparent to the political power consolidated by Robinson over three decades. Adkins used this power to reach the governor's mansion in 1941. He also used this power to fire J. William Fulbright from his post as University of Arkansas president. Fulbright eventually had the last laugh, however, during the U.S. Senate race of 1944. He defeated Adkins and launched a career in Congress that would last for 30 years. (Arkansas History Commission.)

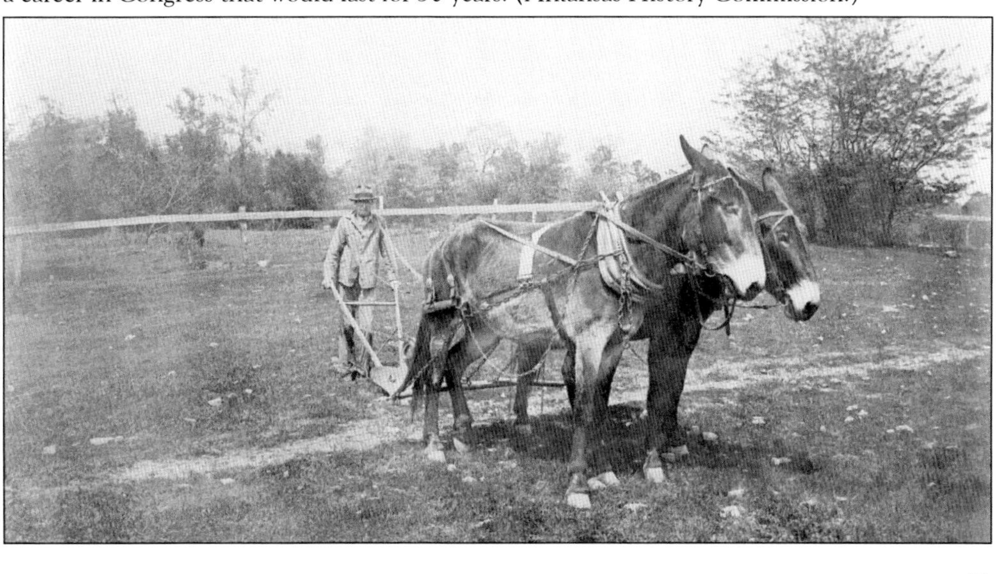

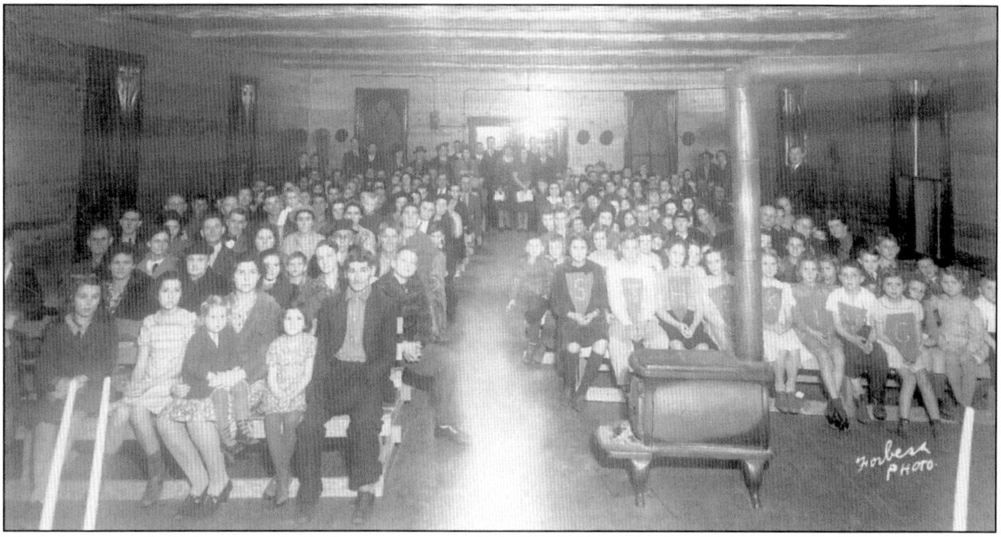

THE CONGREGATION IN THE SANCTUARY OF THE CHURCH OF THE NAZARENE. Members of the congregation enjoyed the heat from the Dudley wood stove. One pastor at the church was Rev. Tom Davis. (Arkansas History Commission.)

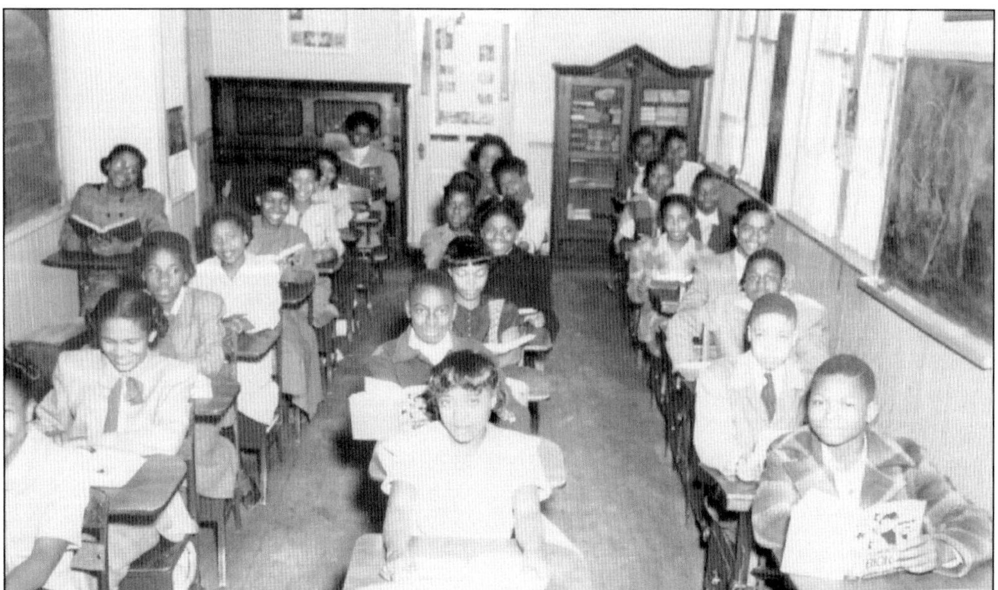

CLASSROOM IN ST. BARTHOLOMEW'S SCHOOL IN LITTLE ROCK. This photograph was taken on February 10, 1949. (Arkansas History Commission.)

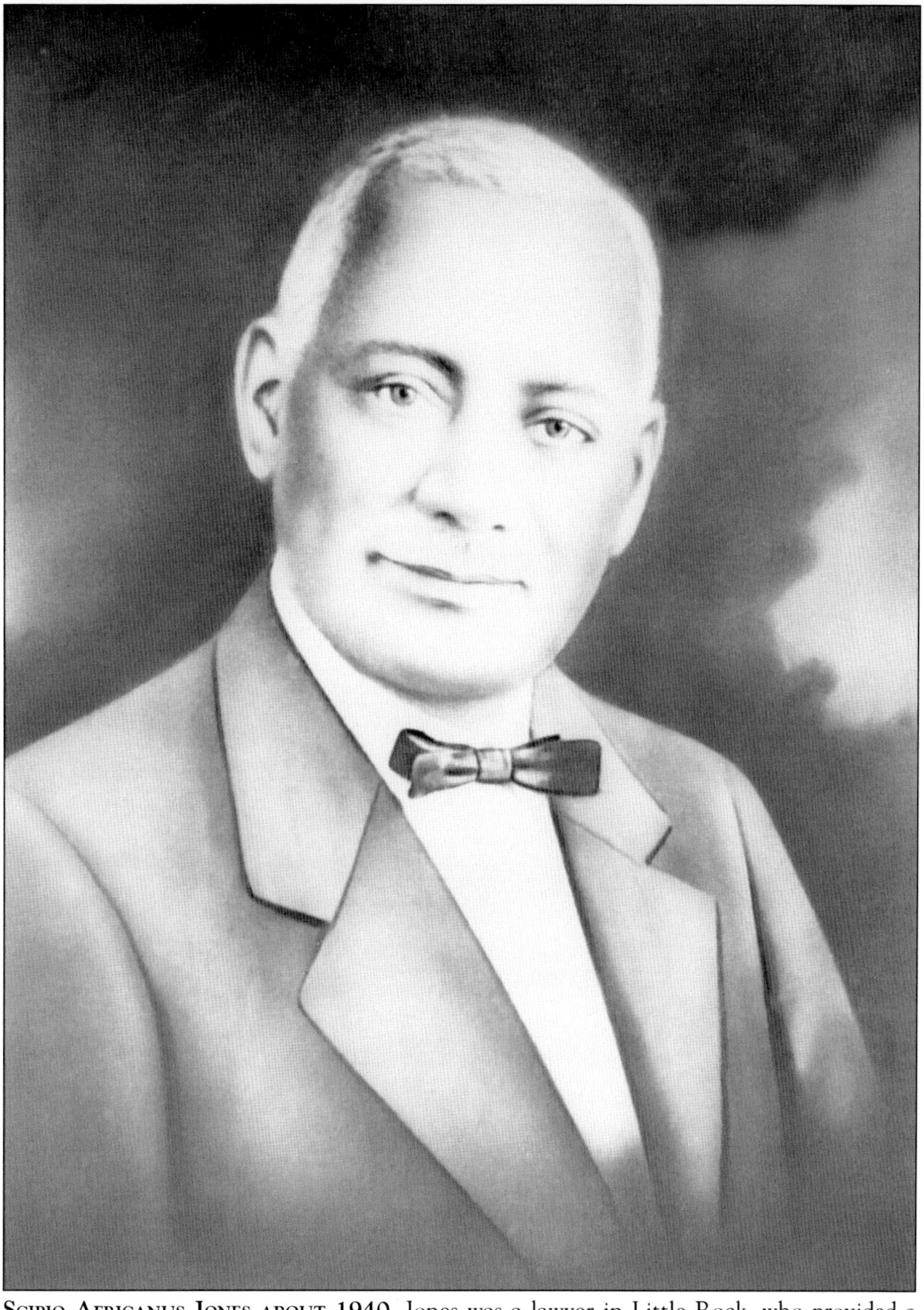

SCIPIO AFRICANUS JONES ABOUT 1940. Jones was a lawyer in Little Rock, who provided a powerful voice for Arkansas blacks in the late 19th and early 20th centuries. Perhaps his most noteworthy accomplishment was convincing Attorney General Jeff Davis, who was an unrepentant racist, that Arkansas needed to reform its scandalous prison system. (UCA Archives.)

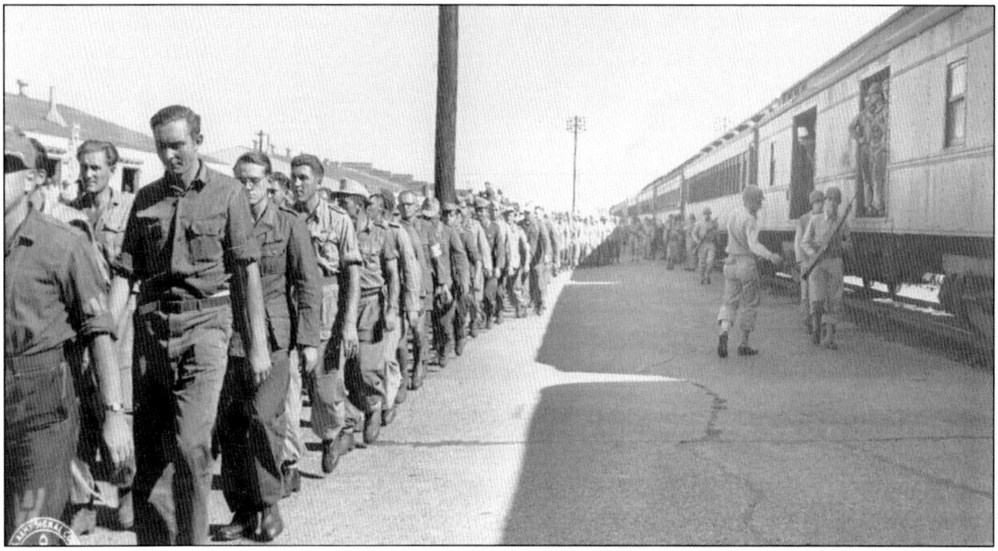

New arrivals from Africa. These German war prisoners came by train to Camp Joseph T. Robinson in August 1943. About 3,000 Germans, mainly veterans of General Erwin Rommel's Afrika Korps, were held in the 300-acre prisoner of war camp until the end of World War II. The prison camp closed in May 1946. (Arkansas History Commission.)

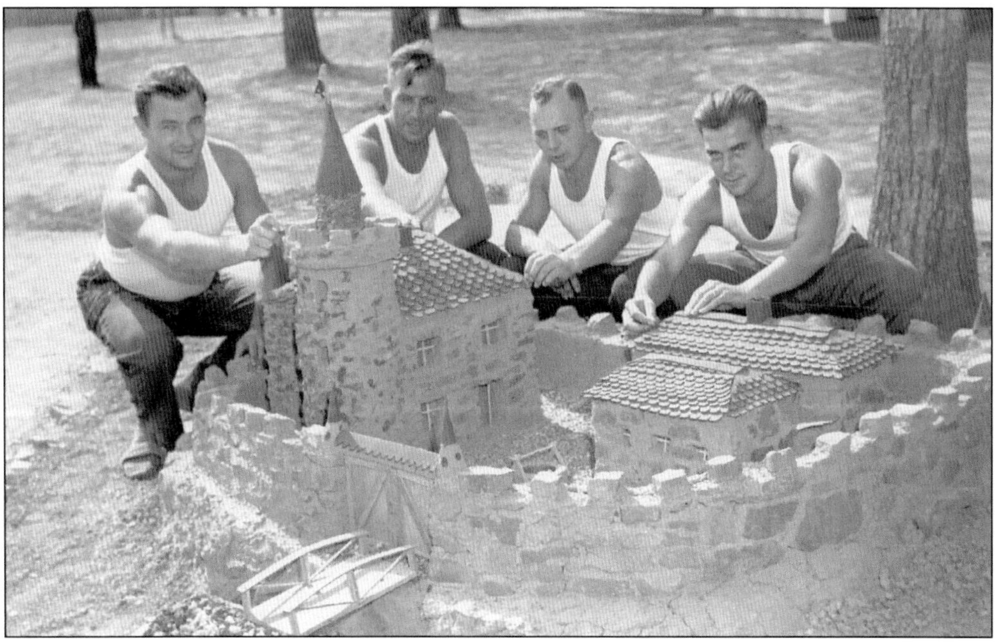

Model Castle Built by German Prisoners of War to Pass the Time. Soccer was the most popular diversion for the prisoners. They also organized orchestras and bands, taught English lessons, and produced plays. Many prisoners worked as contract laborers on Arkansas farms, cotton gins, and compresses while others cut timber for International Paper, loaded trucks for Big Rock Stone and Material Company, or milled pipe at the Choctaw Pipe Company. (Arkansas History Commission.)

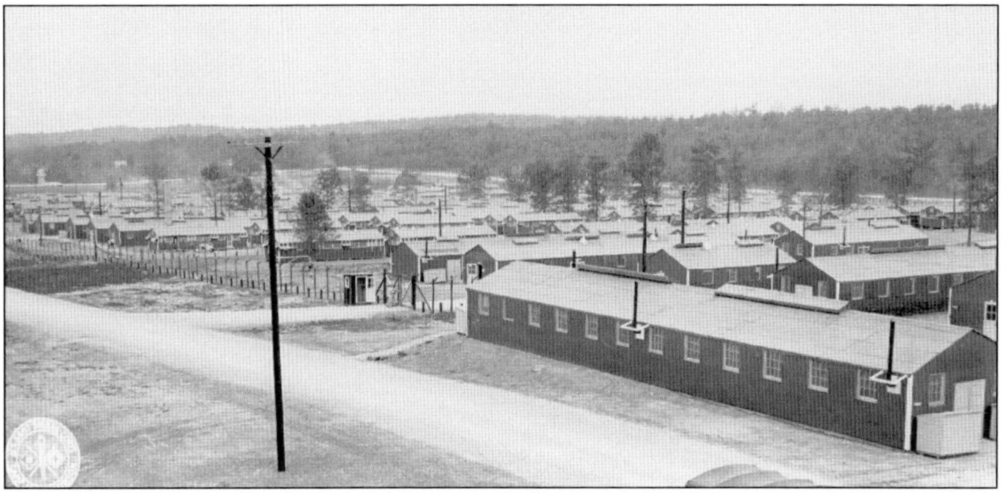

Aerial View of the 300-acre Prisoner of War Camp Inside the 48,188-acre Camp Robinson. During its three-year life span, the facility handled over 10,000 German prisoners, using more than 1,000 guards and support staff. The rest of the post served as a basic training facility, reaching a peak strength of 75,000 men during World War II. (Arkansas History Commission.)

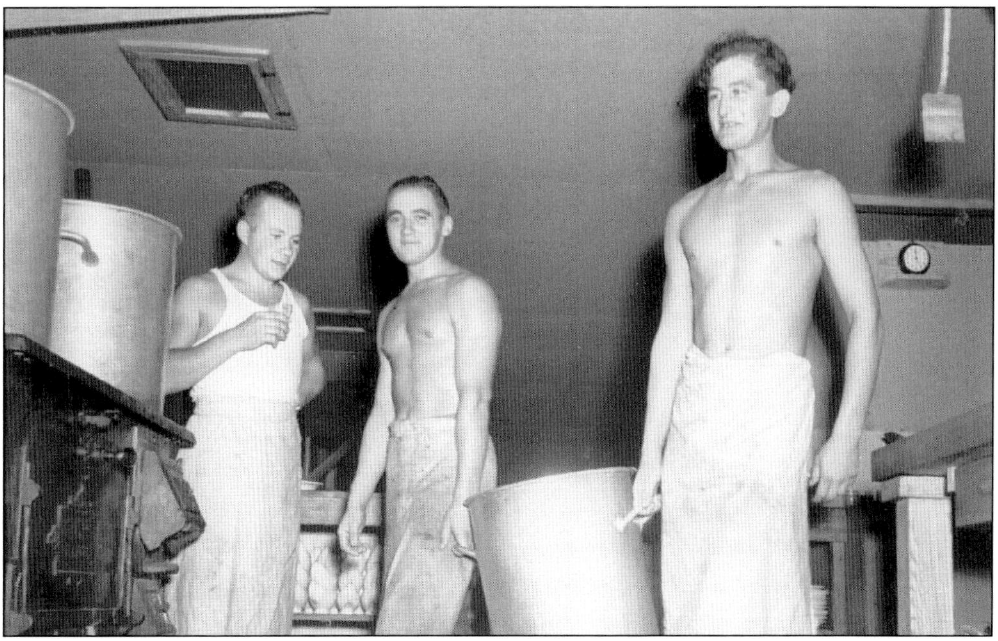

Kitchen Detail at Prisoner of War Camp. The entire kitchen staff was German. Prisoners ate very well, routinely getting such luxuries as eggs, which were strictly rationed to U.S. civilians. Each prisoner also received ten cents per day for use in the camp canteen. People working in the kitchen or at other work details, including contract work outside of the camp, received eighty cents per day. (Arkansas History Commission.)

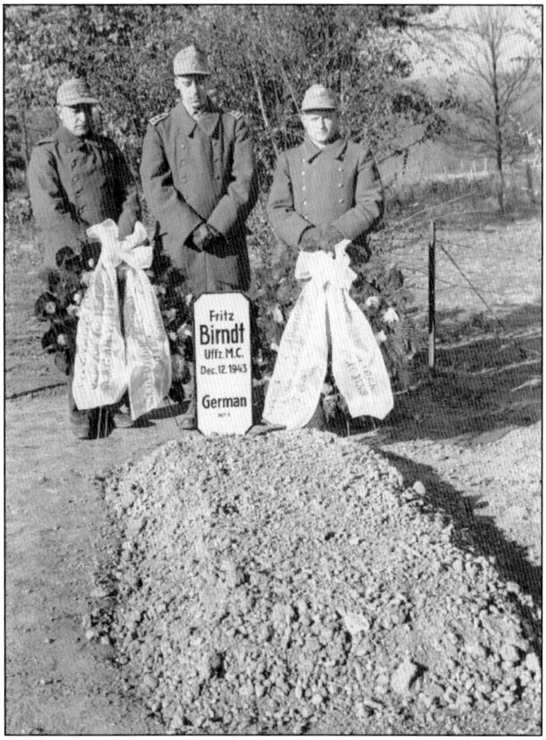

End of the War for a German Prisoner. German prisoner of war Fritz Birndt Uffz. MC. died on December 12, 1943, and was buried in Arkansas by his *Kameraden* (comrades). Only two German prisoners died at the Camp Robinson Prisoner of War Camp, both of natural causes. The camp hospital reserved 120 beds for the prisoners and averaged about 54 patients at any given time. Malaria was the biggest health problem. (Arkansas History Commission.)

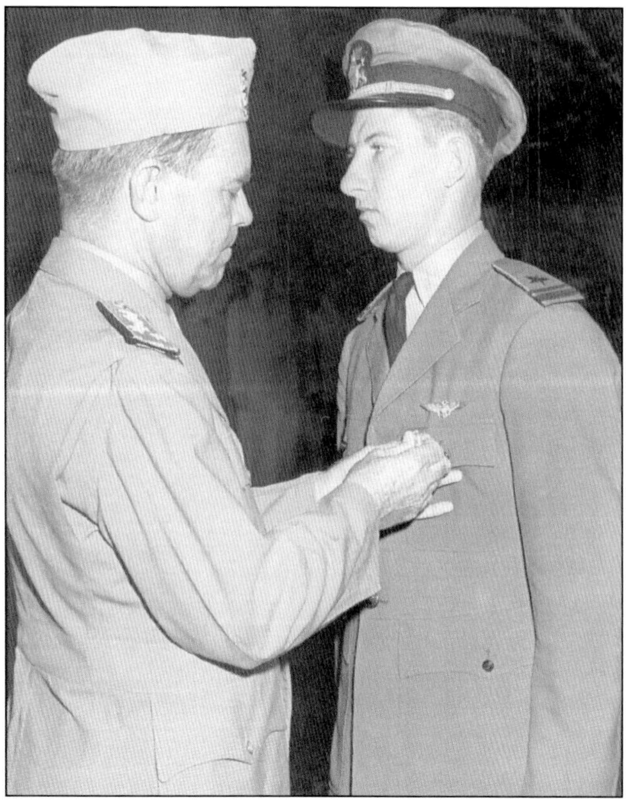

Lt. (j.g.) Norman E. Gaiser, USNR, of Little Rock. Gaiser received the Air Medal from Vice Admiral P.N.L. Bollinger, Commander Air Force, Atlantic Fleet. The twenty-two year old Gaiser distinguished himself by scoring a direct hit on a Japanese cargo ship while he was pilot of a dive bomber. He went on active Navy duty December 24, 1942. (Official U.S. Navy photo, Arkansas History Commission.)

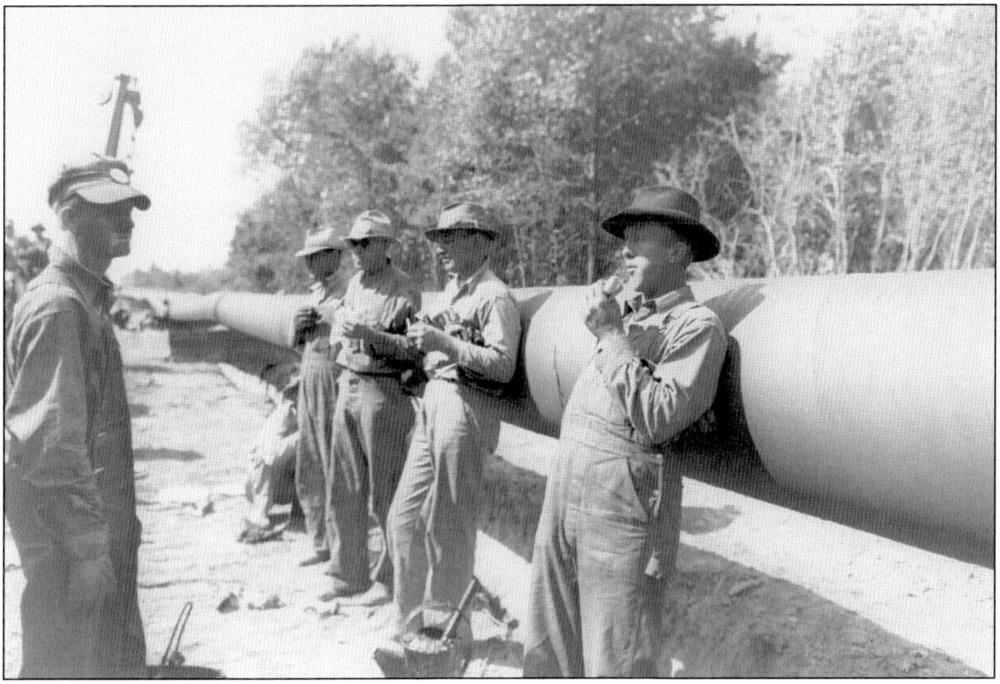

PIPELINE WORKERS. Laying a pipeline between Little Rock and Missouri in the early 1940s, the workers are seen here taking a lunch break. (Arkansas History Commission.)

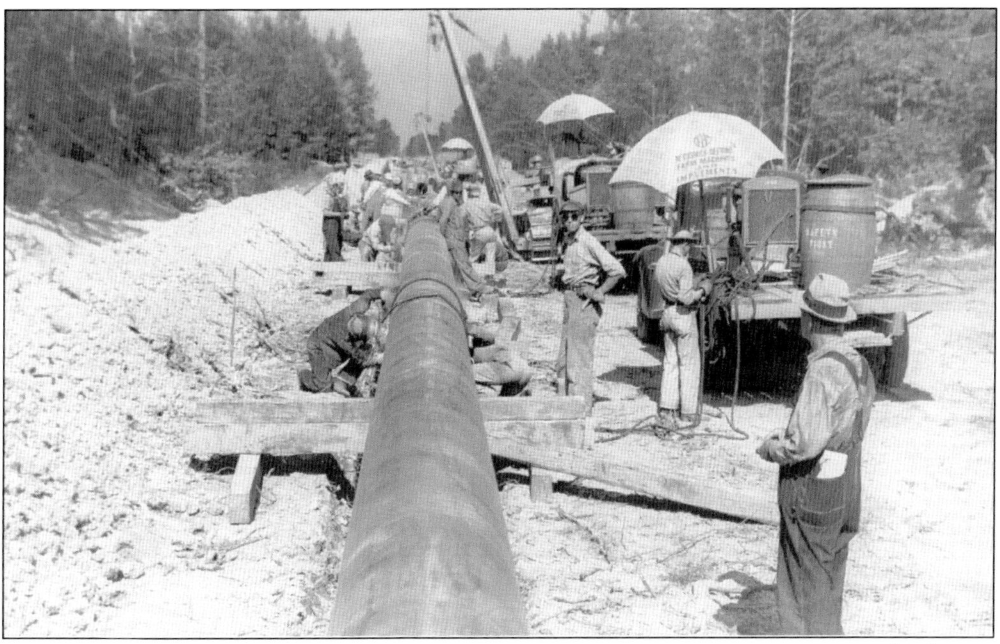

WORKERS LAYING PIPELINE FROM LITTLE ROCK TO MISSOURI IN 1942. (Arkansas History Commission.)

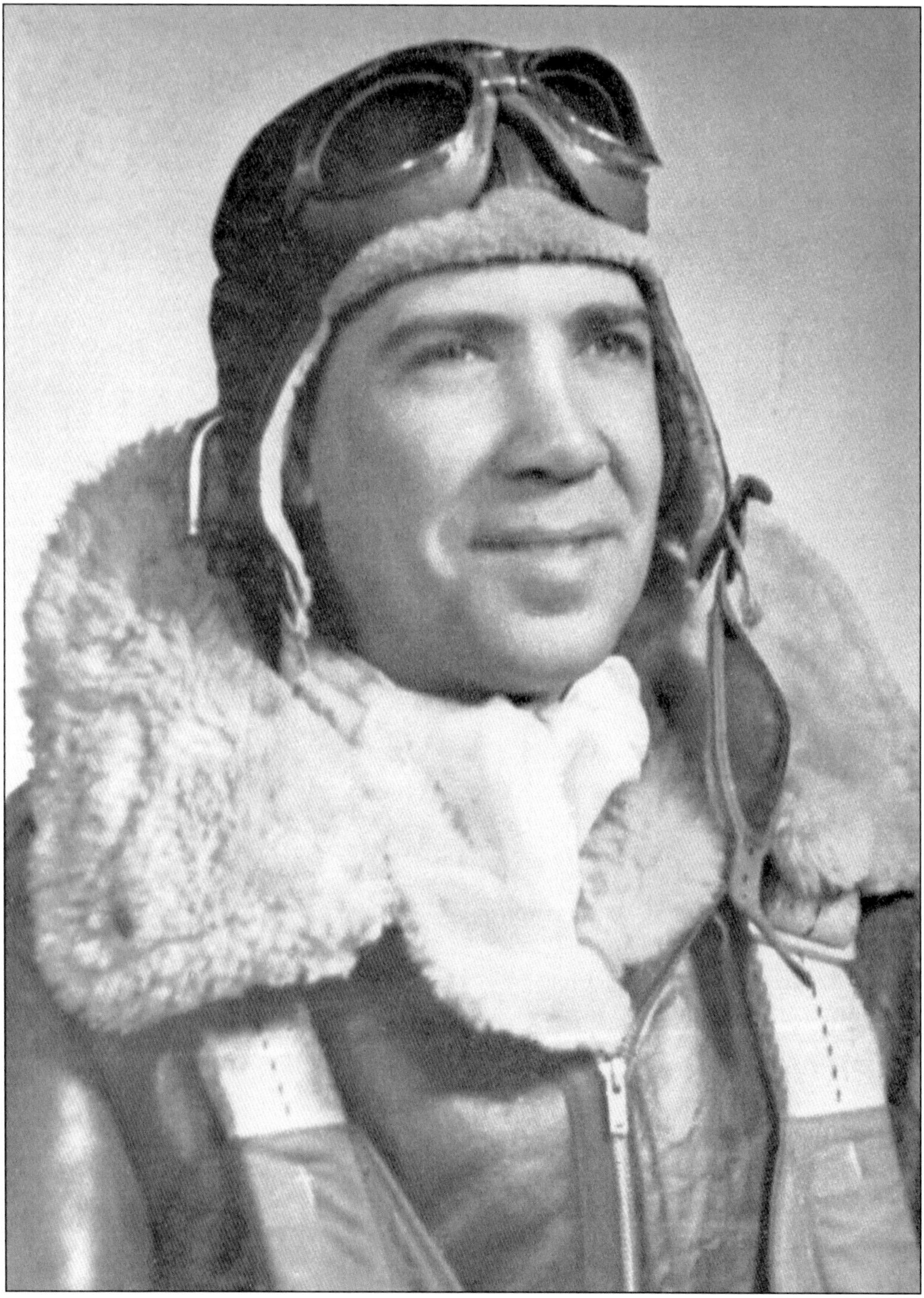

Edwin Lee Baxley. After attending Little Rock Junior College, Draughon's Business College, American Institute of Banking, and Arkansas Law School, Baxley served as a captain in the Air Corps from 1941 to 1946. He was a prisoner of war in Germany for two years. Elected to the state legislature as a representative from Pulaski County, Baxley served for two terms beginning in 1947, later selling life insurance in Little Rock. (Arkansas History Commission.)

Seven

Changing Times

After World War II ended, the aging bonds of segregation began to weaken. While black and white residents still kept pretty much apart, the important stores in Pulaski County removed the "white" and "colored" signs from their drinking fountains, and the Rock Island Railroad stopped seating passengers based on race. Despite these changes, segregation was still the law of the land. But that was about to change.

The U.S. Supreme Court ruled in 1954 that the practice of "separate but equal" schools did not provide equal educational opportunities. Then the court ruled that every school district must desegregate with "all deliberate speed."

The Little Rock school board decided to ease into desegregation by admitting nine black students to Central High. Governor Orval Faubus ordered the Arkansas National Guard to surround the school and keep black students out. Eight of the Little Rock Nine gathered into a group and attempted to enter a side door, but were turned away by guardsmen. The ninth student, Elizabeth Eckford, never knew that the others had formed a group. Utterly alone, she attempted to reach the front door by herself. After being turned away, she once again walked the gauntlet to her bus stop past silent armed guardsmen and a thousand angry whites who screamed abusively at her. Photos of her ordeal, many taken by Will Counts of the *Arkansas Democrat*, appeared throughout the country. The obvious courage of a frightened 15-year-old girl, in the face of such hatred, proved to be the catalyst that began to change white attitudes regarding civil rights.

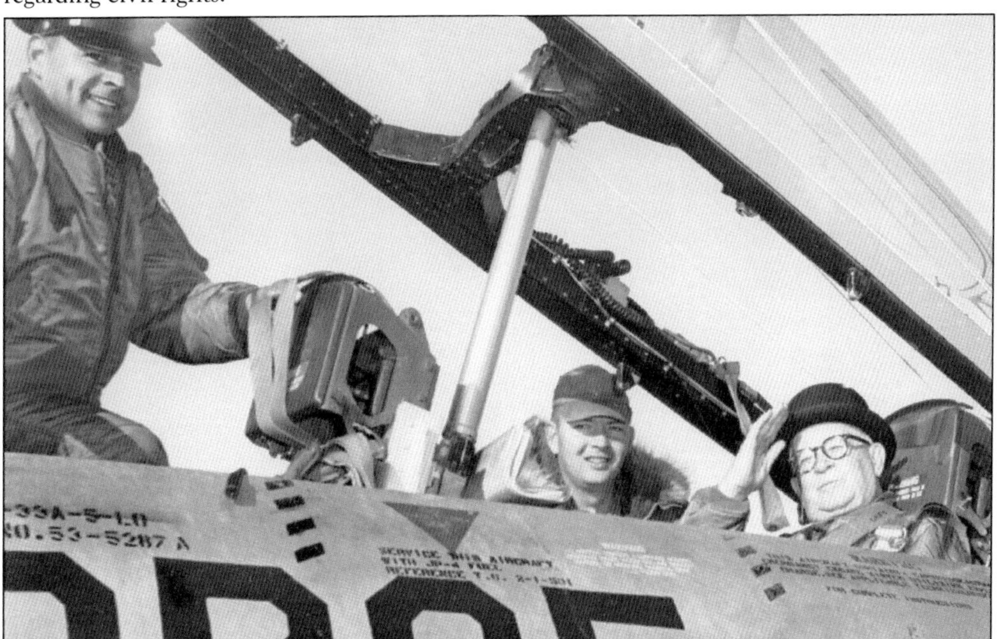

Pulaski County Judge Arch Campbell. Here the judge is preparing for a ride in a U.S. Air Force T33A jet trainer at Little Rock Air Force Base in 1960, two years after he successfully ran for reelection. (Arkansas History Commission.)

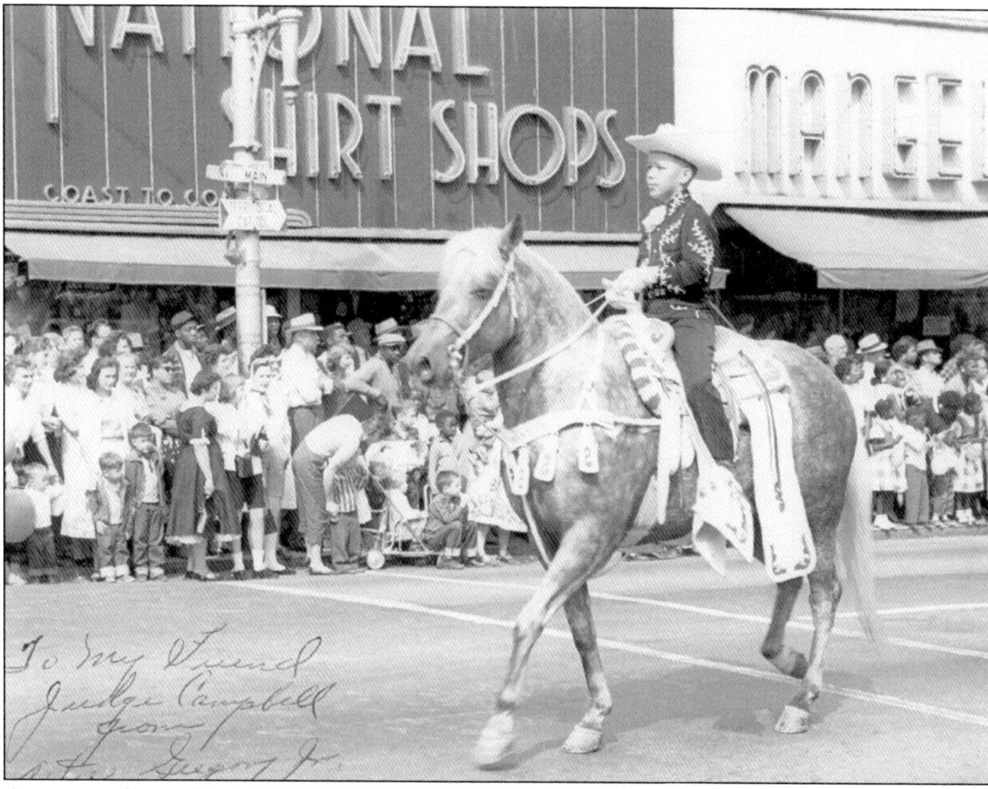

ARKANSAS STATE FAIR PARADE ON MAIN STREET OF LITTLE ROCK, SEPTEMBER 29, 1958. The photograph is autographed "To my friend Judge Campbell from Artie Gregory Jr." (Arkansas History Commission.)

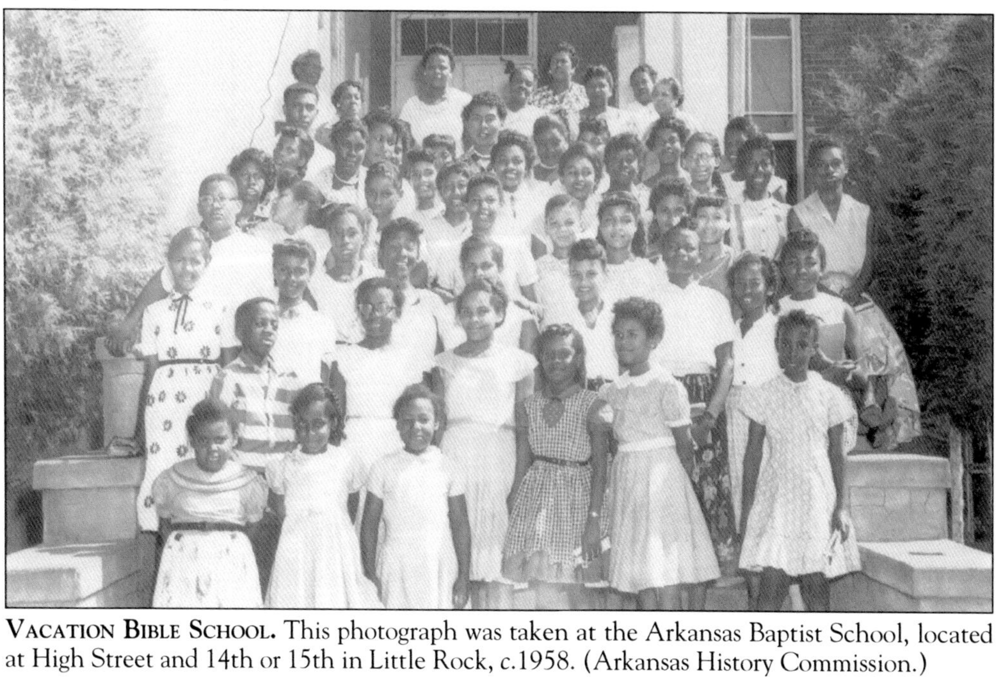

VACATION BIBLE SCHOOL. This photograph was taken at the Arkansas Baptist School, located at High Street and 14th or 15th in Little Rock, *c.*1958. (Arkansas History Commission.)

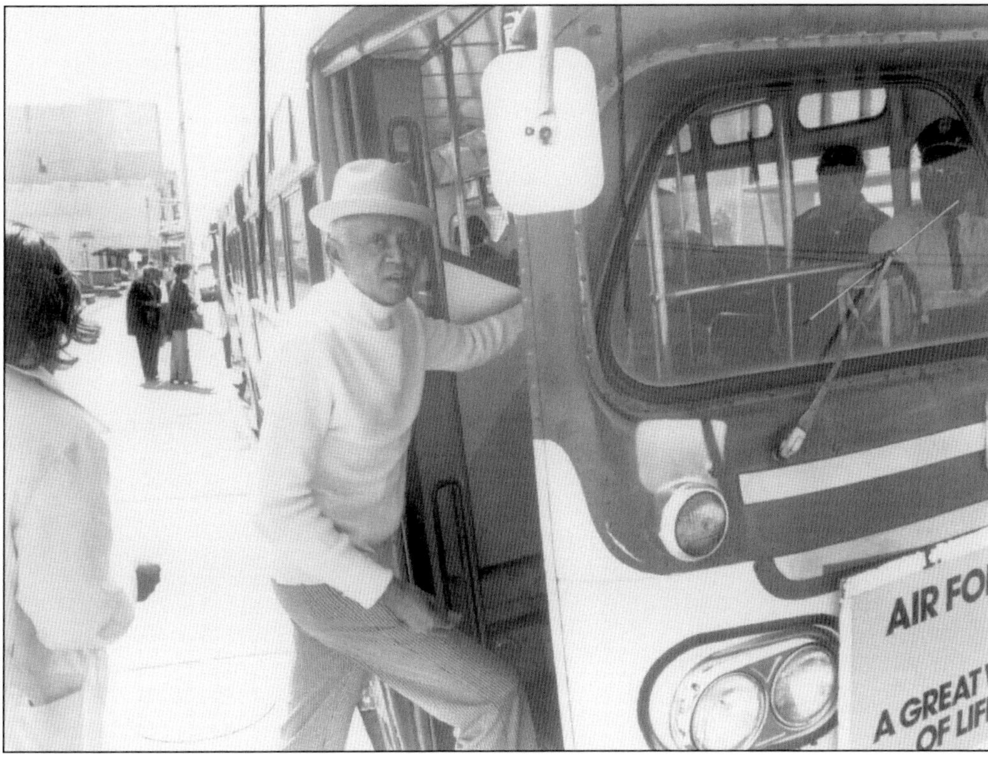

JEFFREY HAWKINS. Hawkins rode the Little Rock transit system for more than 52 years, watching the trolley cars of the 1920s change to modern air-conditioned buses in the 1970s. He also watched the transit system slowly disintegrate from a profitable business to a government-subsidized utility that lost money. Hawkins missed the streetcars. (Arkansas History Commission.)

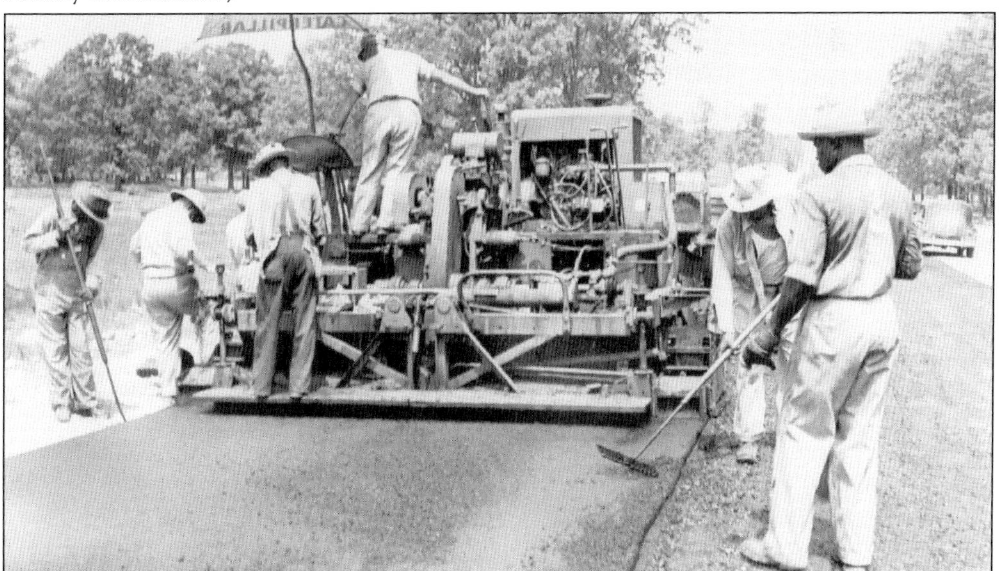

PULASKI COUNTY ROAD CONSTRUCTION CREW, JUNE 26, 1952. (Arkansas History Commission.)

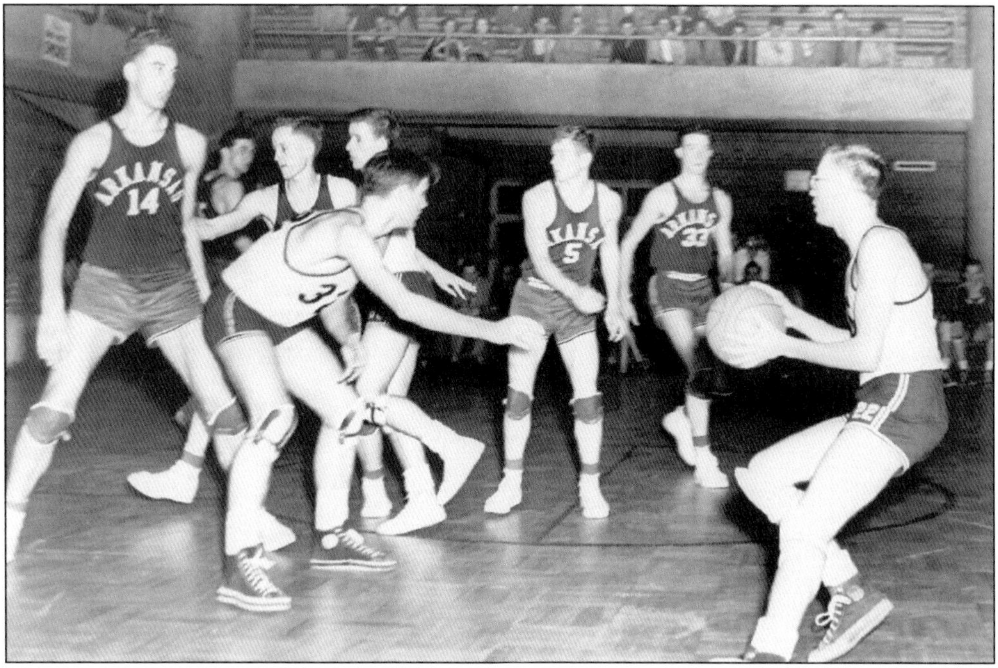

MEMBERS OF THE 1950-1951 TROJAN BASKETBALL TEAM IN ACTION. The Trojans competed for the Little Rock Junior College, which evolved into Little Rock University and then the University of Arkansas at Little Rock. Sydney Moncrief, who played college ball for the Razorbacks in Fayetteville and went on to play professionally with the National Basketball Association, was appointed head coach of the Trojans in 1999. (UALR Library Archives.)

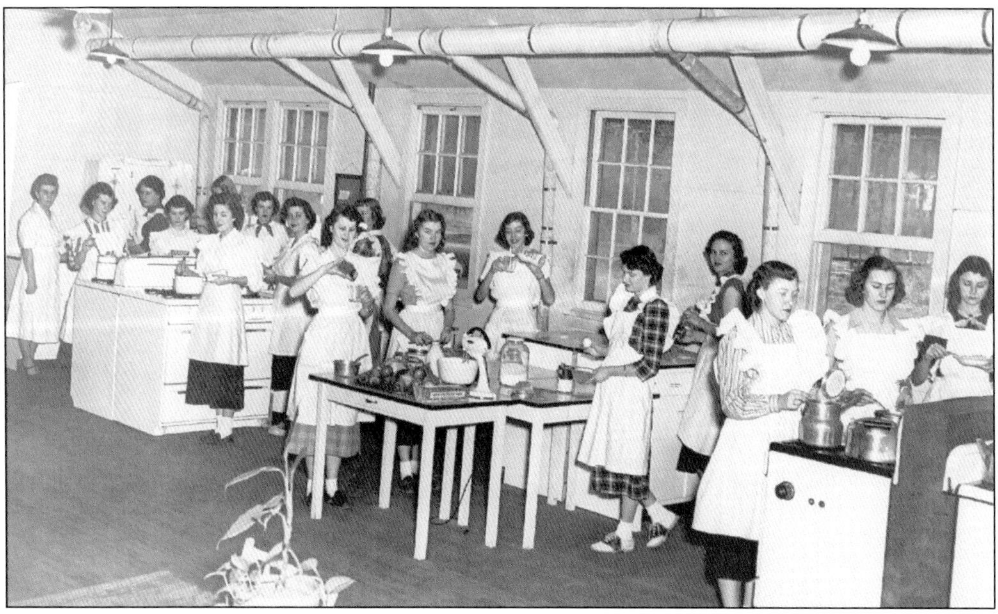

STUDENTS IN A HOME ECONOMICS CLASS AT THE LITTLE ROCK JUNIOR COLLEGE, 1950. Seven years later, LRJC began a four-year degree program, got its independence from the Little Rock School Board with a separate board of trustees, and changed the school's name to Little Rock University. (UALR Library Archives.)

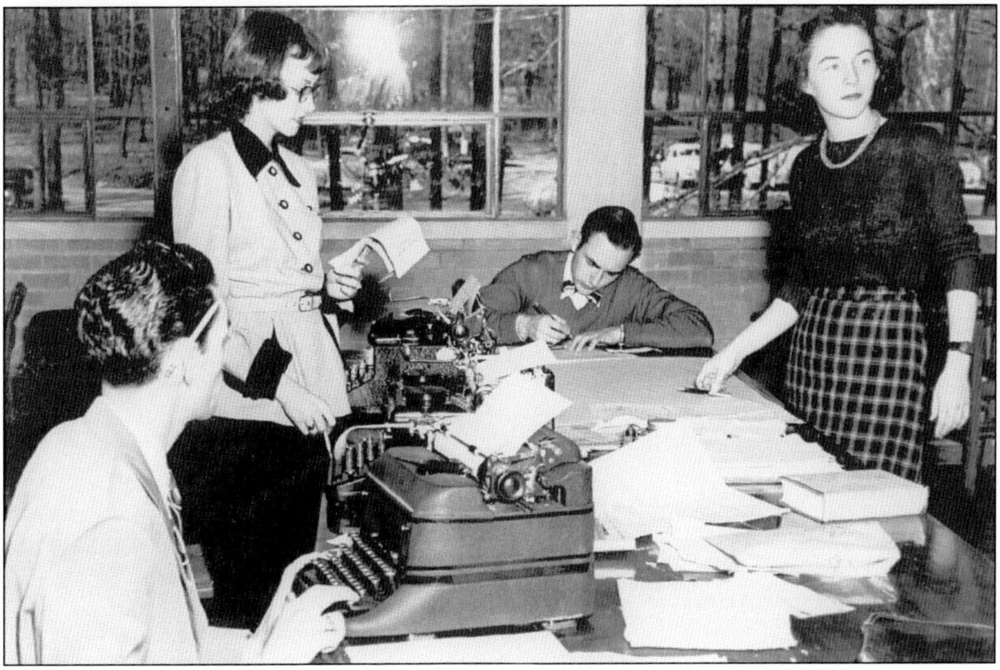

Staff Members Working at the *College Chatter* in 1950. This was the student newspaper of Little Rock Junior College, which served Pulaski County from 1927 until 1956. The college became Little Rock University in 1957 and then grew into the University of Arkansas at Little Rock (UALR) in 1969. This stimulated a period of rapid growth, with student enrollment increasing from 3,500 students and 75 full-time faculty members in 1969 to more than 10,000 students and 400 full-time faculty members in 1998. (UALR Library Archives.)

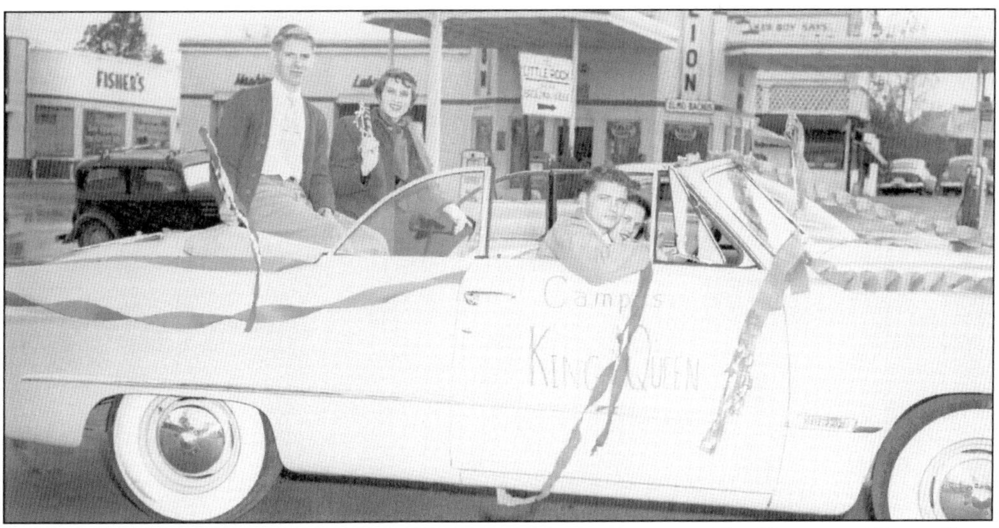

The Little Rock Junior College King and Queen in a 1951 Parade. The college moved to the present location of the University of Arkansas at Little Rock (UALR) in 1949, when local businessman Raymond Rebsamen donated the beautiful wooded site. The name changed to Little Rock University when it became a four-year school in 1957. (Arkansas History Commission.)

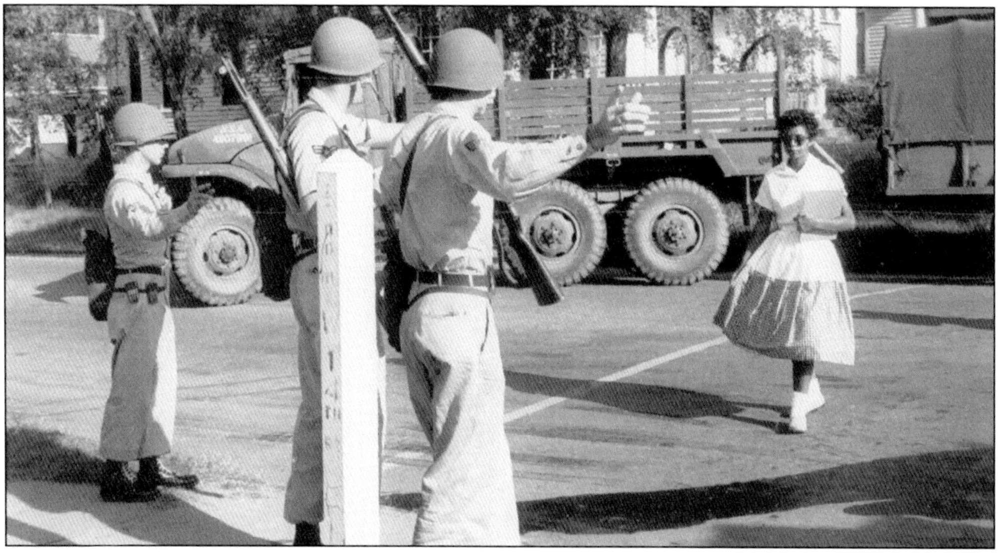

1957 Integration Crisis. Under orders from Governor Orval Faubus, National Guard troops turn Elizabeth Eckford away from Central High School. Will Counts of the *Arkansas Democrat* took the photograph at 16th and Park on September 3, 1957. (Arkansas History Commission.)

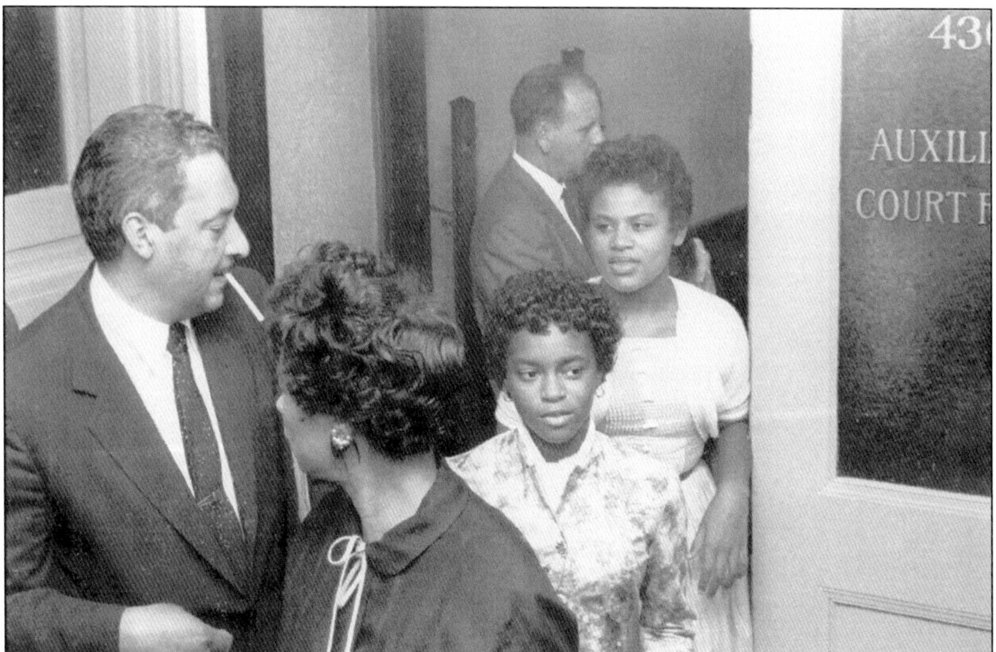

Courting a Solution to the Integration Crisis. Three girls are coming out of a court room with future U.S. Supreme Court Justice Thurgood Marshall (the man with the cigarette). In 1957, Marshall and Wiley Branton were attorneys for the National Association for the Advancement of Colored People. They successfully appealed to the U.S. District Court for an injunction barring Governor Faubus from using guardsmen to impede integration at Central High. (Arkansas History Commission.)

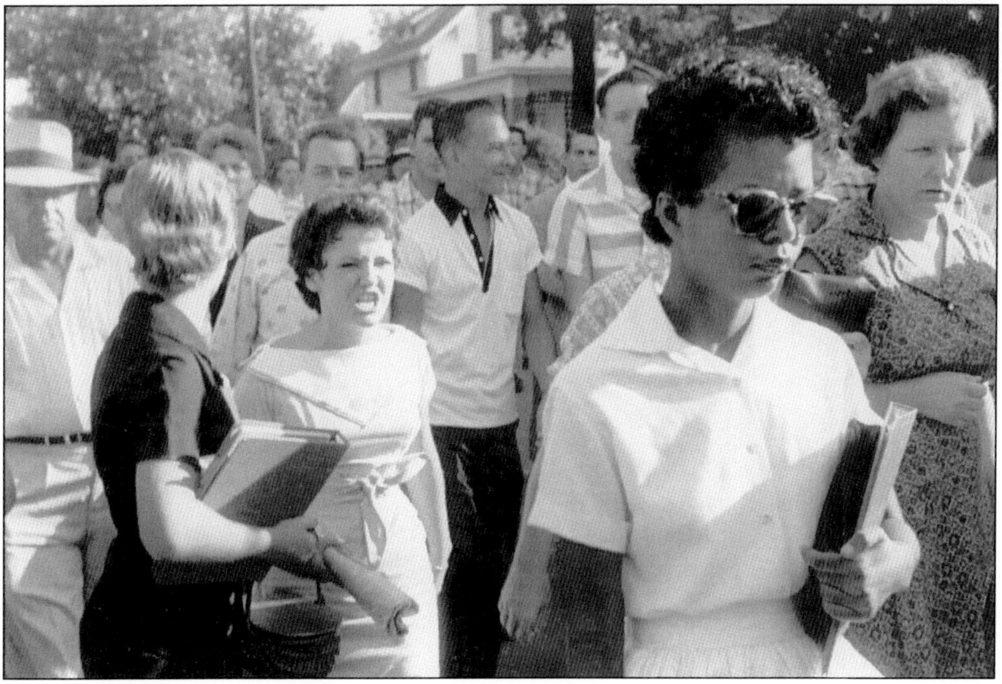

Integration Crisis, September 4, 1957. Hazel Bryan screams at Elizabeth Eckford while a crowd of angry whites follows and taunts the 15-year-old Eckford as she walks away from Central High. Six years later, Bryan phoned Eckford and apologized. While both continued to live in Little Rock, they had no further contact until 1997, when they had an amicable visit at Eckford's home on the 40th anniversary of the Central High crisis. (Arkansas History Commission.)

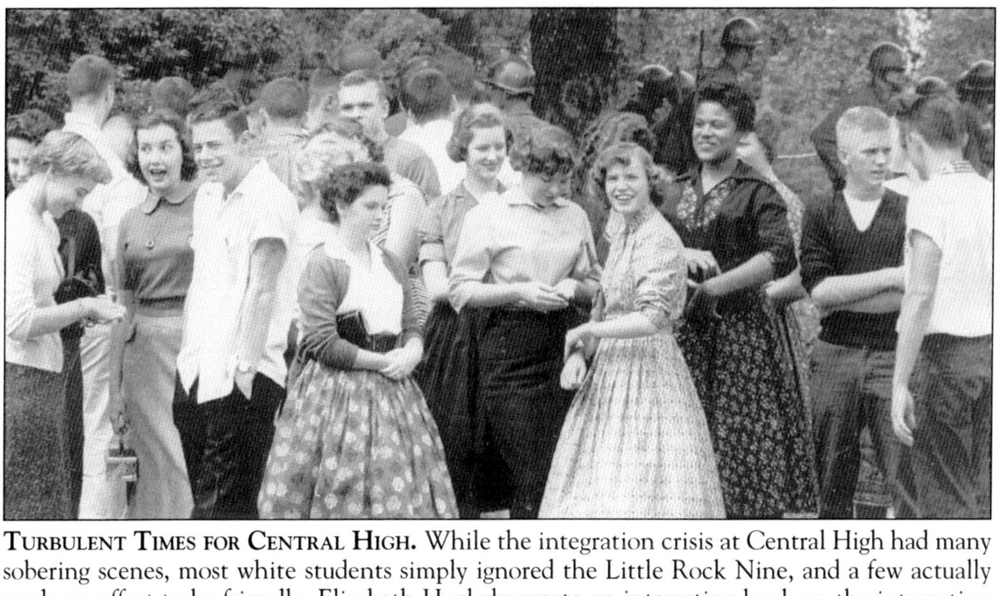

Turbulent Times for Central High. While the integration crisis at Central High had many sobering scenes, most white students simply ignored the Little Rock Nine, and a few actually made an effort to be friendly. Elizabeth Huckaby wrote an interesting book on the integration crisis which was entitled *Crisis at Central High: Little Rock 1957-58.*

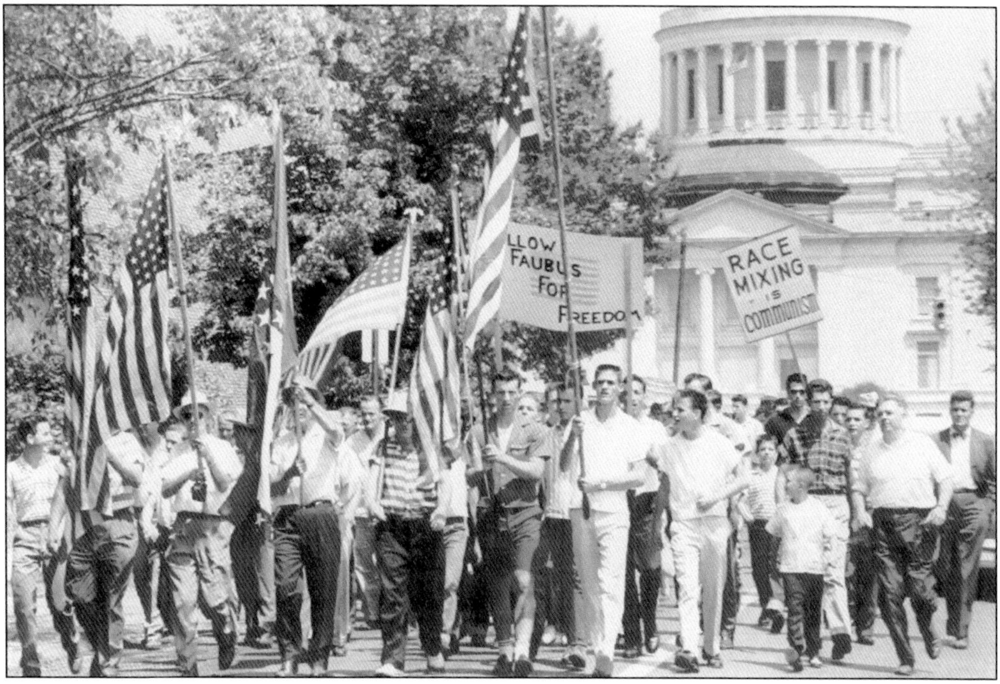

POLICE STEP IN AT CENTRAL HIGH. When a group of angry whites marched on Central High in an effort to keep black students from entering in September 1957, local police stopped them short of their objective. (Arkansas History Commission.)

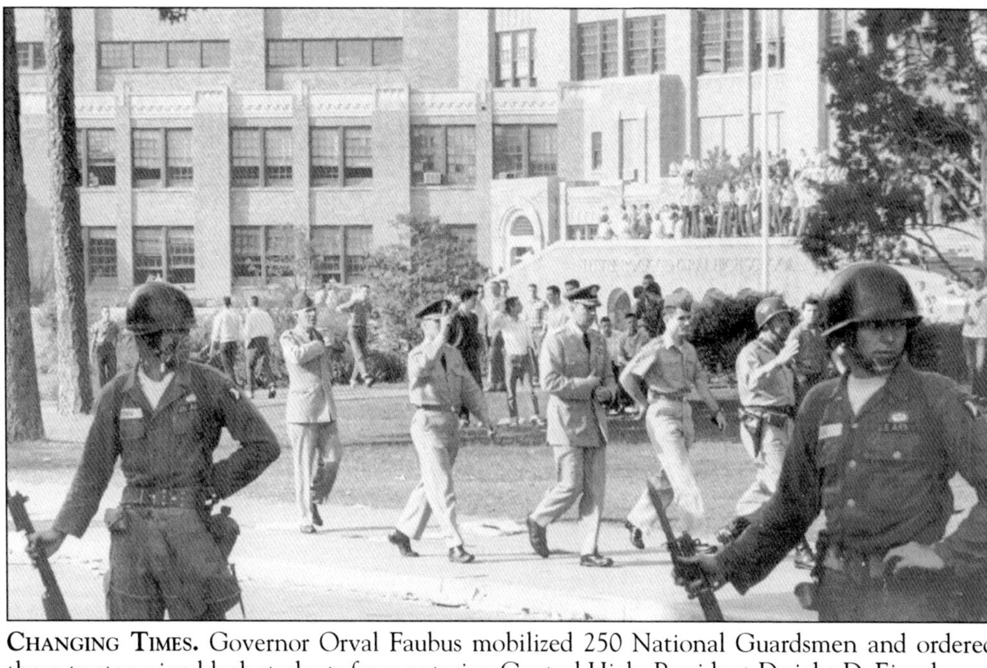

CHANGING TIMES. Governor Orval Faubus mobilized 250 National Guardsmen and ordered them to stop nine black students from entering Central High. President Dwight D. Eisenhower then sent paratroopers from the U.S. Army's 101st Airborne Division into Little Rock to uphold the authority of the federal court. It was not a graceful beginning to desegregation, but it was a beginning, nonetheless. (Arkansas History Commission.)

DAISY AND L.C. BATES. Civil rights leaders who led the struggle to integrate Little Rock, thc Bates are seen here in January 1959. Daisy Bates went on to publish a black-oriented newspaper, the *Arkansas State Press*, as well as a book on the Central High crisis called *The Long Shadow of Little Rock*. (Arkansas History Commission.)

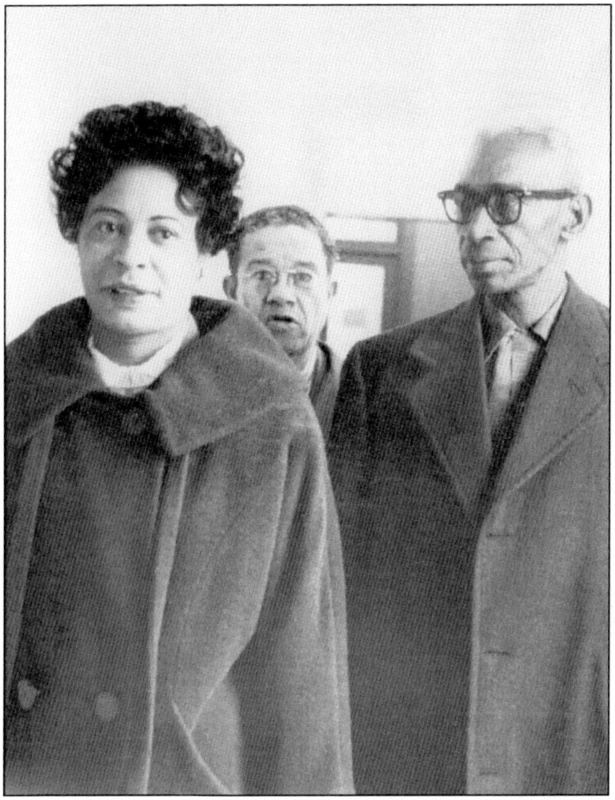

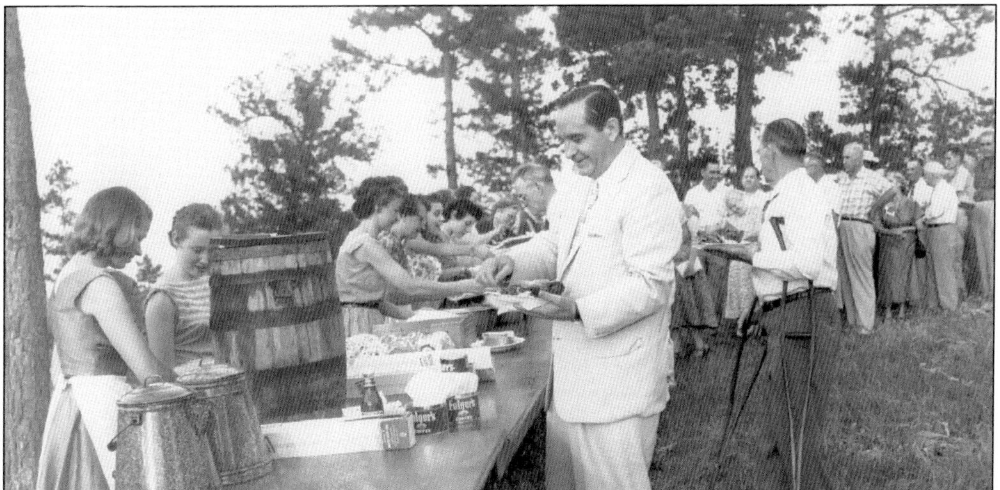

ORVAL E. FAUBUS AT A PICNIC SUPPER, C.1966. It was at this time that Faubus decided not to seek reelection to the governor's office. Democratic gubernatorial candidate James D. Johnson, a staunch segregationist, lost the 1966 race to Republican Winthrop Rockefeller, although the legislature remained solidly Democratic. Only a handful of Republicans were elected to the legislature. (Arkansas History Commission.)

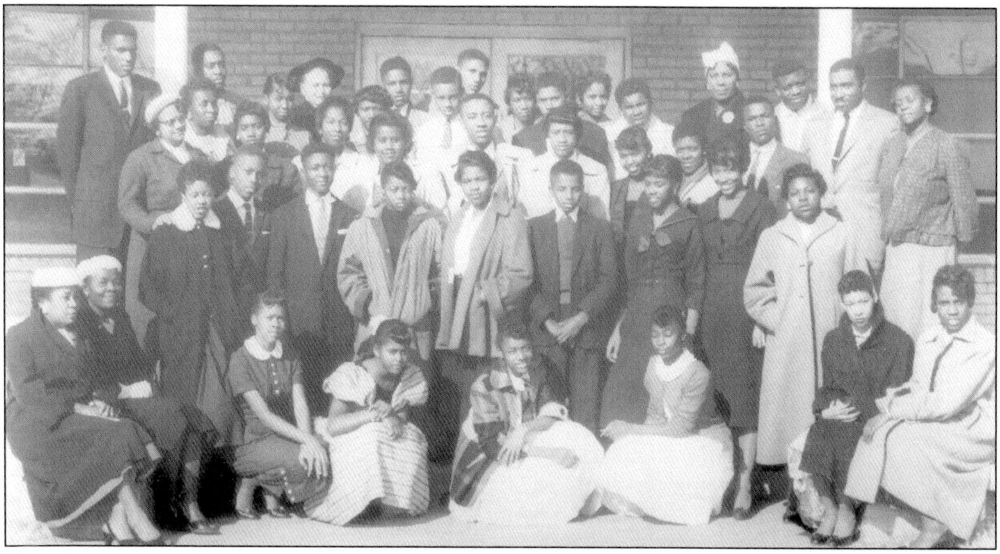

THE ARKANSAS NEGRO CHAPTER OF THE NATIONAL HONOR SOCIETY, 1957. The chapter was quite active, frequently drawing as many as 200 delegates and sponsors to the chapter's general assemblies, meetings, and dinners. This photo shows a planning meeting at Jones High School in North Little Rock, c.1957. Membership was restricted to students with an average grade of B or better. (Arkansas History Commission.)

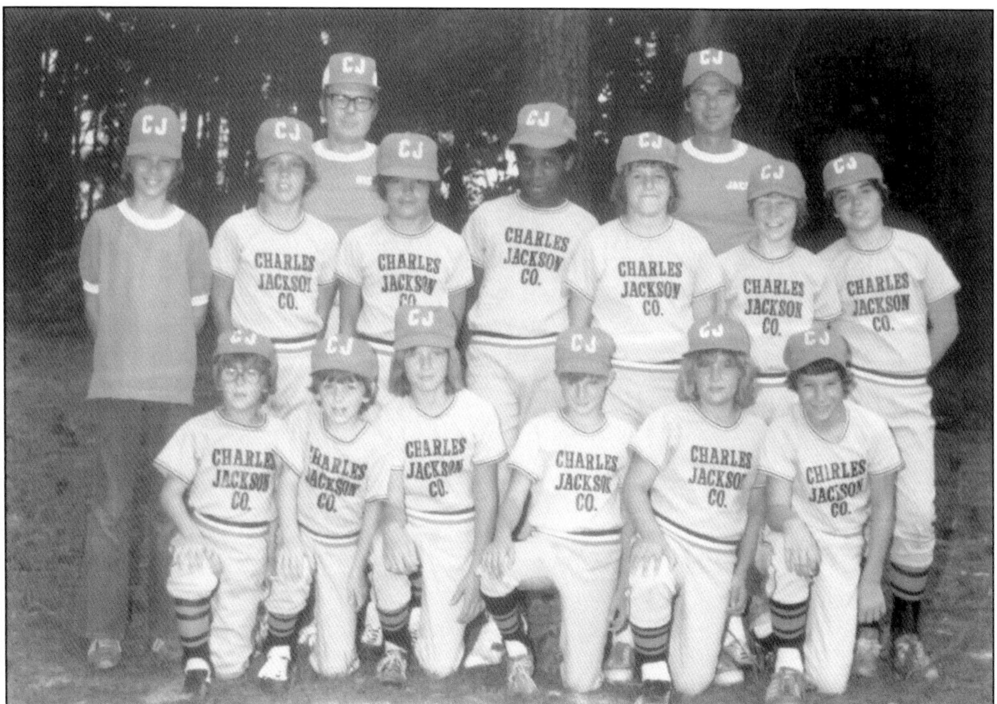

A LITTLE LEAGUE TEAM IN SOUTHWEST LITTLE ROCK, 1978. The team was sponsored by the Charles Jackson Company. (Arkansas History Commission.)

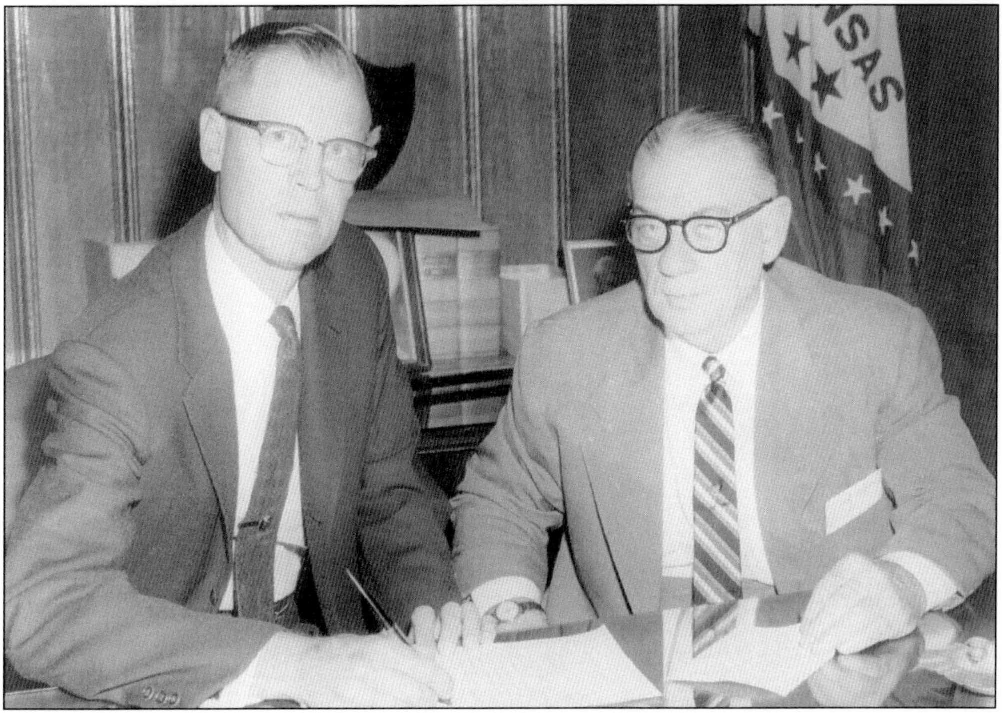

JUDGE JAMES H. PILKINTON AND C.G. CRIP HALL. Here Arkansas Secretary of State Pilkinton is registering to run for governor in 1958. He later withdrew from the race after Governor Faubus created the integration crisis at Central High in Little Rock, and went on to ramrod the preservation and restoration of historic Washington. (Southwest Arkansas Regional Archives.)

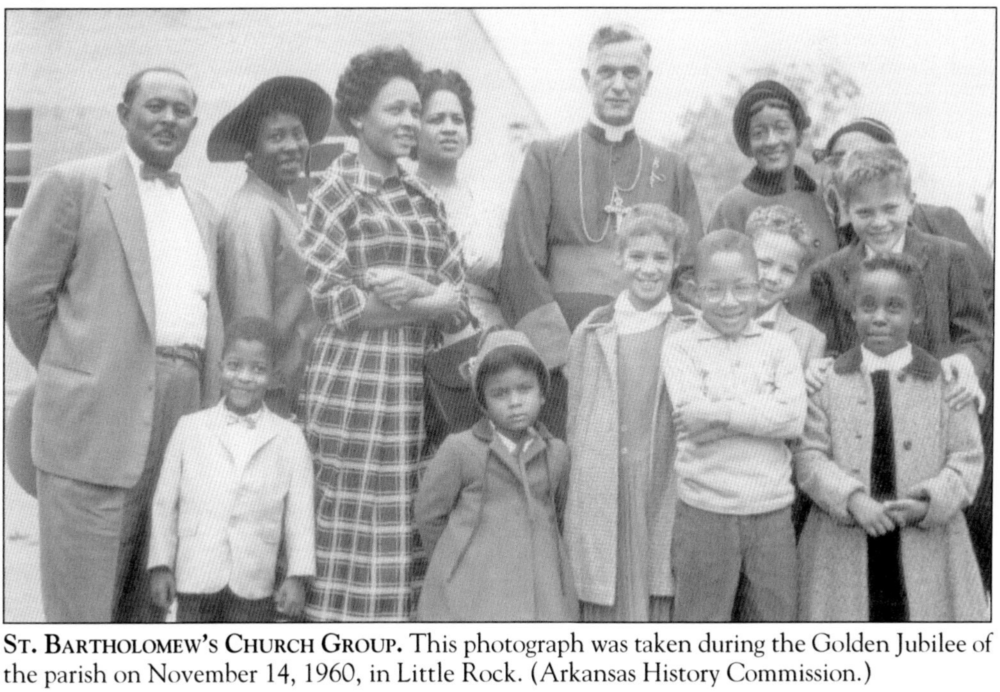

ST. BARTHOLOMEW'S CHURCH GROUP. This photograph was taken during the Golden Jubilee of the parish on November 14, 1960, in Little Rock. (Arkansas History Commission.)

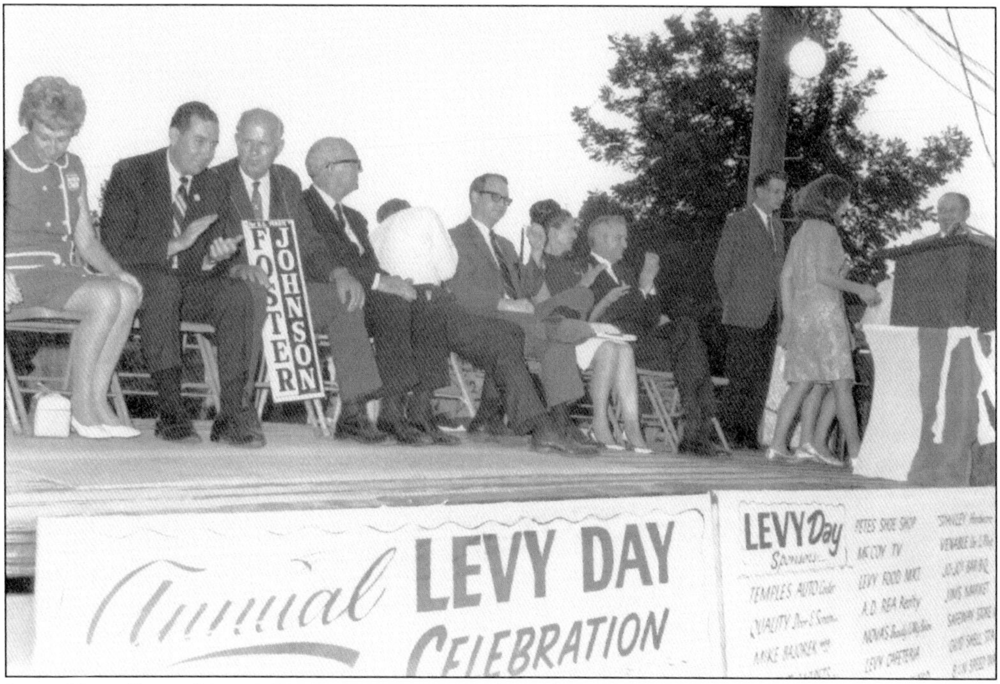

LEVY DAY, JULY 20, 1968. Levy was a "rough and roaring rendezvous" for off-duty soldiers from Camp Pike during 1917 and 1918 according to the WPA guidebook entitled *Arkansas: A Guide to the State*. After the conclusion of the Great War, Levy became a bedroom community for Camp Robinson (formerly Camp Pike) and Little Rock. This photo was taken by R.E. Van Tuyle. (Arkansas History Commission.)

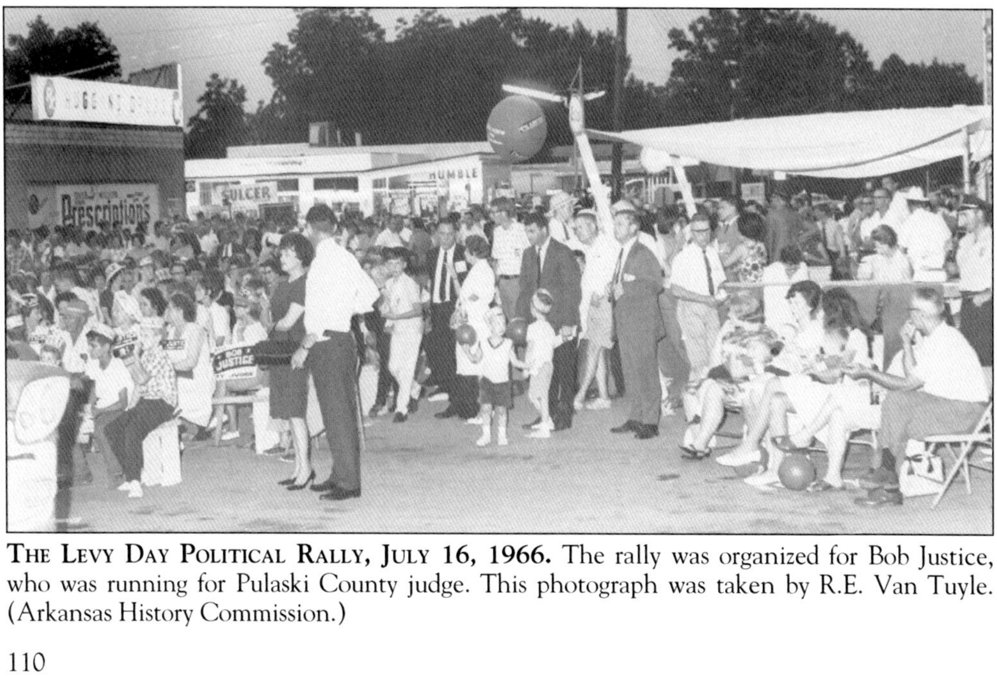

THE LEVY DAY POLITICAL RALLY, JULY 16, 1966. The rally was organized for Bob Justice, who was running for Pulaski County judge. This photograph was taken by R.E. Van Tuyle. (Arkansas History Commission.)

Orval Faubus, May 1974. The photograph is autographed "To Jim Johnson with admiration for your diligence, devotion, and many other qualities. Orval E. Faubus, 1974 campaign, May 28, 1974." (Arkansas History Commission.)

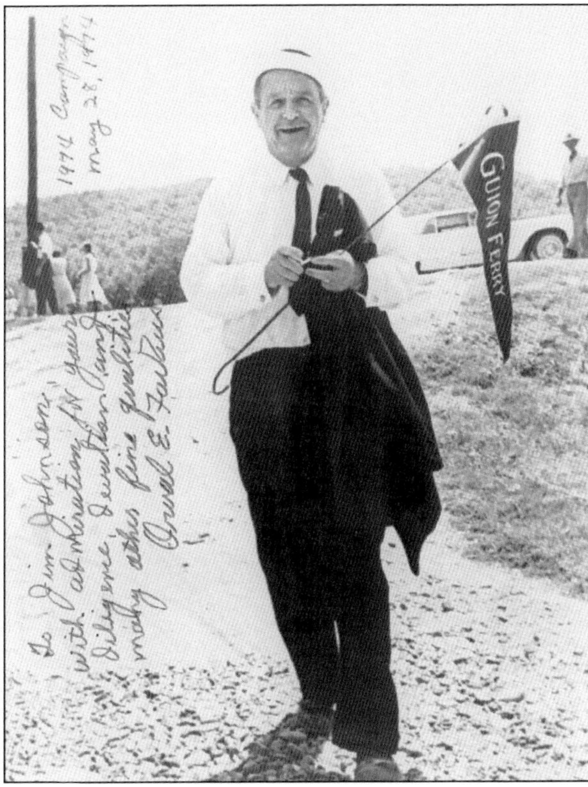

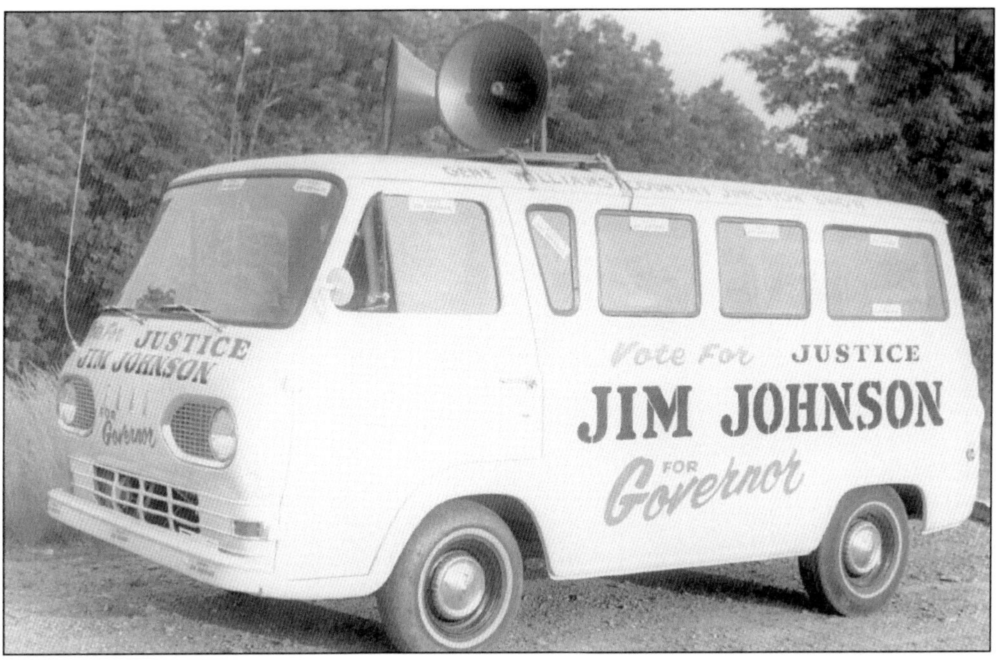

Campaign van for Justice Jim Johnson during the Gubernatorial Race of 1966. (Arkansas History Commission.)

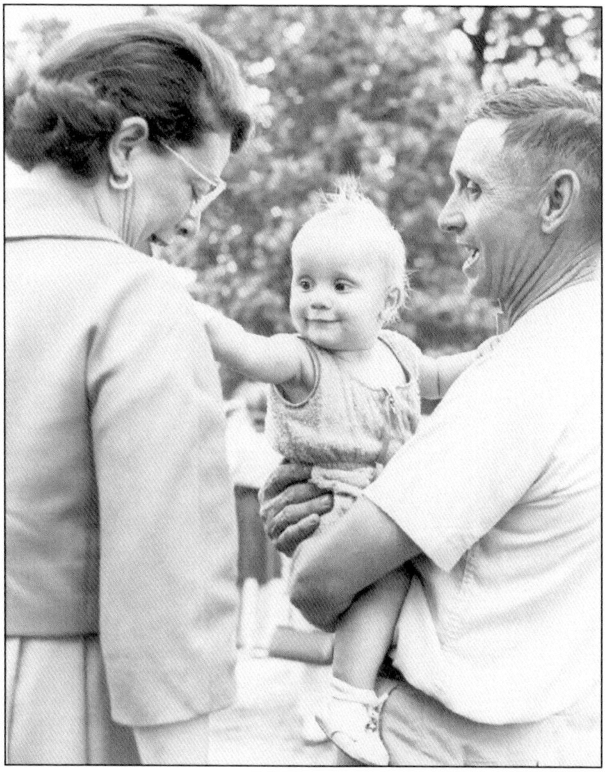

Jeanette Rockefeller. Mrs. Rockefeller was photographed greeting a youngster while campaigning for her husband during the 1966 gubernatorial race. (Arkansas History Commission.)

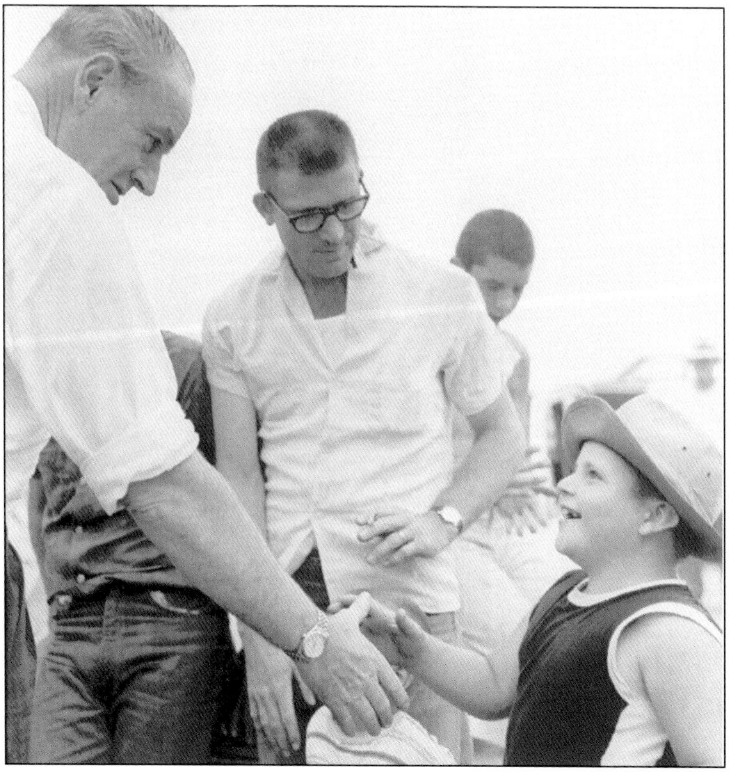

Winthrop Rockefeller Campaigning During the 1966 Gubernatorial Race. He became the first Republican governor of Arkansas since Reconstruction. He is remembered for his prison reform, eliminating illegal gambling, ramroding passage of the state's first minimum wage law, and providing free textbooks to public school students. (Arkansas History Commission.)

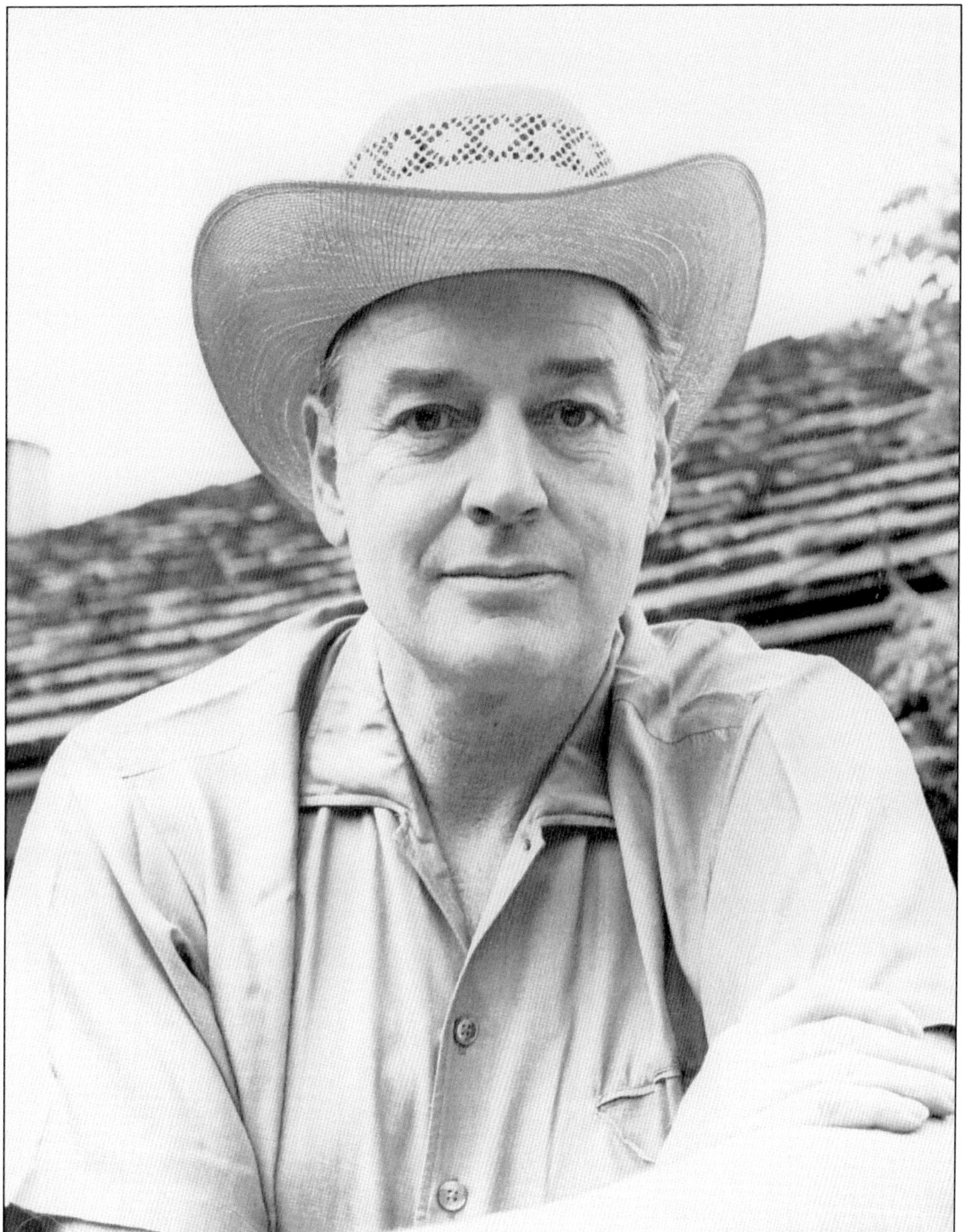

GOVERNOR WINTHROP ROCKEFELLER. Having established a world-renowned cattle ranch in central Arkansas called Winrock Farm, Rockefeller's gubernatorial campaign in 1966 brought Arkansas into the modern era with a media blitz that was fueled by a lot of money, informed by polls, and organized with computers. He also took the unprecedented step of directly appealing to the growing number of black voters for their support. (Arkansas History Commission.)

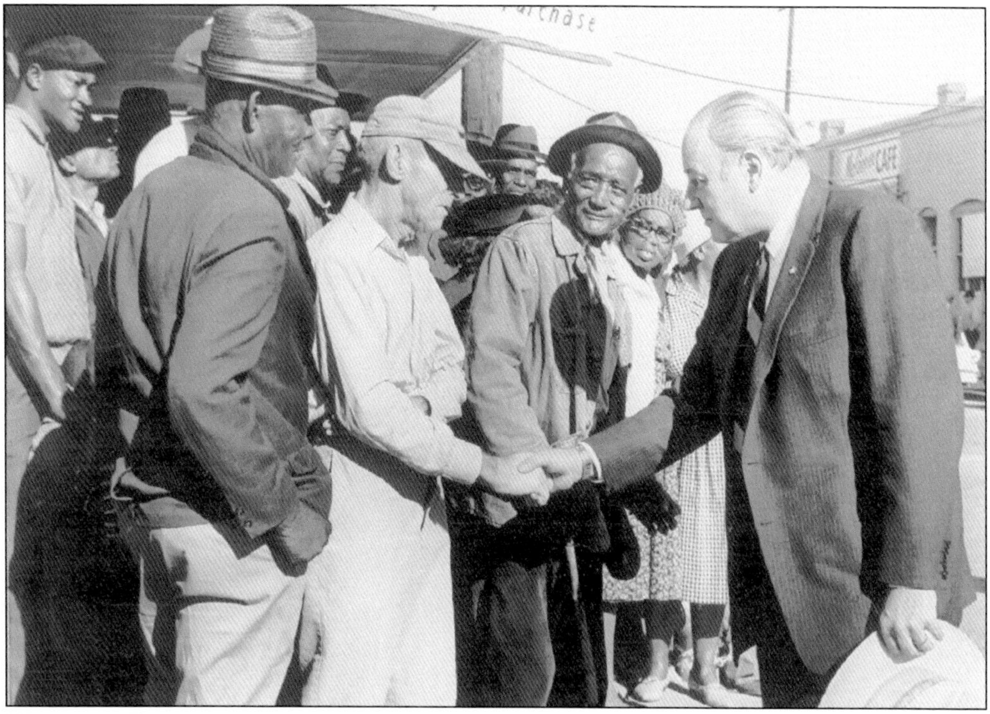

Winthrop Rockefeller During the 1966 Governor's Race. His campaign against Jim Johnson provided a logical conclusion to the falling out Rockefeller had with Governor Orval Faubus and Jim Johnson over the issue of desegregating Central High a decade earlier. Despite some personal shortcomings such as poor administrative skills and a drinking habit, Rockefeller did effect some important improvements to life in Arkansas. (Arkansas History Commission.)

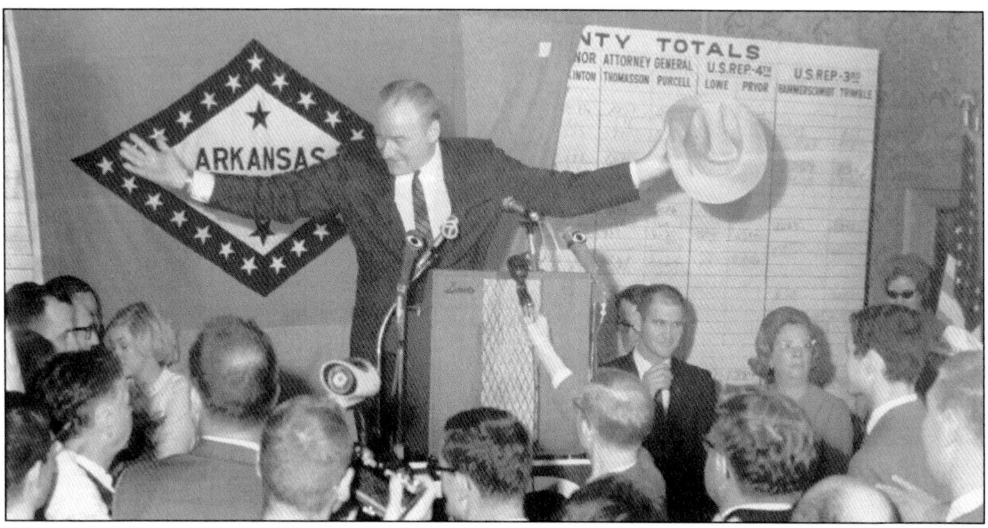

Winthrop Rockefeller Wins the Race for the Governor's Mansion. Perhaps the most enduring legacy of Rockefeller's victory was that support for civil rights became politically acceptable among a broad spectrum of white politicians. (Arkansas History Commission.)

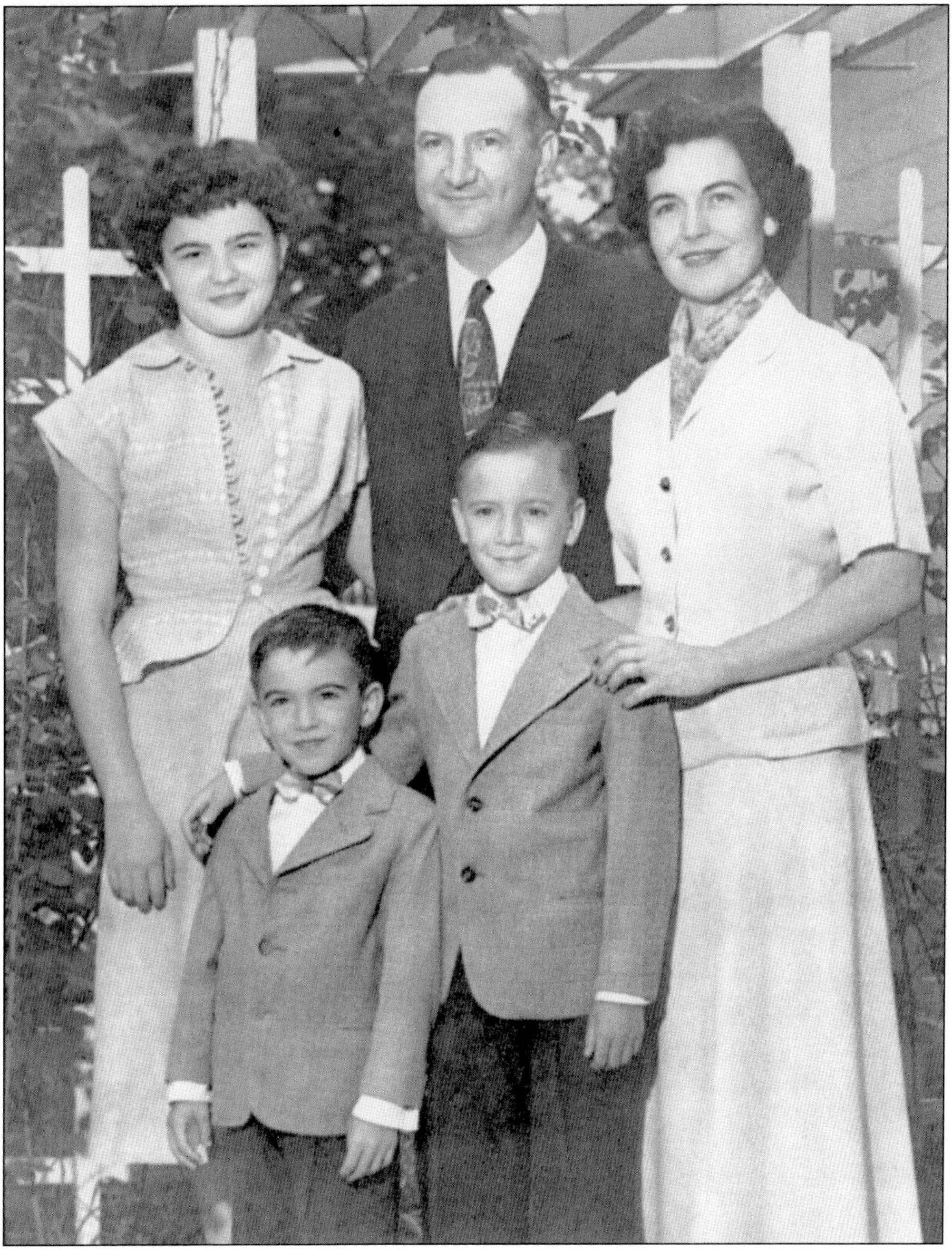

Franklin E. Loy Family. This was a campaign postcard used during his race for Little Rock's mayoral seat. The reverse side of the card extolled Loy's virtues and detailed the planks of his campaign platform. Loy was a 35-year resident of Little Rock when this family photograph was taken. Also seen from left to right are Diana, Franklin Jr., Richard, and Mrs. Loy. Loy was an alderman for 12 years. (Arkansas History Commission.)

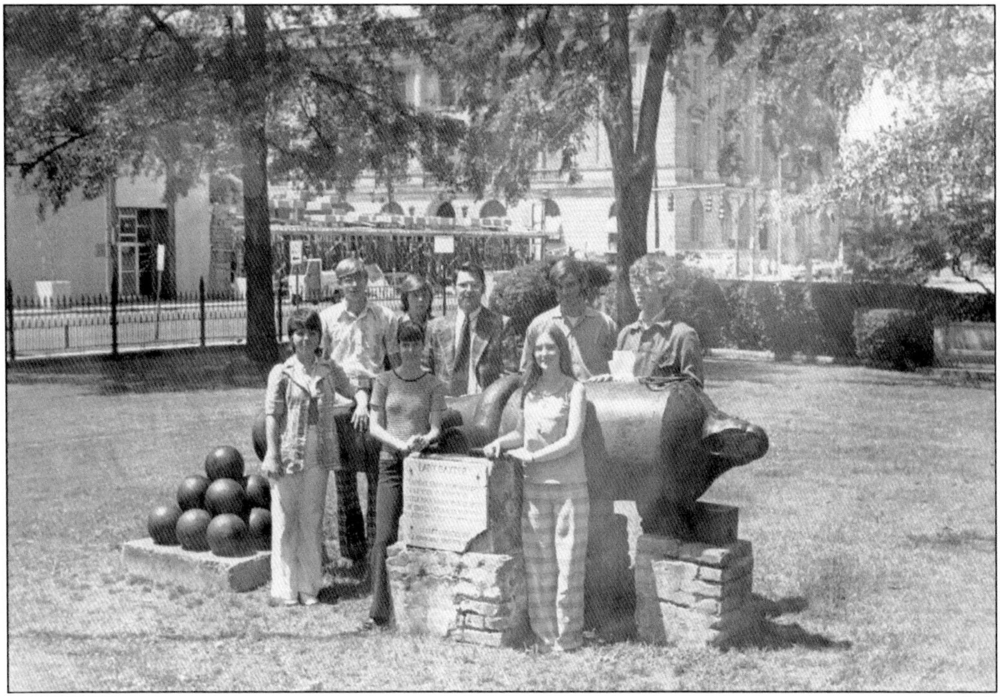

RUSSIAN HIGH SCHOOL HISTORY CLUB. This photograph was taken at the Old State House about 1978. (Arkansas History Commission.)

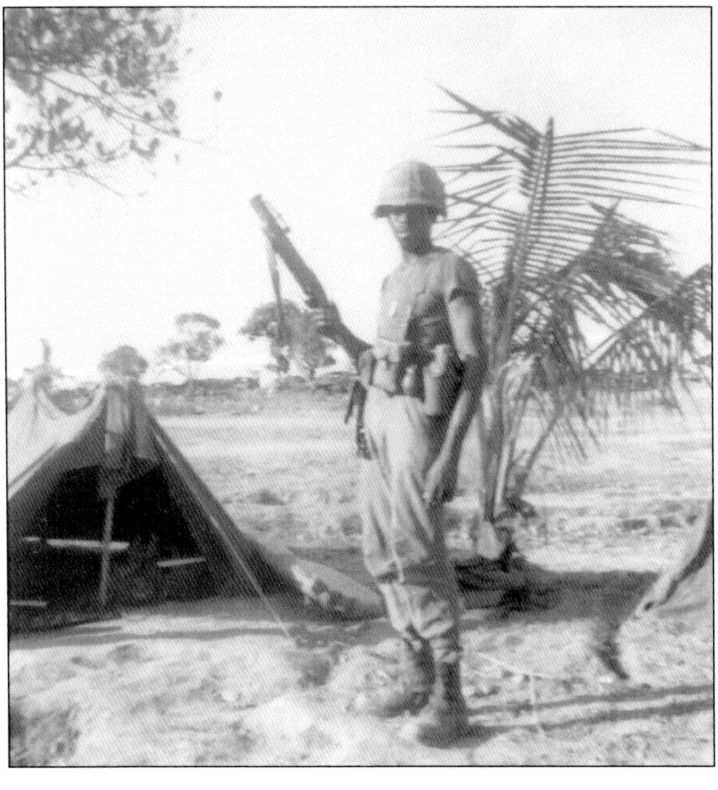

PVT. CLARENCE YOUNG OF LITTLE ROCK IN VIETNAM. He served in the reconnaissance outfit of the 1st Cavalry Division of the U.S. Army at Anke in 1966, about 300 miles north of Saigon. (Arkansas History Commission.)

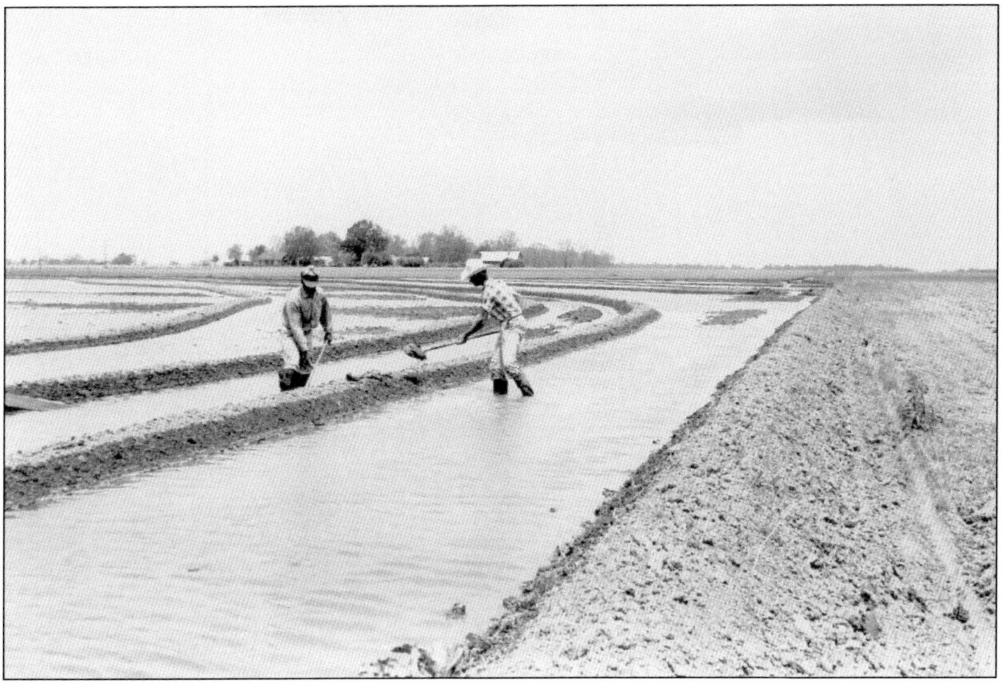

Preparing a Field for Rice Planting near Little Rock. (Arkansas History Commission.)

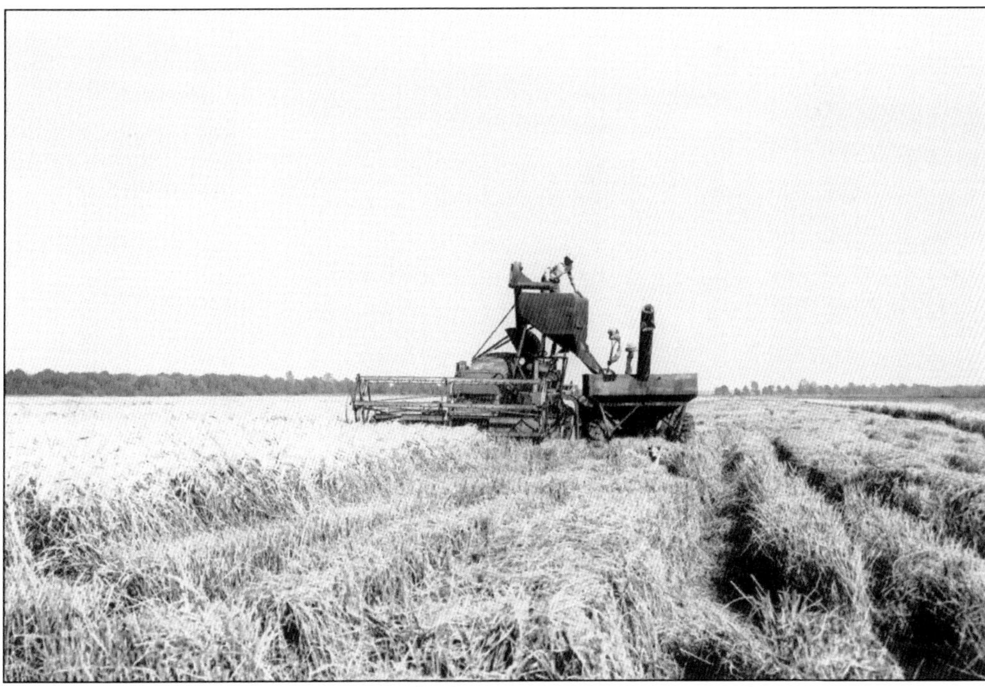

Rice Harvesting near Little Rock. (Arkansas History Commission.)

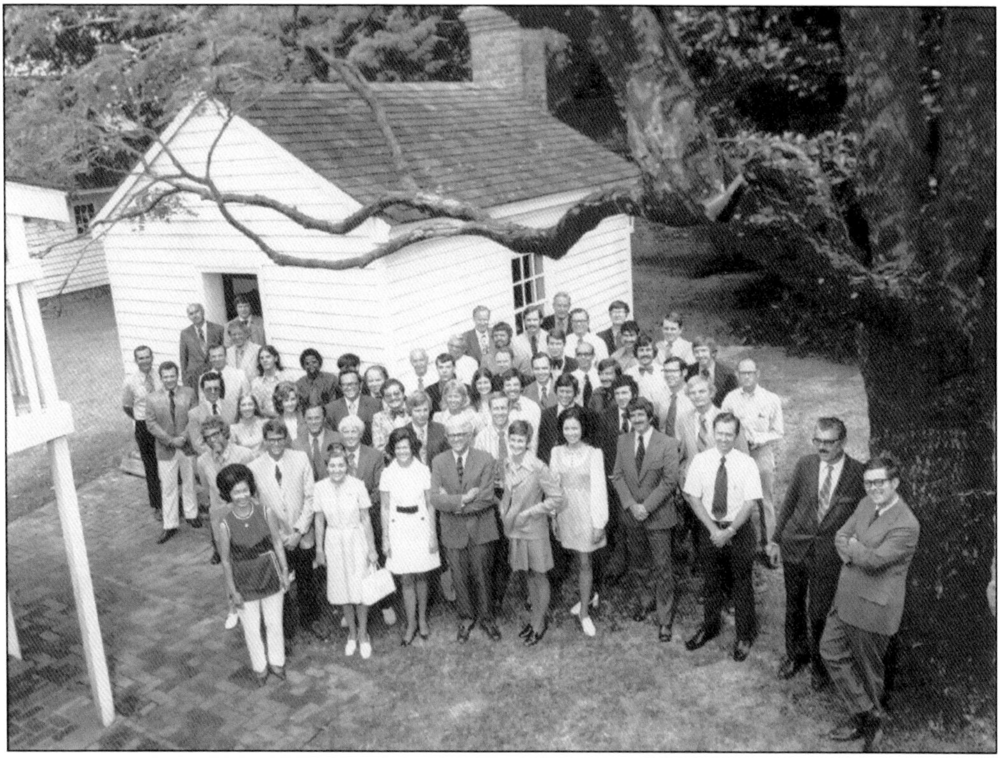

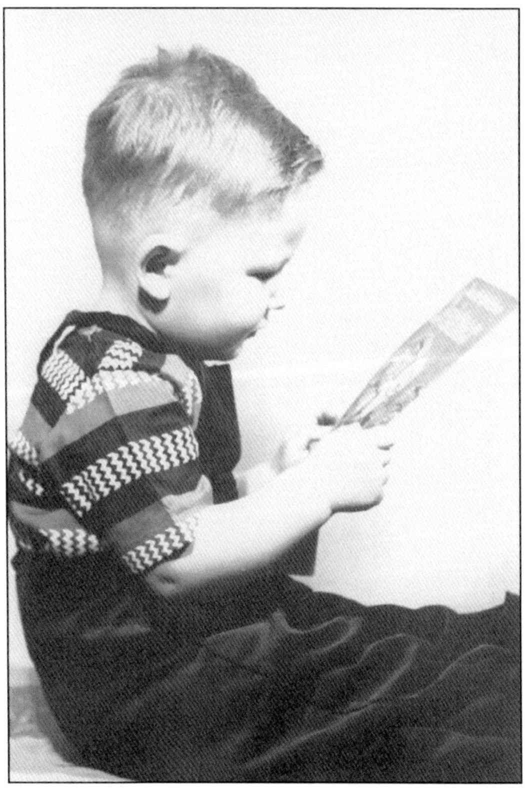

Staff of Cromwell, Neyland, Truemper, Millet and Gatchell, Inc., Architects. Staff members gathered for this portrait about 1975 in front of the Arkansas Territorial Restoration in Little Rock. (UCA Archives.)

Charles Frederick, Age Two Years. The photo is inscribed "Love to Momma Albridge, 1950." (Arkansas History Commission.)

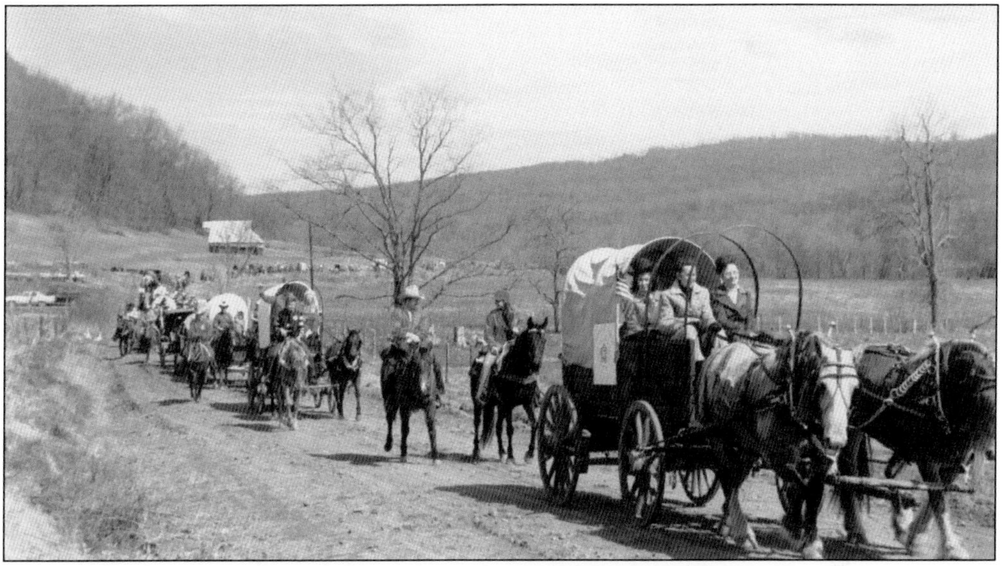

BICENTENNIAL WAGON TRAIN'S PILGRIMAGE TO PENNSYLVANIA. The wagon train is seen here traveling through northwest Arkansas toward Little Rock. (Arkansas History Commission.)

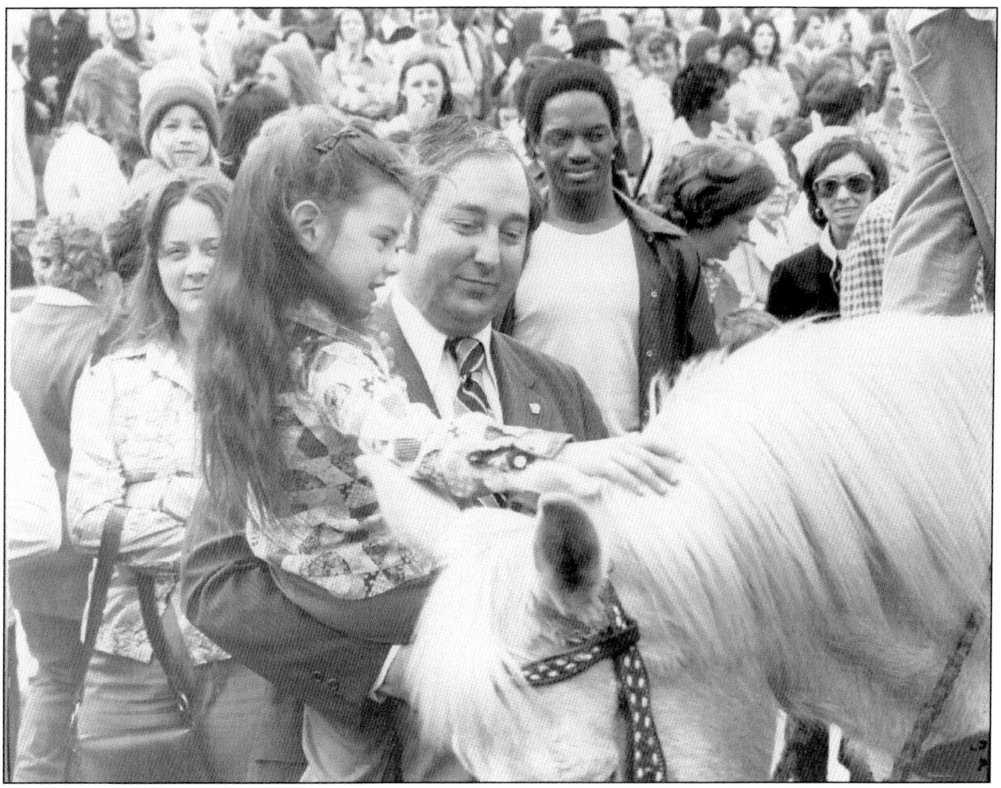

BICENTENNIAL WAGON TRAIN IN LITTLE ROCK ON MARCH 19, 1976. Secretary of state George O. Gernigan Jr., holding an unidentified girl near a horse, participated in the festivities. (Arkansas History Commission.)

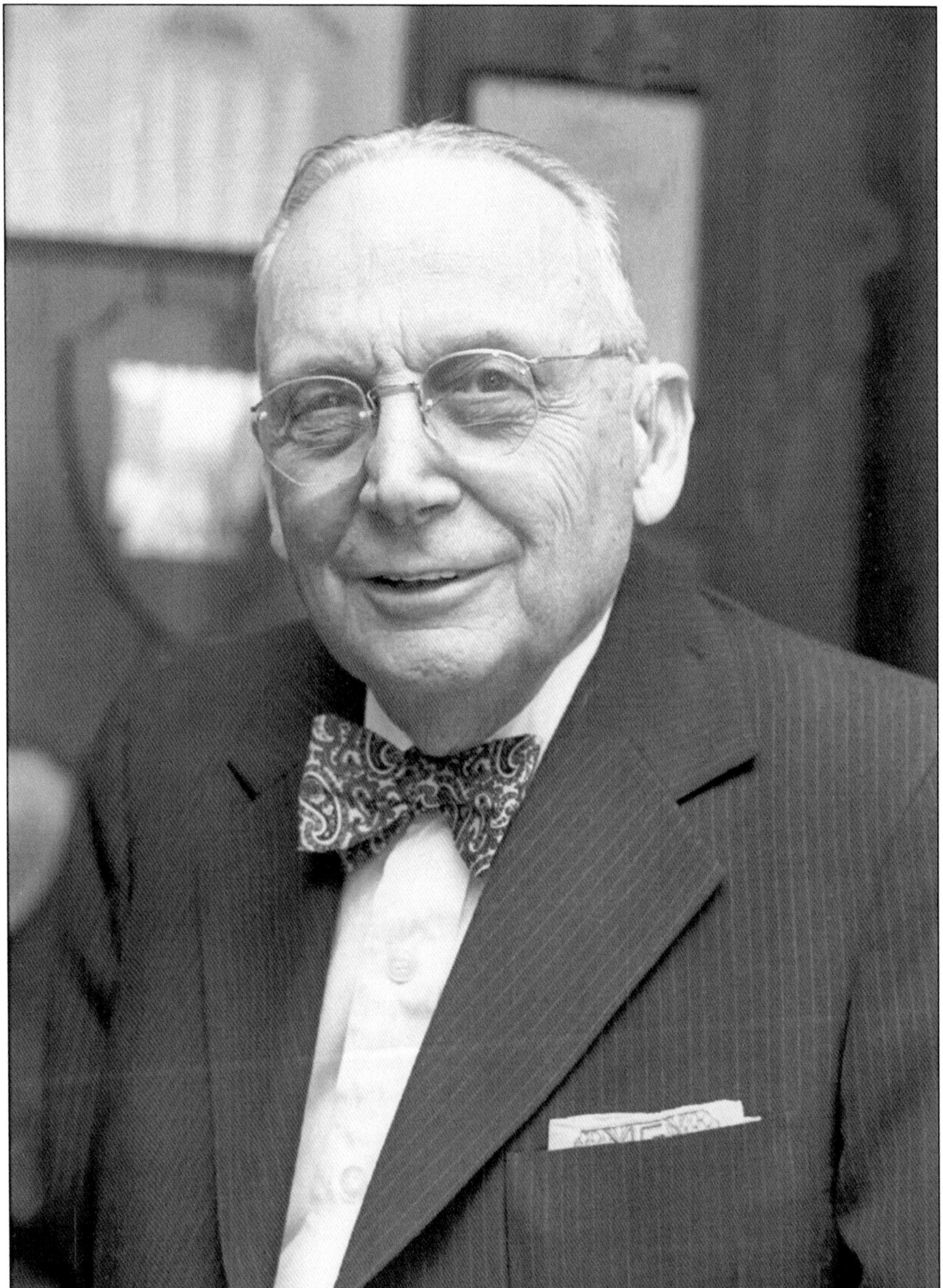

Gus Ottenheimer. He was the chair of the citizen's task force that paved the way for transforming Little Rock Junior College into a four-year school called Little Rock University in 1957. Ottenheimer also served as a longtime member of the school's board of trustees. The Ottenheimer Library, near UALR's campus core, was named to honor this important friend of higher education in Pulaski County. (UALR Library Archives.)

Eight

Revitalizing the Riverfront

As the dawn of the 21st century appeared on the horizon, the riverfront districts of Little Rock and North Little Rock were getting tired, with empty buildings and waning interest in the area. Once the lifeblood of Pulaski County, the vitality of this link between the two communities finally bottomed out. In response, the governments of Pulaski County, Little Rock, and North Little Rock began a collaborative effort to revitalize the riverfront. Numerous and diverse organizations joined the effort to preserve the history and integrity of the area's urban characteristics, while helping to promote economic growth.

Preservation of the Old State House and revitalization of Riverfront Park were followed by the opening of the popular River Market in the 1990s. That was soon followed by construction of an impressive new city library just a block away. On the opposite shore of the Arkansas River, construction began on the Alltel sports arena. Then the Little Rock city council voted to rename a section of Markham Street for President William Jefferson Clinton, in anticipation of building the Clinton Presidential Library there. Revitalization of the waterfront continues to gain momentum as this is written.

While the waterfront will not return to the raucous exuberance it enjoyed during the heyday of the steamboat era, it should provide a valuable resource that the residents of Pulaski County can enjoy and view with pride. As the century and the millennium draw to a close, the prospects for the riverfront and for Pulaski County seem to be getting better and better.

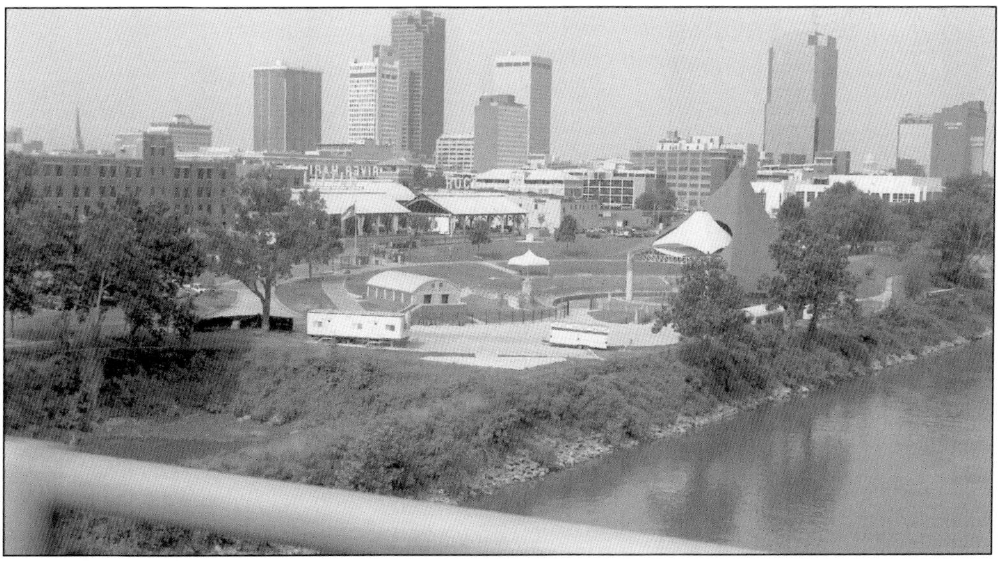

River Market and Riverfront Park. Numerous and diverse organizations from Little Rock and North Little Rock have joined the effort to preserve the history and integrity of the riverfront's urban characteristics, while helping to promote economic growth. (Polly Walter.)

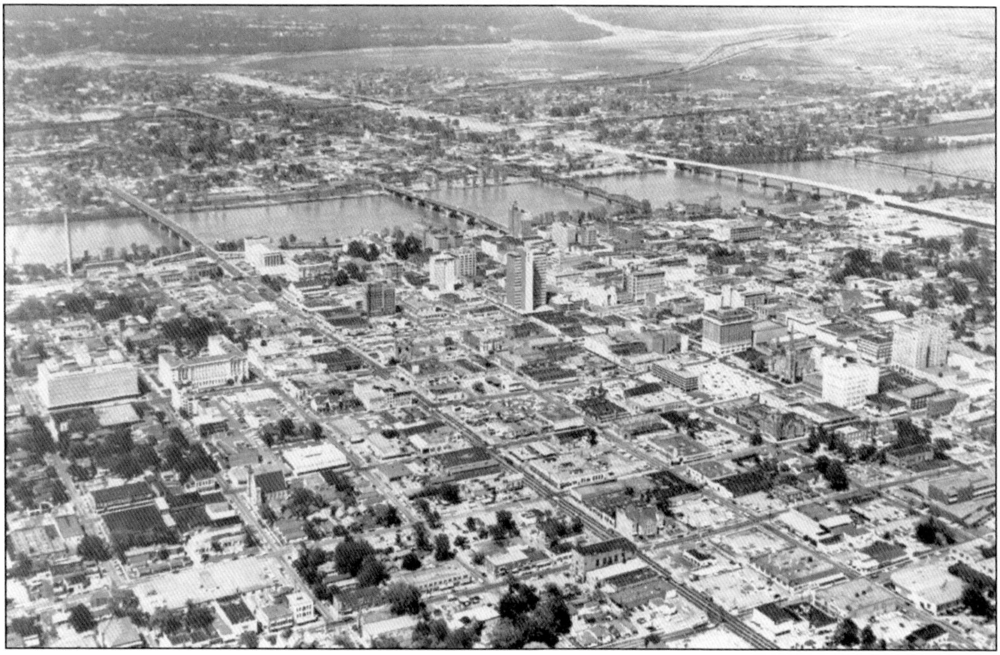

AN AERIAL PHOTOGRAPH OF LITTLE ROCK AND NORTH LITTLE ROCK. This image was taken about 1970 according to notes archived at the Arkansas History Commission. It shows how the Twin Cities grew nearly together. The estimated 1999 population of the Twin Cities exceeded 237,000. (Arkansas History Commission.)

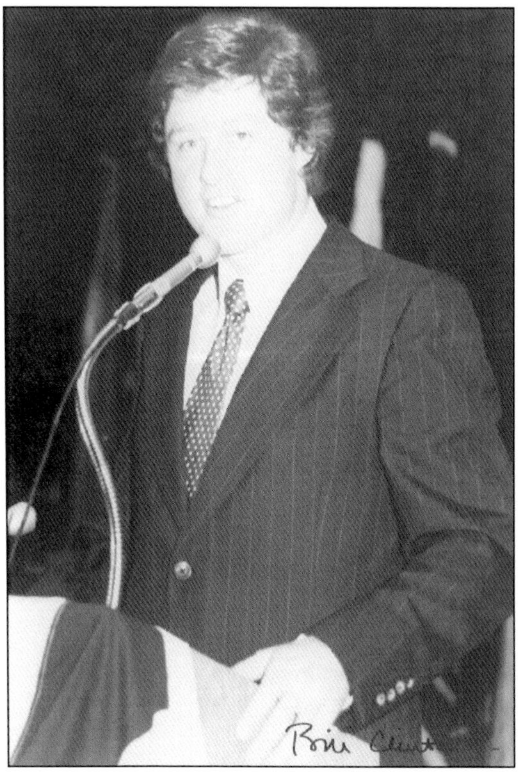

GOVERNOR BILL CLINTON. After serving as attorney general, Clinton won the gubernatorial election in 1978 at the age of thirty-two, becoming the youngest governor in the country. Although he lost his bid for reelection in 1980, he returned to that office in 1982, where he would remain for the next ten years. (Arkansas History Commission.)

THE ARKANSAS HISTORY COMMISSION, MARCH 5, 1987. Pictured here from left to right are: (row one) Dr. John L. Ferguson; (row two) Ruth Tate; (row three) Robert Harvey, Doyle Webb; (row four) Winston Chandler, C. Calvin Smith; and (row five) Ernie Deane and Lee Williams. (Arkansas History Commission.)

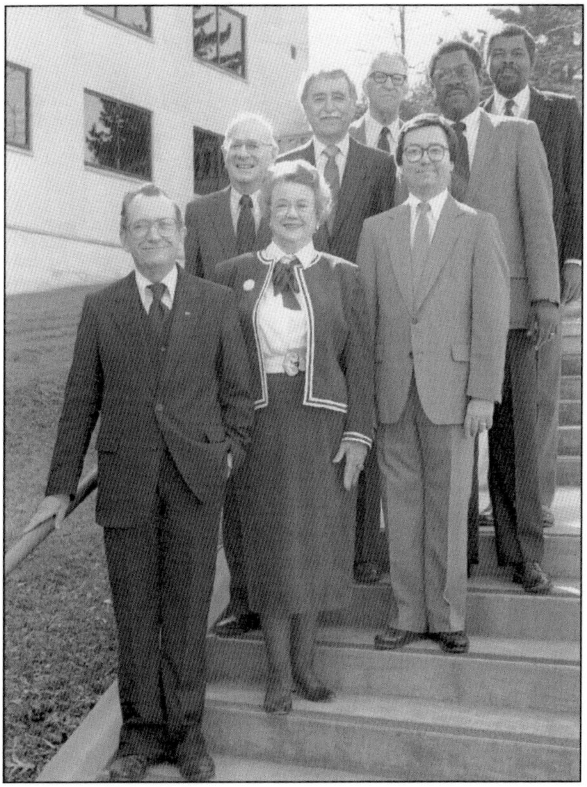

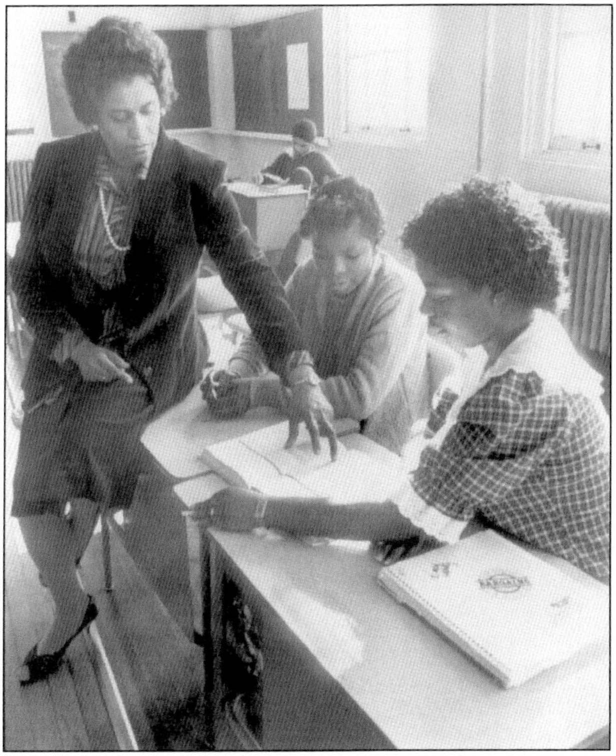

MRS. IRENE HOLCOMB. Mrs. Holcomb goes over a lesson with students. The photo includes Anita Hampton (center) and Zina Henson (right), who were attending the Little Rock School District Transition School. The date of this picture was January 29, 1984. (Arkansas History Commission.)

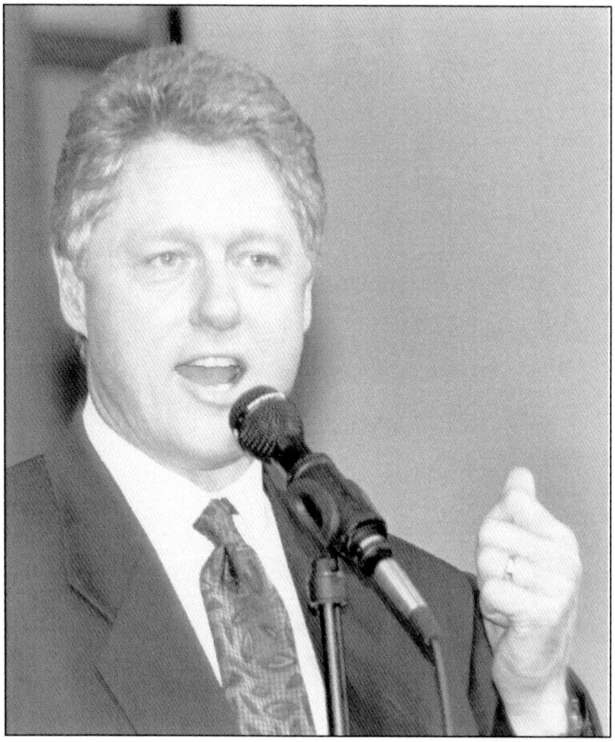

PRESIDENT BILL CLINTON. President Clinton is seen here speaking after his victory ball at the Excelsior Hotel in Little Rock the night of his election to the Presidency in 1992. The forty-second governor of Arkansas became the forty-second president of the United States. (Polly Walter.)

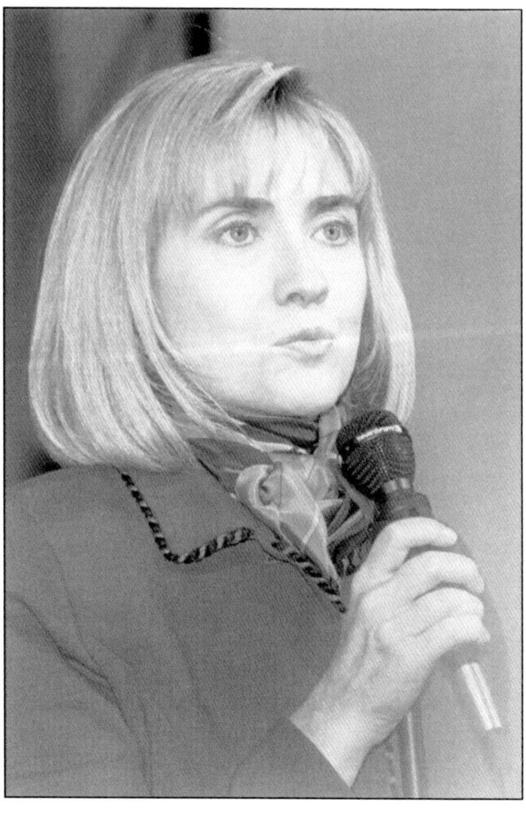

HILLARY DIANE RODHAM CLINTON. She was the first lady of Arkansas long before becoming the first lady of the United States. A graduate of Yale Law School, Hillary Rodham Clinton worked as a staff lawyer for the Children's Defense Fund in Washington, and on the staff of the Nixon impeachment committee in Congress before coming to Arkansas. Her goal while in Arkansas was to enhance education, and her husband appointed her head of one state education program. At the time this book went to press, she was considering a bid for a U. S. senate seat from New York. (Polly Walter.)

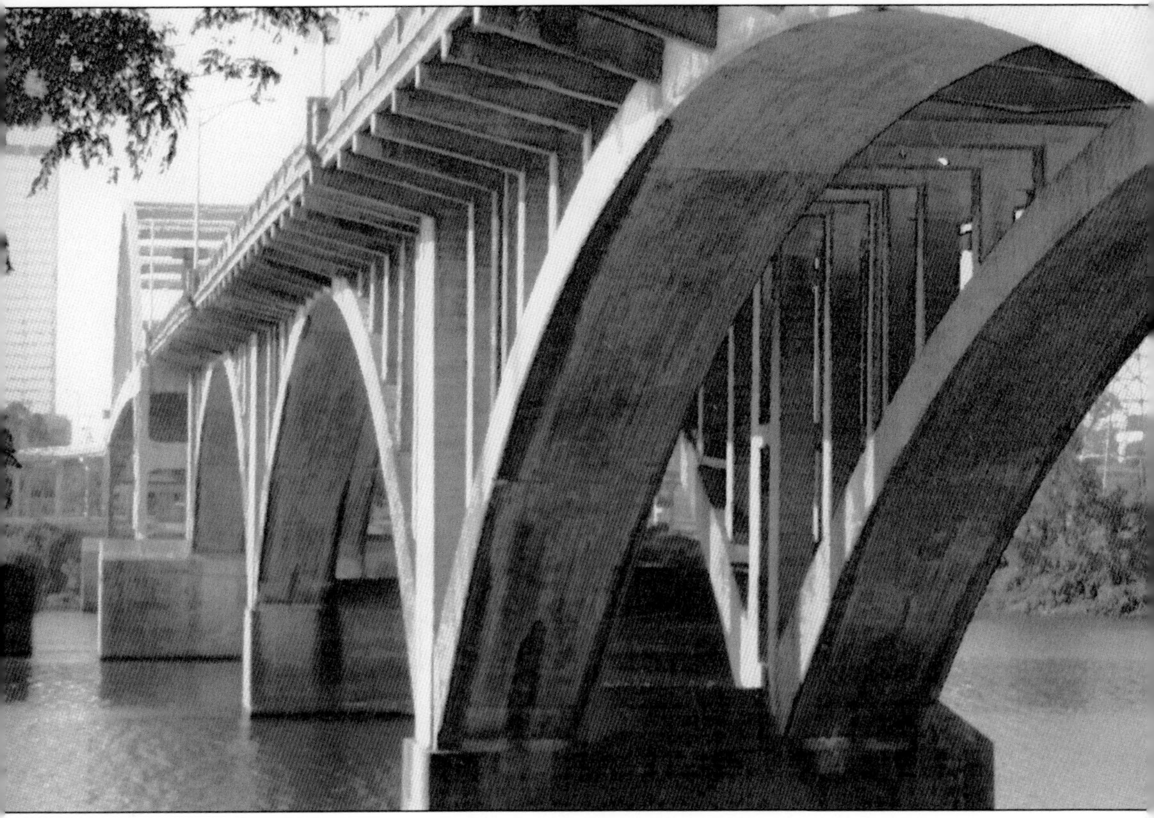

The Broadway Bridge. This is one of six bridges linking Little Rock and North Little Rock along Pulaski County's historic riverfront district. This 1998 photograph—taken from the North Little Rock side of the Arkansas River—first appeared in the traveling Six Bridges Photographic Exhibit, which was produced by UALR Donaghey Scholar Henryetta Vanaman. The exhibit also included work by other area photographers. Note that five of the six bridges connecting the two cities can be seen in the upper photograph on page 122. (Henryetta Vanaman.)

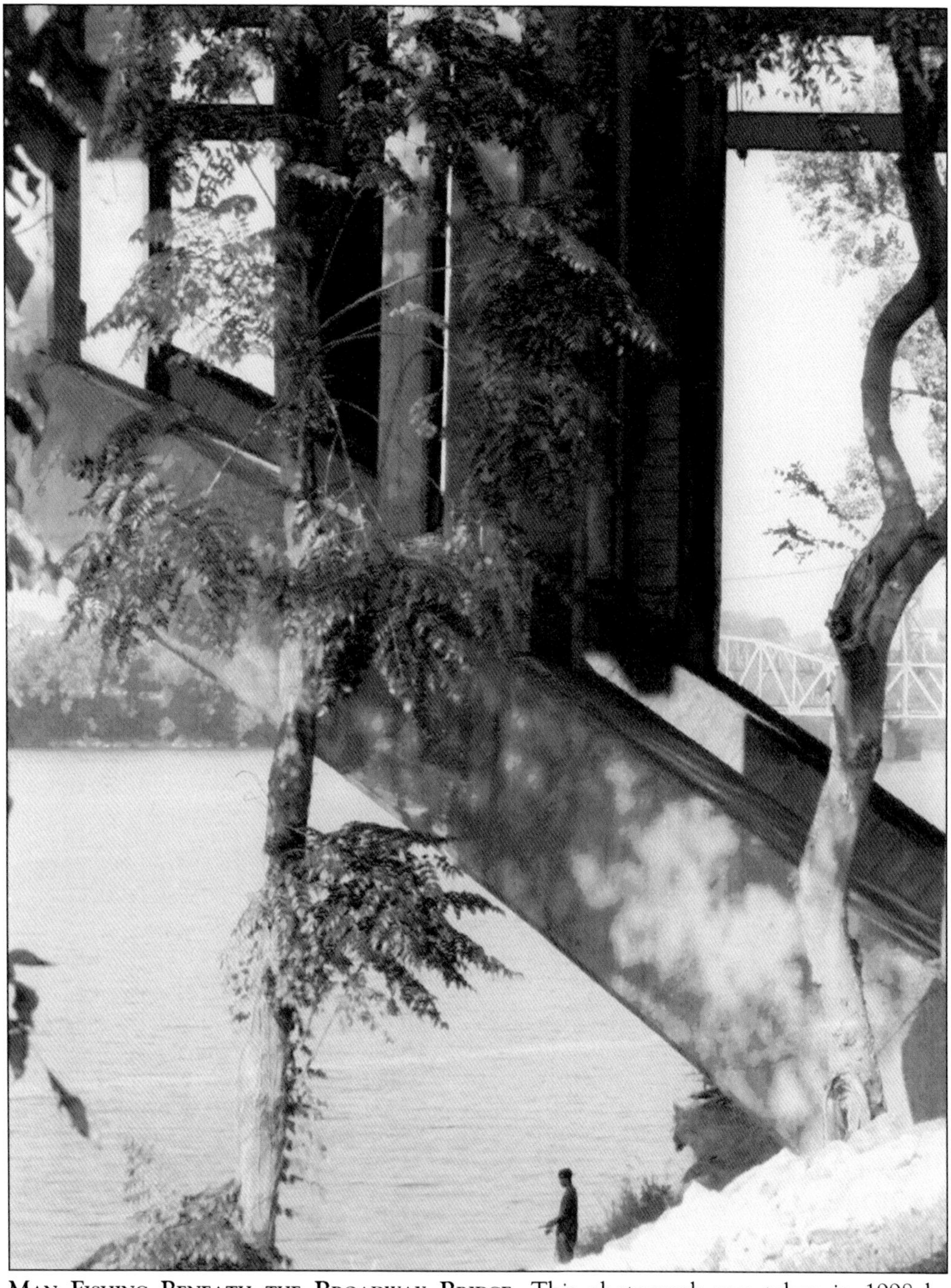

Man Fishing Beneath the Broadway Bridge. This photograph was taken in 1998 by Donaghey Scholar Henryetta Vanaman while participating in the Six Bridges District riverfront planning project, which was directed by George Wittenberg of UALR's Donaghey Project for Urban Studies & Design. The project's goal was to produce a unified plan for Little Rock and North Little Rock, offering suggestions for urban design, governmental jurisdiction, law enforcement, continued growth, historic preservation, coordinated development, and methods for revitalizing the downtown riverfront.

INDEX